Mushrooms in Forests and Woodlands

Mushrooms in Forests and Woodlands
Resource Management, Values and Local Livelihoods

Edited by

Anthony B. Cunningham and Xuefei Yang

publishing for a sustainable future

London • Washington, DC

First published in 2011 by Earthscan

Earthscan Ltd, Dunstan House, 14a St Cross Street, London EC1N 8XA, UK
Earthscan LLC, 1616 P Street, NW, Washington, DC 20036, USA

Earthscan publishes in association with the International Institute for Environment and Development

For more information on Earthscan publications, see www.earthscan.co.uk
or write to earthinfo@earthscan.co.uk

ISBN 978-1-84971-139-5

Typeset by JS Typesetting Ltd, Porthcawl, Mid Glamorgan
Cover design by Susanne Harris

A catalogue record for this book is available from the British Library

Library of Congress Cataloging-in-Publication Data
Mushrooms in forests and woodlands : resource management, values, and local livelihoods / edited by Anthony B. Cunningham and Xuefei Yang.
    p. cm.
  Includes bibliographical references and index.
  ISBN 978-1-84971-139-5 (hardback)
  1. Edible mushrooms–Ecology. 2. Edible fungi–Ecology. 3. Forest ecology. 4. Applied ethnobotany.
I. Cunningham, A. B. II. Yang, Xuefei.
  QK617.M819 2010
  579.6'1632–dc22

                          2010024248

At Earthscan we strive to minimize our environmental impacts and carbon footprint through reducing waste, recycling and offsetting our CO_2 emissions, including those created through publication of this book. For more details of our environmental policy, see www.earthscan.co.uk.

Printed and bound in the UK by TJ International, an ISO 14001 accredited company. The paper used is FSC certified and the inks are vegetable based.

Mixed Sources
Product group from well-managed forests and other controlled sources
www.fsc.org Cert no. SGS-COC-2482
© 1996 Forest Stewardship Council

Contents

Figures, Tables and Boxes

FIGURES

TABLES

BOXES

Preface

Anthony B. Cunningham

From prehistoric times to the present, people have used fungi. For centuries, mushrooms – the fruiting bodies of fungi – have been used, not only for food, but also for stupefying bees in the process of getting honey (*Calvatia gigantea*), and as tinder (*Fomes fomentarius*), medicines (such as *Cordyceps sinensis*, *Ganoderma lucidum* and many others), dyes (*Pisolithus tinctorius*) and hallucinogens in religious rituals (such as *Claviceps purpurea* and *Psilocybe cubensis*). The 'Tyrolean ice-man', who died 5000 years ago on an alpine glacier, carried bits of the medicinal polypore *Piptoporus betulinus* on a leather thong and tinder fungus (*Fomes fomentarius*) in his girdle bag (Peitner et al, 1998).

As a child growing up in southern Africa, it was always a great joy to find edible mushrooms in late spring and early summer. The same is true in China, Estonia, Finland, Malawi, Russia, Sweden or Zambia, where generations of people have enjoyed being outdoors, collecting mushrooms and eating them. Given this widespread interest, why is mycology an 'orphan' science?

In his recent call for a mega-science forum on mycology, Hawksworth (2009) suggests that a reason for this neglect was that Carl Linne (Linnaeus) included fungi with plants in his *Species Plantarum* (1753). Yet, whatever the cause, it is true that despite their value and incredible diversity, fungi are rarely considered in national conservation actions, nor are they part of any international conservation agreements at this stage, such as the Bern Convention and Habitat Directive (Senn-Irlet et al, 2007). Today, we know one thing which Linnaeus did not: fungi are in their own separate kingdom, which diverged from plants and animals over 1500 million years ago (Wang et al, 1999). Given Linnaeus's error, why should a book dealing with fungi in forests and woodlands be found in People and Plants International's Conservation series? We have several reasons for including this book in a series that has always had a strong focus on interdisciplinary approaches to conservation and local community involvement.

Firstly, as Eric Boa points out in Chapter 1, there is a need for integrated approaches in mycology. These can give us a better understanding of links between fungi and people's livelihoods and of the values of fungi compared to other forms of land-use (such as logging), as Susan Alexander and her co-authors describe in Chapter 4.

Secondly, although fungi and plants are in different kingdoms, there are very close links between them, particularly through mycorrhizae, which result from co-evolution between plants and fungi. One well-known example is the importance of mycorrhizae to orchids. Another is the close relationship between ecotomycorrhizal fungi and many tree species, as Cathy Sharp discusses in Chapter 6. Less well-known are cases where links between fungi and plants extend further up the food chain. An example of the latter is Goverde et al's (2000) experimental work, which shows that caterpillars of the common blue butterfly (*Polyommatus icarus*) were smaller and failed to mature when their food-plants had no mycorrhizae.

Thirdly, we felt that this book would contribute to recent efforts to align conservation of fungi with the Global Strategy for Plant Conservation (GSPC), which has identified 'Important Plants Areas' as one of the steps in implementing the GSPC. In 2002, the GSPC was endorsed by the conference of parties to the Convention on Biological Diversity (CBD). Concurrently, Evans et al (2002) used a similar approach, indentifying 'Important Fungus Areas' in the UK as a way of implementing a conservation strategy for fungi. This approach and follow-up within Europe by Senn-Irlet et al (2007) are discussed in more detail in Chapter 9.

Finally, as the GSPC and previous books in this series recognize, working with local people can provide important insights into practical conservation strategies and priorities in a number of ways, including the most basic step: knowing what fungi are out there and something about their ecological relationships. Methods for studying fungal diversity are well established (Schmit and Lodge, 2005). The problem is who will do the work when we know that mycology faces a 'taxonomic bottleneck', with very few mycologists to deal with mega-diversity of fungi. Hawksworth (2003), for example, has pointed out that at 'the current rate of description of new fungi is only about 1100 species each year, a total inventory is impractical within any reasonable time scale; 1290 years at the current rate. Further, the problems of inventorying all fungal species in a particular site is daunting, requiring teams of mycologists with complementary expertise working over decades'. One method for gaining a better idea of where to focus conservation efforts is to take a 'higher-taxon approach' with macro-fungi (Balmford et al, 2004). Another is to get the benefits from 'citizen science'. In Europe and Australia, for example, interested amateur mycologists played an important role in resource management and conservation strategies for macro-fungi. Tropical forests are more of a challenge, as are montane coniferous forests, both having high fungal species diversity yet being remote and visited by few (or no) formally trained mycologists. Local people often have a good knowledge of macro-fungi, their habitat preferences and how they respond to disturbance such as from fire or logging. In Chapters 3 and 4, Egleé and Stanford Zent describe methods used in ethnobiology that are applicable to ethnomycology. Mushroom harvesters, often on the margins of mainstream, urban-oriented societies are also rarely consulted on issues of tenure, resource management needs or marketing opportunities.

Earlier in this International Year of Biodiversity (2010), at an expert workshop planning a new strategy for the Convention on Biological Diversity (CBD) between 2011 and 2020, it was recognized that we continue to lose the world's biodiversity at an unprecedented rate (Djoghlaf, 2010). Stronger links between biodiversity, ecosystem services and people's well-being will be an important component of the post-2010 CBD strategy. They are certainly an important component of this book, which we hope can make a useful contribution to habitat management, fungi conservation and resource use and policy reform, improving people's livelihoods through closer partnerships between researchers, resource users and policy-makers.

REFERENCES

Balmford, A., Lyon A. J. E. and Lang, R. M. (2000) 'Testing the higher-taxon approach to conservation planning in a megadiverse group: the macrofungi', *Biological Conservation* 93, pp209–217

Djoghlaf, A. (2010) *Statement at the informal expert workshop on the updating of the Strategic Plan of the Convention for the post-2010 period*, London, 18 January 2010, Secretariat of the Convention on Biological Diversity, www.cbd.int/doc/speech/2010/sp-2010-01-18-london-en.pdf, accessed 16 June 2010

Evans, S. E., Marren, P. and Harper, M. (2002) *Important Fungus Areas: a provisional assessment of the best sites for fungi in the United Kingdom*, Plantlife, London

Goverde, M., van der Heijden, M. G. A., Wiemken, A., Sanders, I. R. and Erhardt, A. (2000) Arbuscular mycorrhizal fungi influence life history traits of a lepidopteran herbivore, *Oecologia* 125, pp362–369.

Hawksworth, D. L. (2003) 'Monitoring and safeguarding fungal resources worldwide: the need for an international collaborative MycoAction Plan', *Fungal Diversity* 13, pp29–45

Hawksworth, D. L. (2009) 'Mycology: a neglected mega-science', Chapter 1 in *Applied mycology*. M. Rai and P. D. Bridge (eds) CAB International, Wallingford

Peintner, U., Pöder, R., Pümpel, T. (1998) 'The iceman's fungi', *Mycological Research* 102 pp1153–1162

Schmit, J. P. and Lodge, D. J. (2005) 'Classical methods and modern analysis for studying fungal diversity', in J. Dighton, J. F. White, and P. Oudemans (eds) *The Fungal Community: Its organization and role in the ecosystem*, Taylor and Francis, Boca Raton, pp193–214

Senn-Irlet, B., Heilmann-Clausen, J., Genney, D. and Dahlberg, A. (2007) *Guidance for Conservation of Macrofungi in Europe*, Prepared for the Directorate of Culture and Cultural and Natural Heritage, Council of Europe, Strasbourg

Wang, D. Y.-C., Kumar, S. and Hedges, S. B. (1999) 'Divergence time estimates for the early history of animal phyla and the origin of plants, animals and fungi', *Proc. R. Soc. Lond*, B 266, pp163–171

Acknowledgements

This book would not have been possible without the support of The Ford Foundation office in Beijing, China, which provided support through the Kunming Institute of Botany (KIB) to enable production of this book. In particular, Irene Bain (Program Officer for Environment and Development at The Ford Foundation) is thanked for her encouragement and patience. We would also like to thank the Center for International Forestry Research (CIFOR), and in particular Bruce Campbell, for supplementary funding in support of this book. Fiona Paumgarten and Madeleen Husselman at the CIFOR office in Zambia are thanked for enthusiastically providing a range of cover photo options for this book. Åsa Dahlgren is thanked for generously providing information on migrant workers picking berries in Sweden.

At KIB, we would like to thank Professor Yongping Yang for all his support, especially in organizing things at an early stage, and Jiankun Yang for doing the artwork of the *Cordyceps* life-cycle and the links between fungi and forest disturbance ecology.

In China, Ms Bei Hong is thanked for her translation of several chapters from Chinese into English. In the USA, David Arora is thanked for his interesting ideas and discussions on the ecology of harvested fungi during a meeting in Kunming.

As editors, we would also like to thank our friends and families for their support during the book production process. In particular, Anthony would like to thank Michelle Cunningham for her help and his colleagues at People and Plants International (PPI) for being part of a great knowledge network.

Most of all, this book is dedicated to all people who love the many aspects of fungi – whether they are recreational harvesters, commercial collectors, food enthusiasts, researchers or artists enjoying them for their beauty.

Contributors

Dr Susan J. Alexander, US Department of Agriculture, Forest Service, Region 9, PO Box 21268, Juneau, AK 99802, USA

Dr Eric Boa, CABI Europe–UK, Bakeham Lane, Egham, Surrey, TW20 9TY, UK

Dr Anthony B. Cunningham, People and Plants International, 84 Watkins Street, White Gum Valley, 6162 and School for Plant Biology, University of Western Australia, Nedlands, 6009, Western Australia

Cheryl Geslani, University of Hawaii at Manoa

Dr Jun He, ICRAF–China, Kunming, Yunnan, China

Dr Eric T. Jones, Institute for Culture and Ecology, PO Box 6688, Portland, OR 97228, USA

Arpad Kalotas, PO Box 170, Mundaring, WA 6073, Australia

Dr Rebecca J. Mclain, Institute for Culture and Ecology, PO Box 6688, Portland, OR 97228, USA

Dr Sonja N. Oswalt, US Department of Agriculture, Forest Service, Southern Research Station, Forest Inventory and Analysis, 4700 Old Kingston Pike, Knoxville, TN 37919, USA

David Pilz, Lassen National Forest, 2550 Riverside Drive, Susanville, CA 96130, USA

Mr Paul Pirot, 10 Rue des Peupliers, B-6840 Neufchateau, Belgium

Dr Brian E. Robinson, Nelson Institute for Environmental Studies, University of Wisconsin–Madison, USA

Dr Cathy Sharp, Stornaway Cottage, P.O. Box 9327, Hillside, Bulawayo, Zimbabwe

Dr A. F. S. Taylor, Macaulay Research Institute, Macaulay Drive, Craigiebuckler, Aberdeen, AB15 8QH, Scotland, UK

Prof. Dr. Annemieke Verbeken, Department of Biology, Group Mycology, Ghent University, K.L. Ledeganckstraat 35, B-9000 Gent, Belgium

Prof. Xianghua Wang, Kunming Institute of Botany, Chinese Academy of Sciences, No. 132 Lanhei Road, Kunming, China (650204)

Dr. Xuefei Yang, Kunming Institute of Botany, Chinese Academy of Sciences, No. 132 Lanhei Road, Kunming, China (650204)

Prof. Zhu L. Yang, Key Laboratory of Biodiversity and Biogeography, Kunming Institute of Botany, Chinese Academy of Sciences, No. 132 Lanhei Road, Kunming, China (650204)

Dr Eglee L. Zent, Venezuelan Institute for Scientific Research (IVIC), Caracas, Venezuela

Dr Stanford Zent, Anthropology Center, Venezuelan Institute for Scientific Research (IVIC), Caracas, Venezuela

Prof. Yongchang Zhao, Institute of Biotechnology and Germplasm Resources, Yunnan Academy of Agricultural Sciences, 9 Xueyun Road, Wuhua, Kunming, Yunnan, China (650223)

Abbreviations

ABS   Access and Benefit Sharing
AM   arbuscular mycorrhizal
ASEAN   The Association of Southeast Asian Nations
BLM   Bureau of Land Management
C:N   carbon:nitrogen
CBD   Convention on Biological Diversity
CCM   cultural consensus model
CFSI   Cultural Food Significance Index
CIFOR   Center for International Forestry Research
CITES   Convention on International Trade in Endangered Species
CSI   Cultural Significance Index
DRC   Democratic Republic of Congo
ECCF   European Council for the Conservation of Fungi
EMCSI   Edible Mushrooms Cultural Significance Index
FL   fidelity level
FS   Forest Service
FSC   Forest Stewardship Council
GDP   gross domestic product
GIS   Geographic Information System
GNP   gross national product
GPS   Global Positioning System
GSPC   Global Strategy for Plant Conservation
GTI   Global Taxonomy Initiative
HS   Harmonized System (Harmonized Commodity Description and Coding System)
IAR   Informant Agreement Ratio
ICBN   International Code of Botany
IFA   Important Fungus Area
IMA   International Mycological Association
IUCN   International Union for Conservation of Nature
KOH   potassium hydroxide solution
N   nitrogen
NMDS   non-metrical multidimensional scaling
NTFP   non-timber forest product
PCA   principal components analysis
PCLG   Poverty and Conservation Learning Group
PEN   Poverty and Environment Network
ROP   rank order priority

RPL   relative popularity level
RVD   recreation visitor day
SBSTTA   Scientific, Technical and Technological Advice to the Convention on
          Biological Diversity
SIPPO   Swiss Import Promotion Programme
WEF   wild edible fungi

CHAPTER 1

From *Chipho* to *Msika*: An Introduction to Mushrooms, Trees and Forests

Eric Boa

ALL ABOUT PEOPLE

Tumbuka is a Bantu language spoken by around 2 million people who live in Malawi, Tanzania and Zambia. *Chipho* means 'the place where *bowa* grow'. *Bowa* are edible mushrooms and they are collected, sold and consumed widely in all three countries, as well as most neighbouring ones. The main *chipho* occur in miombo woodlands found in eastern and southern Africa (Campbell, 1996). The *bowa* are collected for personal consumption but most are sold at markets (*msika*), some by the side of the road nearest to the forest, and others in towns, where higher prices can be obtained (Figure 1.1).

This chapter examines the sequence of events that occurs from the harvesting of wild mushrooms to their sale and describes the characteristics of the production chain, illustrated with examples from around the world. The miombo mushrooms have attracted a lot of attention but they are only one of many regions where wild mushrooms are important to people (see Table 1.1).

This account is based on information and ideas arising from a previous attempt to summarize what we know about wild mushrooms ('wild edible fungi') and their use and importance to people (Boa, 2004). Mushrooms are among the most valuable of wild-gathered foods, yet there is a poor appreciation of their economic importance and

Table 1.1 *Mushroom tradition in 210 countries according to FAO-defined regions*

Region	Countries	Strong mushroom tradition	Weak mushroom tradition	No information
Africa	55	10 (18%)	28 (51%)	17 (31%)
Asia	51	15 (30%)	18 (35%)	18 (35%)
Europe	37	14 (62%)	9 (29%)	3 (9%)
The Americas	47	7 (15%)	11 (23%)	29 (62%)
Oceania	20	1 (5%)	3 (15%)	16 (79%)
TOTAL		47	69	83

Note: Tradition refers to cultural use and collecting to sell
Source: Adapted from Boa (2004)

Figure 1.1 *Typical roadside stalls selling edible mushrooms* (bowa) *near Liwonde in Malawi*

Photograph: Eric Boa

relevance to rural livelihoods. There is no shortage of interest in wild mushrooms as defined by research discipline: mycologists and anthropologists are two leading groups who have published widely on biology, ecology and culture in different countries. But we lack integrative accounts that go beyond form and function and national boundaries and consider wild mushrooms in the wider economic and trade context. This is an attempt to redress this omission.

THE ROOT OF THE MATTER

The journey from *chipho* to *msika* begins with the mycorrhiza, the fungus-root associations that allow trees and forests to establish and survive. The majority of fungus species that produce edible mushrooms are mycorrhizal. The journey ends with the sale of edible mushrooms; it is the value of this trade that defines their key importance to people. We know a lot about mushrooms, but much less about their importance to rural livelihoods. Without this information, attempts to show how wild mushrooms can tackle poverty alleviation and food security will falter. The importance of wild mushrooms is self-evident to researchers and enthusiasts, but much less so to those who fund international development projects.

Fortunately more is known about wild mushrooms now than in the past, and more support is available for action and investigation. These advances in knowledge are relatively recent. Miombo woodlands were disregarded by professional foresters for many years and non-timber forest products (NTFPs) more or less ignored. A landmark book on miombo woodlands (Campbell, 1996) contained few details about edible mushrooms despite the strong tradition and history of collection and consumption. An earlier paper on wild mushrooms (Morris, 1984) failed to attract attention beyond the readers of mycological journals. In addition to Morris's (1984) work on mushrooms in Malawi, mycologists and natural resource managers are encouraged to read the seminal studies carried out in the miombo of Zambia (Piearce, 1982) and Tanzania (Härkönen, 1995).

Pioneering studies by Wasson and Wasson (1957) on the widespread importance of wild mushrooms, by country and groups of people, helped to stimulate subsequent studies on human use. There is little mention of the extent or value of trade and less about the contribution of wild mushrooms to human livelihoods. A history of mycology briefly hinted at global use of wild mushrooms (Ainsworth, 1976). But while information about the incomes earned from mushrooms has significantly improved, publications on wild mushrooms are still widely scattered: they appear in different disciplines (mycology, forestry, anthropology and medicine) and those from developing countries have a restricted distribution. In addition to the miombo mushroom studies mentioned above, landmark publications include a collection of papers published as *Mycology in Sustainable Development*, which focuses on North American Northwest and Mexico (Palm and Chapela, 1997). More recently, a special edition of *Economic Botany* (vol 62, 2008) brought together an eclectic mix of original contributions on wild mushrooms; it has proved invaluable in updating the information presented in this chapter.

A GLOBAL VIEW

Information on wild mushrooms is widely dispersed and accessing papers and articles is often difficult, particularly those from the poorest forest communities. This limits our ability to obtain a representative overview that transcends the boundaries of discipline and nation and avoids a bias towards information published in the US and Europe. A weak appreciation of the global situation explains many people's surprise at the size of global trade in wild mushrooms, conservatively estimated at US$2 billion (Hall et al, 2003). Economic liberalization and open trade policies in China have greatly increased exports of wild mushrooms and cultivated species (USDA, 2009). Comprehensive data are only available for cultivated mushrooms: from 1988 to 2007 production increased five-fold to 1.5 million tonnes. There should be no doubt that wild mushrooms are important around the world (Table 1.1) and that many people depend on the income they generate. Cultural biases exist because people often associate mushrooms with natural history, a discipline with its own established traditions, which shaped the perception of mushrooms in developed countries (Allen, 1991). The British and French Mycological societies have existed for over 100 years, and most European countries have their own societies. In China, researchers have described the incredible diversity of species found across China (Mao, 2000) and are beginning to address more of the applied problems concerning contributions to livelihood and management of natural resources (see Chapters 2, 7, 8 and 9).

The money earned from collecting and selling is a vital part of people's income in countries as far apart as the US and Canada (Redhead, 1998), Scotland (Dyke and Newton, 1999), rural Spain (de Román and Boa, 2006) and China (e.g. Arora, 2008). Exports of wild mushrooms make significant contributions to national economies in Bhutan and North Korea (Boa, 2004), which both benefit from demand from a rich country (Japan). However, trade figures can be misleading: the bulk of so-called Italian porcini (*Boletus edulis*) originate from outside Italy (Sitta and Floriani, 2008).

People collect mushrooms because it is often one of few opportunities to make money in rural areas (Arora, 2008). Wild mushrooms are a potential 'pathway out of poverty', though few collectors get rich from the proceeds. Good transport networks and competition between buyers are important, as are efficient supply chains. Some edible mushrooms are fragile and easily damaged in transit. It is no coincidence that the most widely-traded species are the relatively robust ones, able to survive long journeys from poorer rural areas with mushroom-rich forests to richer towns and cities where the highest prices can be realized.

Mushrooms make extraordinary journeys from the many remote regions which supply extensive international trade. Italian companies constantly seek new sources of porcini to satisfy global demand, shipping mushrooms from Latin America, Asia and Africa to northern Italy, resulting in new economic opportunities. The trade can also affect local practices if, for example, forest concessions exclude people from traditional mushroom collecting areas.

A global overview of wild mushrooms addresses all aspects of supply and demand as well as use and management of forests and woodlands for other purposes. Forests are used by many groups of people whose contrasting priorities may cause conflict. Wood carvers in Malawi and bark collectors (for medicinal products) use the trees that produce mushrooms; people who hunt with guns for wild animals in Italian woodlands are a potential threat to truffle hunters.

Constructing a global overview has two major benefits. It encourages sharing of experiences and knowledge between countries and it highlights themes common to the collection of different types of wild-gathered products in relation to the management of natural resources: ownership; rights; access; integrity of supply; and so on. Lessons learned from one product can be applied to others. This chapter aims to expand the perspective from which we analyse and reflect on mushrooms in forests.

SETTING THE SCENE

This account draws on information obtained from studies of wild mushrooms in developed and developing countries. Both groups share common features: collecting is carried out by less wealthy people in poorer rural areas where employment opportunities are limited. These shared characteristics allow researchers to use findings from Africa to inform practice and policy in Europe and vice versa.

I have given selected references to original sources of information. A more comprehensive bibliography appears in Boa (2004) and is available online via the FAO website (www.fao.org/docrep/007/Y5489E/y5489e00.htm).

My aim is to outline the available knowledge on all aspects of wild mushrooms which are important to people and forests, with an emphasis on the potential of mushrooms to improve the lives of poor people. Our knowledge of collecting and trade in developing countries is weak and I will highlight topics that need further investigation. I start with a short description of the main types of mushrooms, their uses and properties, then describe their importance to people and mushroom-related practices and traditions. I conclude with a discussion of management, our overall state of knowledge and what should happen next.

NUMBERS, TYPES AND USES OF MUSHROOMS

Wild edible fungi (Boa, 2004) come in a range of sizes, colours, shapes and – of course – tastes. Table 1.2 briefly introduces major types and the ecological niches they occupy. I have adopted the widely used convention of using 'mushroom' to mean the fruiting body of fungi. Scientifically, they belong to the Basidiomycota and the Ascomycota. The majority of 'true' mushrooms (those with a stalk and a cap) occur in the Basidiomycota, of which there are just over 31,000 species according to the *Dictionary of the Fungi* (Kirk et al, 2008). The two main mushroom families are the Agaricales and the Boletales; these comprise around 14,000 species.

The properties and uses of 2075 useful mushroom species were recorded in a review of published information up to January 2006. Records were obtained from nearly 200 sources and around 90 countries (Table 1.3) and a properties database created. The database also includes poisonous species and mushrooms with medicinal and other 'useful' properties. Around 6 to 7 per cent of all species in the Basidiomycota are either eaten or said to be edible, excluding a small number of edible species which belong

Table 1.2 *Different forms of wild mushrooms and their ecological niches in forests and woodlands, with examples of useful genera (food and medicine)*

	With gills	With pores or spines	Bracket (woody) fungi	Others
Symbiotic (all mycorrhizal except Termitomyces)	*Amanita, Lactarius, Russula, Cantharellus, Termitomyces*	*Boletus, Hydnum*	None	*Tuber, Ramaria*
Saprobic	*Pleurotus, Agaricus*	*Hericium*	*Fistulina*	*Morchella, Lycoperdon*
Pathogenic	*Armillaria, Sparassis, Laetiporus*	none	*Ganoderma*	

Note: Saprobic genera occur outside forests. The mycorrhizal genera occur on trees and shrubs.

Table 1.3 *Reported use and properties of 2705 mushroom species from 90 countries*

Use or property	Number of species	% of total
Food	1118	41
Food (uncertain)	62	2
Edible	530	20
Edible (uncertain)	589	22
Poisonous	354	13
Poisonous (uncertain)	52	2

Note: Information from around 200 named sources. Some reports are equivocal. If it is clear that a species has been eaten without harm then it is 'food'. Of the above species, 154 also have medicinal properties but this is an underestimate. Dai et al (2009) list 540 fungal species with medicinal properties from China.

to the Ascomycota. This increases to around 15 per cent of all species in the two main mushroom families, the Agaricales and the Boletales.

The majority of mushrooms that occur in forests and woodlands form ecto-mycorrhiza and are symbionts. A recent review shows the extent of ectomycorrhizal fungi and hints at the mushroom potential of forests and woodlands around the world (Brundrett, 2009). There are about 6000 ectomycorrhizal plant species in 145 genera. *Termitomyces* spp are also symbiotic (they grow in association with termites) and are found in woodlands as well as more open sites. They are collected in Africa and Asia and frequently sold in markets. Although the trade is local and value low, these species are nutritious, with relatively high amounts of protein. Saprobic species are common in forests and woodlands and grow on dead and decaying organic matter. Most trade in wild saprobic species is local; I am not aware of any substantial exports. There is little incentive to export because valuable saprobic species are widely cultivated for food and medicinal purposes (Stamets, 2000). The third group of edible mushrooms are pathogenic on trees. Examples of genera found in the three main ecological niches are shown in Table 1.2.

All mushrooms provide important ecological services to trees and forests. Ecto-mycorrhizal mushrooms are necessary for the establishment and growth of trees. Saprobic mushrooms recycle nutrients and maintain soil fertility and structure. Edible mushrooms are only a small part of the total diversity of species found in forests, although they have the highest financial value. The 'silent' mycological majority make important contributions to forest health but it is difficult to give them a value. All fungal diversity is conserved to some extent through appropriate management of forests. Effective management of edible species in their natural habitat will also help sustain non-edible species.

Most ectomycorrhizal species cannot be cultivated, with the major exception of truffles (*Tuber* spp). Host trees are artificially inoculated and managed in 'truffières' in countries such as Italy, Spain and New Zealand (Hall et al, 2007). Truffle growing is more accurately described as 'semi-cultivation'. New techniques have helped improve the successful establishment of truffières and their subsequent growth to maturity, but there is still an element of 'wait and pray' before reaping the rewards of a substantial investment of money and time.

EDIBILITY

Useful mushrooms are characterized by uses and properties. It is important to distinguish between mushrooms that can be eaten and those that have been eaten. To be a food is a 'use'; edibility is a 'property'. While field guides use the term 'edible' to imply that a mushroom is eaten, it is often difficult to identify the original source of this information. There are strongly held opinions on what can be eaten. Field guides are a common reference source, yet their advice can be contradictory and misleading (Rubel and Arora, 2008). A weak consensus harms the potential expansion of trade and undermines public confidence in eating wild mushrooms, already influenced by a fear of poisonous species. The properties database contains more than 1000 'edible' species that lack confirmation that someone has eaten them. A few field guides include original observations on eating mushrooms or cite sources; Arora (1991) is a good example.

The confusion about edibility does not end with the decision on whether a so-called edible species has been eaten by an individual without harmful consequences. Descriptions of mushrooms are inconsistent. Field guides refer to species as 'not-edible', 'inedible' and even 'do not eat'. These terms are open to different interpretations. 'Inedible' could mean poisonous (if so, then this should be stated) and 'not edible' could mean difficult to digest. 'Not eaten' is a more accurate description and avoids doubt about poisonous species or those not worth eating. I have eaten *Schizophyllun commune*, described by one leading field guide as 'not edible' (Phillips, 2006). It was an unrewarding experience, yet *S. commune* is sold in several countries. Field guides are also cautious about recommending species that are toxic when raw but edible when cooked.

Index Fungorum (www.indexfungorum.org) is an online database used to confirm the validity of a fungus scientific name. A similar system for edible mushrooms would compare the published descriptions of a species and construct a 'summary judgement' based on the most reliable reports. The properties database contains 9486 records from more than 3000 species. This could be used to create an online system for reviewing and improving 'summary judgements' based on all available knowledge. Such a resource would help resolve disputes about which species could be sold and help doctors treat people who have eaten potentially poisonous mushrooms.

POISONOUS MUSHROOMS

How many poisonous species are there? There is a popular and widespread perception that a significant proportion of mushrooms are poisonous. Table 1.3 shows that around 15 per cent of species are (said to be) harmful if eaten, according to the properties database noted above, although records of poisonous species do not always distinguish between cooked and uncooked specimens. The reactions vary from mild, transitory symptoms to long-term organ damage and death. There are less than 20 'deadly poisonous' species known worldwide.

The properties of many more mushroom species have not been recorded, and therefore it is difficult to say how many more poisonous species might exist. Accounts of mushroom poisonings are routinely published in the US. Although other countries are not so well organized, mushroom poisonings attract a lot of attention and are relatively well-reported. However, the media often lack accurate information about which species are involved. It is unlikely that many more important poisonous species remain to be described. Adventurous (reckless?) pickers in Eastern Europe have inadvertently helped to identify poisonous species which are similar to edible ones. In countries with a weak tradition of collecting mushrooms there is much less likelihood of people eating poisonous species.

The threat of poisonous species casts an unduly heavy shadow over wild edible mushrooms. Rubel and Arora (2008) point out that people eat foodstuffs that are poisonous when raw, yet nutritious and safe once cooked. However, fatalities are a regular event and large-scale poisonings have occurred (Boa, 2004). It is difficult to decide whether the clamour of publicity matches the general risk of collecting poisonous mushrooms as hype gets in the way.

A rational assessment might conclude that there is a lower risk of eating a poisonous mushroom than is suggested by reports in the media. Accidents happen, even in regions with well-established traditions of mycophagy. The eagerness of Russians to collect mushrooms has resulted in more poisonings than might be expected in a country with a long mushroom tradition (Härkönen, 1998).

It is not always clear from reports of alleged mushroom poisonings whether mushrooms are the cause of the observed symptoms. Better reporting is needed as well as assistance in identifying species, preferably before people eat the potentially poisonous species. Mushroom police in Norway and shop displays in France provide such a service. These are good investments, which reduce the number of people who need treatment and help maintain public confidence. When, in Georgia in 2008, adults became ill and three children died after reportedly eating poisonous mushrooms they had collected themselves, wild mushroom selling was banned in Tbilisi, nearly 200km away. The species involved in the poisoning were not confirmed at the time of this ban and wild mushrooms have been sold safely in Tbilisi markets for many years. An important local trade was abruptly halted because of an isolated poisoning incident.

IMPORTANCE OF MUSHROOMS

The first comprehensive review of mushroom traditions appeared in 1957 (Wasson and Wasson, 1957). *Mushrooms, Russia and History* stimulated others to continue ethnomycological studies. Wasson was especially interested in hallucinogenic species and their cultural significance (see Letcher, 2008 for an excellent summary of the cultural history of magic mushrooms and a revision of Wasson's contributions.) Ethnomycological studies have been undertaken in many countries, as shown in Table 1.4. The studies describe the cultural importance of mushrooms; they offer few if any insights on the contribution mushrooms make to nutrition and income in relation to other sources.

In Table 1.1 mushroom traditions are compared and assessed using summaries from 210 countries (Boa, 2004). These traditions were assessed mainly on the extent of collection and its importance for food and income. Less emphasis was given to

Table 1.4 *Ethnoscientific studies of wild mushrooms*

Country	Topic
Australia	Useful (includes edible) species in aboriginal culture
Balkan region	Medicinal species: study of eastern Slavs
Benin	Ethnomycological study
Brazil	Study of Sanama Indians (includes edible species)
Burkina Faso	Decline in use of wild mushrooms (Guisso et al, 2008)
Canada	Aboriginal plant use, including edible and medicinal wild fungi
China	Comparison of Hunan and China (mostly edible species)
Himalaya, eastern	Edible fungi of medicinal value
India, central	Ethno-myco-medicinals
Indonesia	Ethnomycology of the Nuaula (Ellen, 2008)
Japan	Uses of fungi and lichens by Ainu
Malawi	Edible, medicinal and species used for ceremonial purposes
Mexico	Medicinal mushrooms: traditions, myths and knowledge
Nepal	General observations (mainly edible species)
Nigeria	Medicinal practices in Yoruba culture
Papua New Guinea	Mainly concerned with edible species
Peru	Fungi, mostly edible, part of ethnobotanical study
Poland	Polish folk medicine
Russia	Khanty folk medicine
Tanzania	Compares use of wild mushrooms with customs in Hunan in China
Turkey	Edible fungi, part of an ethnobotanical study
Venezuela	Ethnomycology of the Jotï (Zent, 2008)
Zambia	Customs and folklore about mostly edible species

Source: Adapted from Boa (2004), which includes references not noted above

cultural uses. Only a few major conclusions can be drawn: a relatively small number of countries in Africa have a strong mushroom tradition; Europe is well represented because more information is published (only three countries lacked any information about wild mushrooms); a few countries in the Americas have a strong tradition; and China dominates mushroom use and collecting in Asia.

CONTRIBUTIONS TO DIET

How important are wild mushrooms to diet? The composition of a small number of species is known and representative data are shown in Table 1.5. The protein content of some species is good. Although it is often said that mushrooms are 'mainly water', in this respect they differ little from many vegetables. The named species in Table 1.5 give a general indication of what to expect in untested species of a genus, but amounts of protein can vary within species. Many species also have medicinal properties.

The contribution made by mushrooms to diet is difficult to measure without more data on the quantities eaten. A general opinion is that mushrooms are not an essential part of the diet, but they are a 'nutritionally-valuable addition' and that they are more important in times of food shortages (de Román et al, 2006). The Finnish

Table 1.5   *Nutritional composition of some wild mushrooms*

Binomial	Country	Composition, % dry weight			
		Protein	Carbo-hydrate	Fat	Mineral Matter (ash)
Amanita caesarea	France	15	nk	14	10
Amanita rubescens	Mexico	18	nk	nk	nk
Boletus edulis	Turkey and Finland	23–38	47	2–9	1–7
Cantharellus cibarius	DR Congo	15	64	5	13
Lactarius deliciosus	France and Chile	23–27	28	7	6
Lactarius piperatus	Turkey	27	65	2	1
Ramaria flava	Mexico (3)	14	nk	nk	nk
Russula delica	India (9)	17	nk	nk	nk
Suillus luteus	Chile	20	57	4	6
Suillus granulatus	Chile	14	70	2	6
Terfezia claveryi	Iraq (11)	8	17	nk	10
Termitomyces microcarpus	Tanzania and DRC	33–49	29–38	5–10	11–23
Tricholoma populinum	Canada	13	70	9	7
Tirmania nivea	Iraq	14	21	nk	5

Note: Adapted from Boa (2004), which can be consulted for sources of information.

Government went to some lengths after the Second World War to promote the collecting of mushrooms (and other wild-gathered foods such as berries) because of concern about food shortages. Common names were 'invented' for species as part of the campaign although many were already in existence. The campaign appears to have been reasonably successful without necessarily improving already established cultural traditions. A crude line can be drawn from north to south in Finland to separate the Karelians in the east, originally from Russia, who have a strong tradition of collecting mushrooms, with the much weaker tradition in the west among inhabitants of Swedish origin (Härkönen, 1998).

It is difficult to invent new traditions. It is much easier to lose them. In Malawi, people who moved to the cities lost their knowledge of wild mushrooms and became suspicious of species that did not come with the implicit safety approval of a shop. Sabitini Fides, a mushroom trader, said:

> *In order to find customers I would walk around residential areas such as the police training college, the barracks, Chancellor College and also the suburbs such as Mponda Bwino and Chikanda, selling from house to house. At first I found the householders reluctant – 'maybe they are poisonous' 'maybe they are not good'. Patiently I would persuade the buyers (mainly women) to try them – tasting some myself in order to demonstrate lack of poison. One might buy. Then the next time others would have observed that the one who bought enjoyed their purchase and they would follow suit. Gradually I would build up his regular customers who eventually would buy without fail.* (Boa, 2004)

MUSHROOMS AS A SOURCE OF INCOME

The global trade in wild mushrooms is worth at least US$2 billion (Table 1.5). This estimate does not include related species worth substantial amounts in trade: *Tricholoma magnivelare* is exported to Japan from the Pacific Northwest of the US and Canada; morels are exported from India and Nepal; Turkey has a notable export trade in wild mushrooms. Wild mushrooms provide regular, although seasonal, employment for large numbers of people in many countries.

Many people collect on a small scale for personal consumption or local trade. The amounts earned may be modest but it can make a difference in personal finances. During a study of níscalos (*Lactarius deliciosus*) in Castilla Léon, Spain (de Román and Boa, 2006) the authors were warned not to be fooled by people who said that collecting was a hobby. A family of four could make a profit of between €5600 and €8400 a season, around 40 per cent of the average family annual income for this region. In northwest Yunnan people built houses and occasionally bought cars with the proceeds from selling matsutake (*Tricholoma matsutake*) (Arora, 2008). In Oaxaca, the poorest state of Mexico, I watched small children earn between $20 and $30 a day collecting *Tricholoma magnivelare*.

The number of countries in which substantial amounts of money can be earned from wild mushrooms is relatively small. For every well-documented case of mushroom riches there are thousands more examples of people earning much more modest sums. Women in Malawi spend several hours in the miombo woodland before walking up to 10km to market to earn a few dollars (Lowore and Boa, 2001). Export trade data suggest the scale and importance of collections (Boa, 2004). North Korea earned US$150 million from exports of matsutake to Japan between 1993 and 1997. The annual export of morels from India (mainly to Europe) was reckoned to be between US$50–60 million. Annual exports of chanterelles from Turkey ranged from US$11–375 million between 1989 and 1999. Harvests are unpredictable and prices vary.

The commercial trade in mushrooms offers opportunities for employment, which often attract people from outside the areas where the mushrooms are found. Mushroom collecting in Europe and North America employs immigrants from southeast Asia and Mexico, some of whom have little or no tradition of collecting wild mushroom (Redhead, 1997). The demand from restaurants in Britain has helped to establish a small wild mushroom industry in Scotland and attracted collectors with no previous experience (Dyke and Newton, 1999). The potential dangers are that people new to mushrooms collect the wrong species and fail to observe best harvesting practices.

Table 1.6   *Approximate world market value for mycorrhizal mushrooms*

Type	Approximate in-season retail value in USD
Porcini (*Boletus edulis*)	> $250 million
Chantarelle (*Cantharellus cibarius*)	$1.62 billion
Matsutake (*Tricholoma matsutake*)	$500 million
Truffles (*Tuber melonosporum*, *T. magnatum*)	> $300 million

Source: Adapted from Hall et al (2003)

Buyers check quality and identity of species, reducing the risk of mis-identification, but have little or no influence on how mushrooms are picked.

An individual who buys fresh chanterelles, dried porcini or dried morels in a Belgian supermarket will rarely have any idea of where the mushrooms were picked. Collectors in Bulgaria, China and India would be intrigued to find out how much the mushrooms sell for. For the consumer in Belgium wild mushrooms are a culinary delight; for collectors they are a way of living. The benefits of natural resources are rarely shared equally, especially when their value is high, and the poor often benefit least. Yet the amounts earned by collectors can play an important part in sustaining rural livelihoods, and the value of the trade demonstrates the importance of developing integrated forest management plans that give due prominence to mushrooms.

MANAGEMENT

Wild-gathered mushrooms are difficult to manage. The ownership and right of access to forests is often unclear, frequently contested and difficult to police. The discovery of a valuable mushroom or increased trade opportunities often adds to the existing challenges in resolving the needs and priorities of diverse communities of forest users. The nature conservationist in California believes that mushroom harvesting threatens the health of forests (Arora, 2008b); physical violence erupts when villages compete for matsutake in China (Yeh, 2000); and influxes of collectors from outside an area challenge open-access policies to Scandinavian forests (Paal, 1999).

Forest authorities may be reluctant to acknowledge the importance of mushroom collecting and dismiss the rights of local collectors because of encroachment – such fears were expressed in Malawi. Power struggles and vested interests drown out the voice of the poorer rural communities who live next to the forests and whose activities are often blamed for forest losses. However, mushrooms are an opportunity to enhance the value of forests and increase the incentives to maintain standing trees. This is easier said than done: it is more convenient to maintain the ignorance of forest users than enter into long negotiations on how their needs and rights can be accommodated within forest management plans.

Concerns about mushroom collecting centre on its consequences for future harvests. Long-term research in Switzerland shows that mushroom picking does not impair future harvests (Egli et al, 2006), contrary to widely held beliefs. The effect of mushroom collecting on tree health is less well known, but the Swiss research suggests that collecting has little impairment on growth of ectomycorrhizal fungi. A more likely consequence of intense harvesting is damage from trampling. However, the Swiss study also shows that these effects are reversible and the yields recover once pressure from collecting is removed. The implications for mushroom management are clear: rotate areas where collection is permitted.

WHERE DO MUSHROOMS OCCUR?

There are limited data on distribution of mushrooms. Although the general locations where valuable species occur are known, these often cover large areas. The links between ectomycorrhizal mushrooms and trees suggest a novel way to manage mushrooms in forests. Collectors use folk knowledge of where species are likely to occur to locate potential sources of different mushrooms. When plantation forests are established with trees that are known to support edible mushroom species, the value of the forests may increase, although there is no certainty that the edible species will 'grow'. Trees have multiple associations with ectomycorrhizal mushrooms and the conditions which favour one species are poorly understood.

Information about known ectomycorrhizal associates of tree species is sparse. Protocols for validating the associations between a tree and a fungal partner are well established (Brundrett, 2009). The association between known ectomycorrhizal mushrooms and tree species has been summarized in a Canadian study and selected data are shown in Table 1.7. Unpublished data by de Román from the miombo woodlands are shown for comparison in Table 1.8. *Pinus* and *Eucalyptus* are the most planted forestry species and both have endomycorrhizae. *Boletus edulis* in Malawi is an introduction and is not a native species. It is not eaten locally. In neighbouring Tanzania, where many wild mushroom species are eaten, mushrooms with pores are generally avoided (Härkönen et al, 2003).

FOREST USERS

Successful management of mushrooms balances the impact and effects of collection and harvesting against the wider aims of forest management. These aims are influenced

Table 1.7 *Number of mushroom species that form ectomycorrhizae on tree genera in Canada, with edible examples*

Tree	# Fungi	Edible examples
Abies	8	*Lactarius deliciosus*
Alnus	15	*Gyrodon lividus*
Betula	37	*Russula delica, Leccinium scabrum*
Fagus	27	*Russula mairei*
Larix	10	*Suillus flavus*
Picea	64	*Boletus edulis, Tricholoma sulphureum*
Pinus	44	*Lactarius deliciosus, Tuber aestivum*
Populus	3	*Tricholoma scalpturatum*
Pseudotsuga	45	*Cantharellus formosus, Tuber* spp
Quercus	17	*Tuber aestivum*
Salix	4	none

Source: Ectomycorrhizal descriptions database. www.pfc.forestry.ca/cg-bin/edd/catalog.asp. Accessed 29 February 2010.

Table 1.8   *Mushrooms that form ectomycorrhizae on tree species in Malawi*

Tree	Examples
Brachystegia spiciformis	Cantharellus
Brachystegia utilis	Cantharellus
Bridelia micrantha	'Boletoid'
Pinus keysia	Suillus
Protea angolensis	Lactarius
Uapaca kirkiana	Cantharellus, Lactarius, Russula
Uapaca sansibarica	Lactarius, Russula

Source: Unpublished data from Miriam de Román

by the relative importance of different forest uses and their ability to have their claims accepted. Are wild mushrooms more valuable than other NTFPs, for example, and how do they compare in financial benefits to wood production? Some forests have a strategic as well as economic importance: they protect water catchments and fragile sloping land and they help to conserve biodiversity.

The challenge for planners and policy makers is to balance the competing demands on forests and provide a framework within which forest managers can operate effectively. For wild mushrooms this means minimizing the impact of harvesting (mainly that associated with the physical presence of collectors) while allowing collectors fair and equitable access to forests, and addressing the concerns of those who believe that commercial extraction is unsustainable while allowing local enterprises to develop. The sustainable production of wild mushrooms therefore has social, economic and even political dimensions.

Table 1.9 lists some of the concerns and conflicts that arise between different users. Forest managers want to be paid for the right to collect mushrooms; collectors dispute ownership of the forest, claiming it is a free public resource. As the wild mushroom trade expands it is becoming more visible and conflicts are more common. The loss of forests reduces the earning of local communities while influxes of collectors from other areas increase competition for valuable species. In Italy, the owners of woodlands have traditionally allowed free access to wild truffle collectors. They owned the trees but not the soil. Now some are claiming that they own both, having observed the large amounts of money that collectors can earn, although these are a small minority of all licenses granted in any one year.

There is little direct competition between different wild-gathered products unless these are physically part of a tree, for example charcoal makers cut down the trees needed for mushroom production. It is unlikely that collection itself reduces future harvests, although studies in more countries (see Egli et al, 2006) may be necessary to convince people who draw analogies between harvesting plants and harvesting mushrooms (i.e. the more you harvest the less you'll get next time). Conflicts between conservationists and forest users are doggedly pursued in developed countries, where the political power and determination of an urban middle-class concerned about 'biodiversity' leads to emotional rather than rational debate about how to manage forests (Arora, 2008b).

Similar debates also occur in the miombo woodlands. At first NGOs, development professionals and other proxies for forest users attempted to interpret and represent

Table 1.9   *Multiple use of forests and mushroom collecting*

Use	Concerns	Conflicts	Resolution
Timber	Collection interferes with forest management; no payment to forest owners	Collectors dispute ownership and (free) right of access	Manage access, ensure local communities have priority; issue licenses and permits
Fuelwood, charcoal	Removal of branches reduces tree vigour and production of mushrooms	Competition between different forest user groups	Manage access, ensure local communities have priority; issue licenses and permits
Hunting	Incompatible with collecting	Competition between different forest user groups	Schedule activities at different times
Other NTFPs	No direct adverse consequences between different products	Competition with other forest user groups	Regulate access, ensuring local communities have priority
Amenity	Mushroom collecting depletes resource and 'harms forests'; reduces production and diversity of mushrooms	Different viewpoints: forests as extraction resources (jobs, income); and conserved resources (e.g. ecological services, biodiversity)	Obtain good data on impacts of different uses; propose management plans that balance competing needs

Source: Unpublished data from Miriam de Román

the needs of local communities and balance the needs for utilization and conservation. In the last two decades a stronger representation of local communities in such debates has provided a clear articulation of their priorities based on the need to feed families and improve livelihoods.

Conflict resolution also involves the identification of alternative ways to earn money. Cultivating saprobic mushrooms is a popular rural enterprise in China and technologies have been developed that are suitable for small scale production (Oei, 1996).

Case studies from the US and Canada on management of commercially important wild mushrooms describe in more detail how management schemes have evolved in response to emerging concerns (Pilz and Molina, 2002). These studies are particularly useful in describing collectors and collecting practices and they provide a useful contrast to the few studies carried out for subsistence collections in developing countries (Lowore and Boa, 2001).

Developing management plans for large scale collection of wild mushrooms began in earnest with the growth of the commercial trade in the Pacific Northwest. Rules and regulations have been in place in some countries for many years but these were not designed to cope with the scale of extraction seen in North America. Scandinavia has open access: anyone can pick edible fungi as long as they do not harm property. This policy has been challenged by economic migration from neighbouring countries, from the former Soviet Union and the availability of cheap labour for collecting wild mushrooms and wild berries. Similar changes in Eastern Europe have created new opportunities for commercial harvesting and led to concern about unsustainable harvests and how to regulate collections. In Italy each province regulates who has the right to collect truffles (*Tuber* spp). Collectors have to pass a simple test which confirms that they are aware of how and where to harvest. Around 30,000 licenses (each costing around US$90) were issued in Emilia-Romagna in northern Italy in 2001.

In Winema National Park, Oregon, the sale of permits provides a substantial income, although the returns vary considerably. In 1997 the permits were worth US$366,000; four years later this dropped to US$78,000. It is unclear why there should be a decrease in income from licenses. Possible reasons include decreased yields, the affordability of licenses and availability of better sites (Boa, 2004). In Bhutan, only token amounts are earned from the sale of permits (Namgyel, 2000). Local communities also administer permit schemes to limit access to valuable sites, though this appears to be a less successful way of resolving disputes between neighbouring communities.

In Malawi forest officers were concerned that allowing people to collect wild mushrooms in protected forest areas will lead to greater extraction of wood products (Table 1.9), particularly firewood (Lowore and Boa, 2001). Until 2004 there was no officially registered commercial collecting in Malawi and I am not aware of any attempt to introduce a permit system.

The success of regulation schemes depends on who controls or owns forests. It is a relatively simple matter to regulate collections of *Boletus edulis* in commercial pine plantations of South Africa compared to the more complex problems posed by multiple use of native forests in Malawi. The pressure to regulate access to sites comes from various sources, and not all involved in forestry. A strong conservation lobby has sought to limit commercial harvests in the US (McLain et al, 1998).

Logging bans introduced in China, the Philippines, Canada and elsewhere have opened up new opportunities for collecting wild mushrooms and prompted familiar concerns about over-harvesting. In Siberia, the opposite is the case: an increase in logging activities by foreign companies has made it more difficult for local people to collect wild mushrooms (see Boa, 2004, for original references).

RESEARCH NOW AND IN THE FUTURE

The export of *Tricholoma magnivelare* from the Pacific Northwest to Japan began in the late 1980s. Japan's demand for *T. matsutake* had outstripped the capacity of its own forests. Forest areas declined, in part because of the death of pine trees attributed to the pine wilt nematode. *T. magnivelare* had similar properties to the esteemed Japanese species and found in large quantities in Washington, Oregon and British Colombia, where hardly anyone collected it and only Japanese descendants ate it prior to the start of the export trade. A similar story occurred with *T. matsutake* in countries such as North Korea, China and Bhutan: little valued until Japanese buyers appeared (Arora, 2008).

We know more about wild mushrooms and people than ever before. The growth in commercial trade and a stronger interest in international development and management of natural resources have helped expand the research horizon beyond the rich but narrow topics pursued by ethnomycologists. This is an exciting time to be a development mycologist, combining an interest in mushrooms, people and the environment, seeking new knowledge that helps manage a valuable natural resource.

None of this would have been possible, however, without the strong guidance and innovative research pathways that emerged in response to the growth of commercial harvesting in the Pacific Northwest of North America (e.g. Alexander et al, 2002; Pilz and Molina, 2002). When I first came across the publications from this programme I was initially suspicious of how the results could be applied to a project I managed on miombo mushrooms in 1999. These doubts were dispelled when I saw immediate parallels between mushroom collectors and forest managers in Malawi and Oregon.

It has always been difficult to get research funding, and field mycology and the mushroom trade carries little apparent academic kudos. The surprising news is that much has been achieved in improving our knowledge of wild mushrooms. Mycologists play a prominent part in continuing to develop new technologies (Hall et al, 2007) and our understanding of species continues to expand. Despite the earlier criticism of field guides in their characterization of edibility, they are an invaluable help in identifying species and more are published and updated as interest in mushrooms increases.

However, information is missing about the individuals involved in mushroom collecting: what do they do and why do they do it? Collecting mushrooms is only one way to earn money, and the income is highly seasonal. We need to know more about livelihoods and the strategies poor people use to improve the way they live. We need to combine anthropological research methods with the natural science methods familiar to mycologists. A review by Sillitoe (1998) on indigenous knowledge explains the opportunities for integrating natural and social research. Publications mentioned in the previous paragraph and several chapters in this book describe research procedures. All that remains now is for people to go out and discover.

REFERENCES

Ainsworth G. C. (1976) *An Introduction to the History of Mycology*, Cambridge, Cambridge University Press

Alexander, S., Pilz, D., Weber, N. S., Brown, E. and Rockwell, V. A. (2002) 'Mushrooms, trees and money: value estimates of commercial mushrooms and timber in the Pacific Northwest', *Environmental Management* 30, pp129–141

Arora, D. (1991) *All that the rain promises and more. A hip pocket guide to Western mushrooms.* Berkeley, Ten Speed Press

Arora, D. (2008a) The house that matsutake built. *Economic Botany* 62, pp278–290

Arora, D. (2008b). California porcini: three new taxa, observations on their harvest, and the tragedy of no commons. *Economic Botany* 62, pp356–375

Bandala, V. M., Montoya L. and Chapela, I. H. (1997) Wild edible mushrooms in Mexico: a challenge and opportunity for sustainable development, in M. E. Palm and I. H. Chapela (eds) *Mycology in Sustainable Development: Expanding Concepts, Vanishing Borders.* Boone, NC, Parkway Publishers, pp76–90

Boa, E. (2004) *Wild edible fungi: A global overview of their use and importance to people.* Non-wood Forest Products 17, FAO, Rome

Campbell, B. (ed) (1996) *The Miombo in Transition: Woodlands and Welfare in Africa.* Bogor, Indonesia, Centre for International Forestry Research

Dai, Y.-C., Yang, Z.-L., Cui, B.-K., Yu, C.-J. and Zhou, L.-W. (2009) Species diversity and utilization of medicinal mushrooms and fungi in China (review), *International Journal of Medicinal Mushrooms* 11, pp287–302

De Román, M., Boa, E., Woodward, S. (2006) Wild gathered fungi for health and rural livelihoods, *Proceedings of the Nutrition Society,* vol 65, no 2, pp190–197

Dyke, A. J. and Newton, A. C. (1999) Commercial harvesting of wild mushrooms in Scottish forests: Is it sustainable? *Scottish Forestry* 53, pp77–85

Ellen, R. (2008) Ethnomycology among the Nualu of the Moluccas: putting Berlin's 'General Principles' of ethnobiological classification to the test, *Economic Botany* 62, pp483–496

Guisso, K. M. L., Lykke, A. M., Sankara, P. and Guinko, S. (2008) Declining wild mushroom recognition and usage in Burkina Faso. *Economic Botany* 62, pp530–539

Hall, I. R., Brown, G. T. and Zambonelli, A. (2007) *Taming the truffle. The history, lore and science of the ultimate mushroom.* Portland, OR, Timber Press

Hall, I. R., Stephenson, S. Buchanan, P., Wang, Y. and Cole, A. L. J. (2003) *Edible and Poisonous Mushrooms of the World.* Portland, OR, Timber Press

Härkönen, M., Saarimäki, T. and Mwasumbi, L. (1995) Edible mushrooms of Tanzania. *Karstenia* 35 supplement 92

Härkönen, M. (1998) Uses of mushrooms by Finns and Karelians. *International Journal of Circumpolar Health* 40, pp40–55

Härkönen, M., Niemelä, T. and Mwasumbi, L. (2003) *Tanzanian mushrooms. Edible, harmful and other fungi.* Helsinki, Botanical Museum, Finnish Museum of Natural History

Kirk P. M., Cannon, P. F., Minter, D. W. and Stalpers, J. A. (2008) *Dictionary of the Fungi* [10th Edition], Wallingford, UK, CABI

Lowore, J. and Boa, E. (2001) *Bowa markets: local practices and indigenous knowledge of wild edible fungi,* Egham, UK, CABI (available from Boa)

Mao, X. L. (2000) *The Macrofungi of China,* Zhongzhou, Henan, Henan Science and Technology Press

McLain, R., Jones, E. and Liegel, L. (1998) The MAB mushroom study as a teaching case example of interdisciplinary and sustainable forestry research. *Ambio* 9, pp34–35

Morris, B. (1984) Macrofungi of Malawi: some ethnobotanical notes, *Bulletin of the British Mycological Society* 18, pp48–57

Namgyel, P. (2000) 'The story of Buddha mushroom. *Tricholoma matsutake*', Unpublished manuscript, Thimpu, Bhutan, 14 pp

Oei, P. (1996) *Mushrooms cultivation, with special emphasis on appropriate technologies for developing countries,* Leiden, Tool Publications

Paal, T. (1999) Wild berry and mushrooms resources in Estonia and their exploitation. *Metsanduslikud Uurimused* 31, pp131–140

Palm, M. E. and I. H. Chapela (eds) (1997) *Mycology in Sustainable Development: expanding concepts.* Boon, NC, Parkway Publishers

Phillips, R. (2006) *Mushrooms,* London, Macmillian

Piearce, G. D. (1982) *An Introduction to Zambia's wild mushrooms and how to use them,* Zambia, Forest Department

Pilz, D. and Molina, R. (2002) Commercial harvest of edible mushrooms from the forests of the Pacific Northwest United States: issues, management and monitoring for sustainability. *Forest Ecology and Management* 155, pp3–16

Redhead, S. A. (1997) The pine mushroom industry in Canada and the United States: why it exists and where it is going, in I. H. Chapela and M. E. Palm, *Mycology in Sustainable Development: expanding concepts,* Boon, NC, Parkway Publishers, pp15–39

Rubel, W. and Arora, D. (2008) A study of cultural bias in field guide determinations of mushroom edibility using the iconic mushroom, *Amanita muscaria,* as an example, *Economic Botany* 62, pp223–243

Sillitoe, P. (1998) The development of indigenous knowledge: a new applied anthropology, *Current Anthropology* 39, pp223–252

Sitta, N. and Floriani, M. (2008) Nationalization and globalization trends in the wild mushroom commerce of Italy with emphasis on porcini (*Boletus edulis* and allied species), *Economic Botany* 62, pp307–322

Stamets, P. (2000) *Growing Gourmet and Medicinal Mushrooms* [3rd edition] Berkeley, CA, Ten Speed Press

United States Department of Agriculture (USDA) (2009) *Mushroom industry report,* http://usda.mannlib.cornell.edu/MannUsda/viewDocumentInfo.do?documentID=1395

Villarreal, L. and Gomez, A. (1997) Inventory and monitoring wild edible mushrooms in Mexico: challenge and opportunity for sustainable development, in M. E. Palm and I. H. Chapela (eds) *Mycology in Sustainable Development: Expanding Concepts, Vanishing Borders,* Boon, NC, Parkway Publishers, pp99–109

Wasson, V. P. and Wasson, R. G. (1957) *Mushrooms, Russia and History* (2 vols) New York, Pantheon Books

Yeh, E. (2000) Forest claims, conflicts and commodification: the political ecology of Tibetan mushroom-harvesting villages in Yunnan Province, China, *China Quarterly* 161, pp225–278

Zent, E. L. (2008) Mushrooms for live among the Joti of the Venezuelan Guyana, *Economic Botany* 62, pp471–481

How to Collect Fungal Specimens: Key Needs for Identification and the Importance of Good Taxonomy

Xianghua Wang

INTRODUCTION

This chapter focuses on collecting specimens of fungal fruiting bodies (mushrooms). Compared with plants, which have leaves, flowers and fruits, mushrooms have relatively few features to enable classification. Accurate identification relies on features such as spores (colour, size, morphological forms and grain), epidermis (peridium) and ascidium (pitcher-shaped part), which can be observed under a microscope. It is therefore vital to possess good fungal specimens. Detailed guidelines on how to collect, label, store and maintain collections of fungi are available from various sources, including the manual by Baxter and van der Linde (1999), which can be downloaded from www.spc.int/pps/SAFRINET/fung-scr.pdf.

COLLECTING SPECIMENS OF FRUITING BODIES AND FIELD RECORDING

A good fungal specimen should meet the following criteria:

- Fruiting bodies at each stage from immature to fully mature should be included, but avoid collecting over-mature specimens that are decomposing.
- The specimen should be dried thoroughly, retaining as much of the original shape and colour as possible. This can be done in a drying cupboard or near a heater.
- Additional tissue samples from various parts of the fruiting body may need to be preserved. This can be done using 70 to 90 per cent alcohol or a formalin solution with or without glacial acetic acid (see Hawksworth et al (1995) for further suggested solutions).
- The specimen should be properly labelled with detailed information about its place of origin, habitat and the features of the fresh specimen. Photographs and spore prints can be a useful supplement to this information.

- It is important to prevent the specimen from decomposing or being eaten during the drying process.

Collecting

In natural habitats

When collecting fungal specimens that grow on ground surface, directly pulling out the fruiting bodies should be avoided. It is important to carefully cut the contact part between the fruiting body and stroma with a knife, and then observe whether any part of it is buried under ground or connected with something underground. Some fungi species such as *Termitomyces, Phaeocollybia* and *Oudemansiella* have rhizoids, all or part of which may be left behind in the soil if taken carelessly. The stroma of the *Cordyceps* grows from dead insect bodies. In the case of *Cordyceps sinensis*, the host insects are Hepialid moth caterpillars. These are carefully dug from the ground so that the fungus and the caterpillar are removed intact. Special attention should also be paid when collecting specimens that have sclerotia, such as *Polyporus umbellatus* and *Xylaria nigripes*. It is also important to take bed soil connected with fruiting bodies when collecting specimens which grow on rotten wood or ground litter; this helps to retain their shapes and provides references on their growth habits to aid identification. When collecting specimens of mycorrhizal fungi, samples of branches and leaves of symbiotic or associated tree species may also need to be collected to provide additional information.

When collecting specimens of ectomycorrhizal fungi, knowledge on their relationship with tree species is crucial to finding specimens. As discussed in Chapter 7, these species usually grow under trees such as Pinaceae, Fagaceae, Betulaceae and Salicaceae in northern temperate areas; Dipterocarpaceae and Hamamelidaceae in the tropics or south temperate zones; and Leguminosae in African miombo woodland.

Specimens of hypogeous fungi whose fruiting bodies are partly or fully buried beneath the soil are difficult to collect. Guidance of local people familiar with these fungi may be helpful. On the ground surface where some species of the genus *Tuber* such as *T. melanosporum* and *T. indicum* produce their fruiting bodies a large sheet of brûlé, which looks as if hay has been burned by fire, can be found; this is used to determine whether there is truffle produced or not. Hypogeous fungi are usually food to some animals, so burrows or signs of digging may serve as an indicator of where hypogeal fungi may be located.

When collecting specimens, it is better to carry spacious containers that are not liable to bend such as a bamboo or plastic basket. Relatively large or hard specimens may be placed directly in a basket, or a paper bag before being put into the basket to avoid pressing upon or contaminating other species. Small mushrooms (those with a cap (or pileus) less than 3cm) or fragile specimens can be put in a partitioned plastic container (Figure 2.1.A) or a separate box (Figure 2.1.B). In this way their fruiting bodies will not be damaged or squashed. Slimy specimens or those of fruiting bodies that dehydrate easily may be first put into a small, clean plastic bag and then a larger container placed over the fruiting bodies. During the same field trip, if the fungus grows in symbiotic relations with particular tree species, then botanical specimens may be put in the same bag as the fungal specimen to avoid confusion.

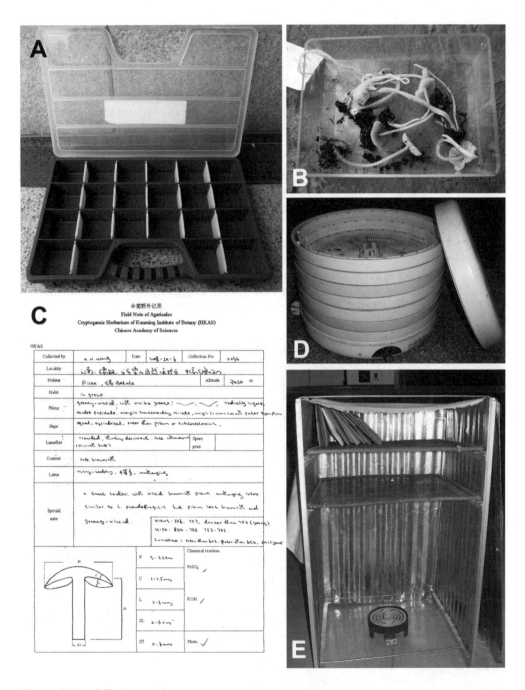

Figure 2.1 *Collecting equipment*

A: Partitioned box for containing small-size specimens; B: Separate plastic box for containing small-size specimens; C: Field record of specimen of the genus Lactarius; D: Temperature-controllable, air-blasting electric drying oven; E: Home-made drying oven using electric heating stove (on the right is the front door of the oven).

During fieldwork, time must be set aside for making records to accompany each specimen. From field experience, when detailed records are required, only four specimens can be dealt with in an hour. Based on this, it can be calculated how much time should be reserved for recording. Normally, when there are many specimens, it is better to finish the collecting and go back to the station no later than 2.00pm. When collecting is finished at dusk and the recording is done in the evening, a poorer quality of record is produced.

In local marketplaces

In many regions in the world, especially areas with high cultural diversity, such as China, Mexico and Thailand, wild fungi are sold in local marketplaces of different sizes (Jones, 1994; Wang and Liu, 2002; Pérez-Moreno et al, 2008). These markets are useful places, not only to obtain specimens, but also for getting to know how local people use fungi (Figure 2.2). From the perspective of scientific research, there is also a chance of coming across rare specimens among the diverse fungi sold in local marketplaces. In the taxonomic literature there are good examples of fungal type specimens discovered in local marketplaces (Chiu, 1948, Petersen and Zang, 1989).

Figure 2.2 *A typical local marketplace in China, where local people are selling a variety of mushrooms*

Photograph: Xinghua Wang

When collecting specimens in markets, in addition to paying attention to the specimens themselves, it is also very important to interview the seller, gatherer or trader to get information on the location and habitat where the specimens were collected. Both fresh and dried specimens are sold in markets. Special attention should be paid when collecting dried material, as fungal specimens do not maintain their original condition after being dried. For example, dried specimens that look as if they belong to only one species may turn out to include specimens of several species. Place of production, purpose of use and name of the location should be recorded from discussions when buying dried specimens in the marketplace. This information can be crucial to identifying them.

Specimens collected in local marketplaces are frequently incomplete, e.g. lacking part of the fruiting bodies such as the cap or stype. For example, in markets in China, the volva of the fruiting bodies of *Amanita* is usually removed, and its volval remnants may easily fall off when touched. The bases of specimens of the genus *Boletus* are also sometimes cut off. This makes examining basal hyphae impossible. Specimens of some species such as *Oudemansiella radicata var. furfuracea* have slimy caps, but the slime may dry off after a long time in the marketplace after collection. All of these factors make identification difficult, so when collecting in marketplaces it is very important to consciously choose specimens that are complete and in good condition. It is also important to collect fruiting bodies at as many stages of maturity as possible.

When surveying fungal resources in markets, normally one is able to identify only some of the species. Beginners may be poorly informed about taxonomical groups. To accurately acquire information such as frequency of appearance, trade volume, name of location, type of use and economic value of different fungi species in markets, a useful methods is to:

* number each fungal species, and record detailed information about them separately; the serial numbers can be replaced with names obtained by identification later;
* record the serial numbers of the photographs as they are taken, and tally them with the specimens (this can be very helpful to identification and later analysis).

If you find differences among specimens but are uncertain whether these are due to them being different species, it is better to collect and number them for correct identification later.

Recording

The recording of fungal specimens includes records of habitats as well as the specimens themselves. Information on growing habits such as types of rotten wood, symbiotic tree species and height above sea level is vital to classification and identification, and should be recorded during collecting in the field. If possible, use a GPS (Global Positioning System) to record information on the collecting location. In addition, because classification of fungi macroscopically is based on features of fresh fruiting bodies, many of which (e.g. colour, texture and size) change when dried, it is necessary to record in detail all the important features while the specimens are still fresh.

The recording of fresh features of fruiting bodies should be done in daylight on the day of collecting, or under white fluorescent light with enough light intensity in the evening. If the texture of the cap surface possesses special features (e.g. sticky or water-soaked) this should be recorded immediately while collecting. Before recording, one may tie a tag on mature fruiting bodies and add a number to it in pencil. The size records of fruiting bodies should be based on mature specimens. For colour records, there are two chromatograms for reference: Kornerup and Wanscher (1967) and Ridgway (1912). The tissue of the fruiting bodies may be tasted when recording, and then spat it out and the mouth rinsed (note: beginners may not know which species are poisonous; it is very important for them to remember this and act accordingly). Spore prints should be collected before or after making records on the day of collecting. Aluminium foil can be used for spore prints, because it does not absorb water, shows colour clearly and can be numbered with a pencil. To make a spore print, the best method is to take part or all of the cap, apothecium or parts connected with the gleba (the fleshy spore-bearing inner part of puffballs and stinkhorns) and turn them upside-down on the foil. Let them stand for 12 to 24 hours, move the tissue, observe and record the colour of the spore print, and then fold the foil and put it in a strong paper bag. For material which does not have thick enough spore powder, it is better to use a pencil to delimit the scope with spore print for later verification (Bridson and Formen, 1998).

Record paper should be in duplicate, one for the gatherer to keep and the other to be placed with the specimen. When recording in field, the record may be photocopied or transcribed in the laboratory. It is best to use a soft (2B) pencil for recording, so that the writing will not fade when soaked or after time has passed. Figure 2.1.C shows a field record of a specimen of the genus *Lactarius*.

Drying

Ideally, the specimens should be dried immediately after recording is completed. Small specimens or those used for extracting DNA may be dried with silica gel, first wrapping the fruiting bodies in absorbent paper and then putting them in a zip-lock bag with silica gel. Sun-drying specimens may seem suitable, but is not recommended: the temperature is not high enough to kill worm ova in the specimens, which may later destroy them.

Unlike collections of plant specimens, which are put in a plant press for drying, fungal specimens must be dried using an electric drier. Hard, tough specimens may be dried whole, while bigger and fleshy ones such as boleti may be sliced vertically into two or more pieces before drying. Small specimens should be placed on tissue paper or packed with it before being put under the drier to prevent them falling off through holes in the grid of the drier. Specimens of *Gasteromycetales* whose spores have already been released should be packed in air-permeable paperbags before being put under the drier to avoid the spores contaminating other specimens. When laying out specimens under the drier, those with distinct features may be put together while those with similar features should be separated to avoid difficulties in distinguishing them after drying.

In choosing drying equipment, a temperature-controllable electric drying oven with an internal fan used for drying fruits (Figure 2.1.D) is a good choice. One may also make a drying oven using an electric heater (Figure 2.1.E). It is better to keep the temperature at around 50 to 60°C; in addition to helping maintain the original shapes of the specimens, this will kill worm ova. The specifications for making a drying oven are that should be 60 to 80cm high with a square cross-section of 30 to 40cm edge length. Four to five layers of metallic grid are inside the drier with a 10 to 12cm space in between. Specimens are placed at a distance of 40 to 80cm from the heater.

When drying, place the drier on even ground and use an electric heater (300W capacity) or a kerosene stove if electricity is not available. Cover the top of the drier with a cloth, and adjust the temperature according to the size of the opening. After drying specimens should be packed in bags immediately and placed in containers that are pressure- and breakage-proof.

Preserving

Specimens should be kept as dry as possible before preservation. Those that are dried in the field, especially big fleshy ones, often get damp when taken back to the laboratory. Therefore, before putting them into a permanent collection, check them to make sure they are sufficiently dry. Some institutes require that specimens be frozen beforehand. It should be kept in mind that specimens need to be packed in air-tight plastic bags before being frozen. When removing them from refrigerators, it is better not to take them out of the bags before the temperature returns to normal level or they are liable to get damp. In most cases, people use paper boxes to contain specimens. These are good for preserving the shapes of fruiting bodies. Placing specimens in paper bags and then putting the paper bags into plastic bags is the preferable technique. This effectively keeps moisture out and ensures that tissues of specimens can be better recovered during observation (Bridson and Forman, 1998). For tiny fruiting bodies, it is better to put them in small bags to prevent them being lost. They can then be placed in the standard sized bags used in the collection.

TAXONOMY

Identification

The purpose of identification is to find a correct scientific name for a specimen. With fungi, however, many species still need to be formally classified. In some cases all that may be possible as an interim measure is to find the name of a closely related species based on the features of the specimen, published literature and cross-checking with lists of current names (such as the *Index Fungorum*, www.indexfungorum.org).

In order to achieve an accurate identification, one should have a good knowledge of taxonomy, detailed records of the specimen's diagnostic characteristics, be able to carry out meticulous microscopic work and have access to as much of the relevant literature as possible. Making records of the diagnostic characteristics of fungi has been discussed earlier in this chapter. Microscopic work and the use of peer-reviewed publications are discussed in the following sections.

Meticulous microscopic work

To identify fungal specimens, microscopic observation and recording are important. In modern fungal taxonomy research, more and more microscopic features need to be observed, and the measurement data about each part of the specimen is getting increasingly accurate. Only through observing the features for classification as fully as possible can current literature effectively help identification. Meticulous microscopic work includes skilled microscopical preparation, thorough observation and recording, and micrography. Figure 2.3 shows a record written during microscopic observation of specimens of *Lactarius.*

Spores are very useful for identification. In many ways they are the 'identification cards' of fungi. Related features of spores include: colour, size, morphological forms and pattern of the surface. In distilled water or potassium hydroxide solution (KOH), colour spores can be directly observed without dying, while colourless spores need to be dyed before observation (Congo red or Melzer's Reagent are normally used for this purpose). Observation should begin strictly from the side of the spore; beginners usually judge the spore to be broader and rounder than it actually is, due to an incorrect observation angle. The epidermis and hymenophore are playing an increasingly important part in identification and classification, so they should also be given attention. In basidiomycetes, clamp connections are also used as index for classification, for example in identifications of specimens of *Amanita, Ramaria, Tricholoma, Cantharellus/Craterellus* and *Sarcodon* (Corner, 1967; Singer, 1986; Petersen and Zang, 1989; Stalpers, 1993; Yang, 2005).

Microscopic observation of fungal specimens does not require complicated slicing methods. Free hand slicing is usually sufficient. Use tweezers to nip a small piece of cap or gleba and put it in the reagent, then it is ready for observation. When slicing for epidermal features of fruiting bodies, such as epidermals of the cap, stipe or peridium, it should be noted that the blade should be perpendicular to the surface, so it is better to slice along the stem or vertically. When it is not easy to separate the hyphae, it is best to use one head of the tweezers to knock lightly on the slide glass. This can help recover shrunken, intumescent hyphae (Yang, 2005).

Spores of fungi are usually small (2–15 (30) μm) and their hyphae and walls are thin, so observations should be carried out under a magnification of 10×100 times. Microscope slides can be prepared for this purpose. Under a magnification of 10×40 times, details normally cannot be seen clearly, resulting in inaccurate measurements of each part. When using a microscope to observe fungal tissue, one should be always attentive to the size of diaphragm of the microscope. A big aperture is useful for observing spores with a grainy surface, but adjustment to a smaller aperture is needed when observing layers of hyphae. An alternative is to use a phase contrast microscope, which can highlight the walls of hyphae or of transparent spores without having to dye them. Microscopic observation should be done quickly, because the shapes of hyphae may change and eventually lose their value for identification when the tissue is placed under the medium for a long time.

BOX 2.1 SOME NOMENCLATURAL PROBLEMS RELATED TO EDIBLE AND MEDICINAL FUNGI

Some of the complexities of naming macro-fungi are illustrated by three Asian examples.

Cordyceps sinensis

The caterpillar fungus, *Cordyceps sinensis*, was described in the 19th century on the basis of a type specimen bought in a local marketplace in China. The stroma of the type specimen was immature and spores could not be seen. This resulted in taxonomic confusion, with descriptions of separate 'species' from different localities such as Gansu, China and Nepal. After comparing several specimens collected in Tibet with type specimens of these 'species' from Gansu and Nepal, Liu et al (2003) believe that the features of these species are not essentially different from those of *C. sinensis*, so these species should be considered as synonyms. A further complication is that *C. sinensis* produces telemorphs and anamorphs (usually in the form of mould). As a result, according to the rules of nomenclature, this species is allowed to have two names to respectively represent its telemorph and anamorph states (*Cordyceps sinensis* is the name for telemorph while *Hirsutella sinensis* is the name for the anamorph). Recent renaming of *C. sinensis* as *Ophiocordyceps sinensis* by Sung et al (2007) adds to this complexity.

Taiwanofungus camphorates

Taiwanofungus camphorates is a rare medicinal fungus found in Taiwan, China. After Zang and Su (1990) published a new species *Ganoderma camphoratum* based on the type of specimen of *Taiwanofungus camphorates* collected in Taiwan, Chang et al (1995) published a new species *Antrodia cinnamomea* T. which also refers to *Taiwanofungus camphorates*. Based on the genealogical research result of DNA sequence, Wu et al (2004) categorized *Taiwanofungus camphorates* in a new genus called *Taiwanofungus* using *G. camphoratum* as type. Thus, *T. camphorates* is the name that should be adopted currently, and *G. camphoratum* is nomenclatural synonym and *A. cinnamomea* is taxonomic synonym.

Tricholoma matsutake

Research found that the well-known and commercially important fungus, *Tricholoma matsutake*, is the same species as *T. nauseosum*, a name now used as the taxonomic synonym. However the former's basionym *Armillaria matsutake* (Ito and Imai, 1925) appeared later than the latter's basionym *A. nauseosum* (Blytt, 1909). Compared with *Armillaria matsutake* S., however, *A. nauseosum* is not widely used. For stable use of names, it is necessary to keep the latter name. Based on this, Ryman et al (2000) proposed to retain the use of *T. matsutake*. This suggestion was adopted by the latest rules of the ICBN (Appendix IV, p424, see Zhang, 2007).

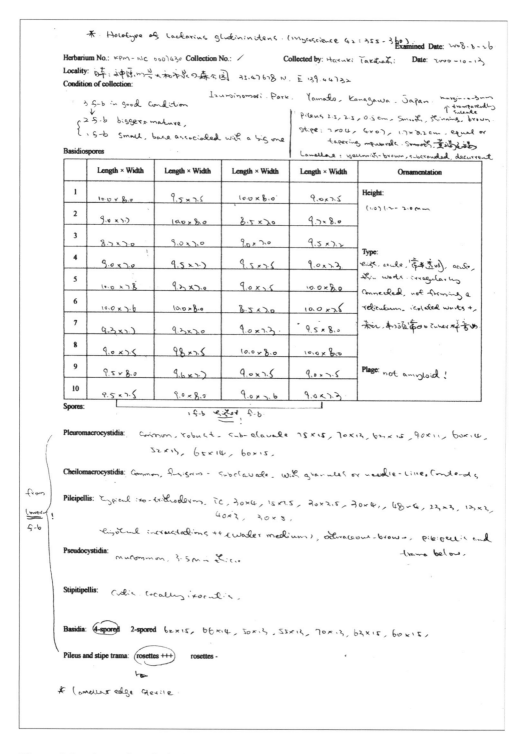

Figure 2.3   *A record made during microscopic observation of specimens of* Lactarius

Drawing pictures of the distinctive microscopic shapes and features of spores is a useful way of recording features that are difficult to describe. Drawing can be done through the diagraph tube installed on the microscope. If there is no such tool, one should check and correct the size drawn on paper through an ocular micrometre from time to time to avoid deviation between the actual image and the drawn one. If drawing spores, the magnification should be between 3000 and 5000 times, i.e. 1cm on paper corresponds to 2–3µm of the object; as for hyphae, 1000–2000 would be better.

Instruments and materials needed for microscopic work on fungi are:

- a microscope with an ocular micrometer;
- a double-sided razor blade for slicing;
- three different reagents: five per cent KOH solution for recovering the tissues of dry specimens; Melzer's Reagent to determine whether there is amylaceous reaction on the surface of spores (see Hawksworth et al, 1995); and Congo Red Solution, with a concentration suitable for observation purpose.

Literature for identification

The amount of literature for identification is enormous, and cannot all be listed here. A short list of recommended literature follows (full citations can be found in the References at the end of this chapter):

- World Fungi: Arora (1986); Laessoe (2002); Hall et al (2004).
- Fungi in China: Ying, J. et al (1982, 1987); Institute of Biology (1979).
- Fungi in Japan: Imazeki et al (1988), Hongo (1957), Hongo (1967) and Hongo & Izawa (1994).
- Fungi in Europe: Jordan and Wheeler (2005); Phillips (2006).
- Fungi in North America: Miller and Miller (2006).
- For keys to identify specimens of *Agarics*, refer to Moser (1983).

Procedure for identification

Identification is a process where one learns through experience. Beginners may learn to categorize some specimens based on their appearance or microscopic features, such as Ascomycetes, Basidiomycetes, Agaricales and *Polyporus*. Referring to the colour of spore prints is very useful in identification of Agaricales specimens. As discussed above, microscopic features can be obtained through microscope observations. One may take both the appearance and the microscopic features of the specimen into consideration and look them up in relevant index forms, and then identify the specimen to the generic level and then, ideally, to species. It often occurs that features for classification described in the literature, such as pattern of epidermis of caps, are not seen in initial phases of microscopic observation. At this point, observation should be started again, as speculation usually leads to incorrect identification. Useful fungi often belong to fairly well-known genera or species, so reading good field guides can speed up the identification process. Following up on the likely species from field guides with other relevant literature, and then carefully comparing the features of the specimens with descriptions in the literature, are useful steps in the identification process.

Nomenclature

Nomenclature is an important part of taxonomy. Scientific names should be adopted according to the current International Code of Botany (ICBN). The purpose of the ICBN is to give each taxonomic group a unique and stable name. Knowledge of nomenclature also has a practical value: it aids understanding the research results of genealogical taxonomy, comparing and analysing different names used in different literatures, and avoiding using outdated names. Problems concerning correct naming of wild fungi are very common. In some cases, as the *Index Fungorum* shows, synonyms are common. Box 2.1 lists some nomenclatural problems related to fungi.

Applications of taxonomy

Taxonomic knowledge is not only important from a scientific point of view, but also has practical applications. A good example is the need to distinguish between poisonous fungi and edible fungi. Most cases of deaths caused by eating fungi in China resulted from toxic *Amanita* species (Yang, 2005). If correctly identified, then many fatalities would be avoided, although some edible species such as *Amanita caesaria* and *A. manginiana* are difficult to identify on account of their similar morphology to other *Amanita* species (Yang, 2005). Among 250 species of *Psilocybe*, 150 have a hallucinogenic effect (Guzman, 2008); knowledge of how to identify them would help people avoid eating these hallucinogenic mushrooms by mistake. Fungi of genetically related groups share similar chemical elements (Liu Jikai, 2004), so it is possible that genetic relationships among different fungi can guide our knowledge of their chemistry. In *Psilocybe*, for example, the species containing the hallucinogen psilocybin can be distinguished from those which do not contain psilocybin based on the genetic relationships within this genus (Moncalvo et al, 2002; Maruyama et al, 2006).

Taxonomic knowledge also enables us to have a better understanding of the ecological habits of numerous fungi. Species of many genus of fungi share the same ecological habits: species of the genus *Termitomyces* live in symbiotic relations with termites; species of *Cordyceps* live in insect bodies (Figure 2.4). Species of Russulaceae, Boletaceae, Cantharellaceae and Tuberaceae are all ectomycorrhizal fungi, and species of Lentinaceae and Polyporaceae (in its narrow sense) are all saprophytes. Taxonomic understanding requires some ecological knowledge of these fungi as well; this can help determine quickly the degree of difficulty and methods of domestication of some fungi and understand the roles these fungi play in terrestrial ecosystems.

Taxonomic research based on accurate identifications also plays a significant part in assessing and comparing the application status of fungi in different communities. It also provides insights through comparisons of useful fungi in different regions of the world. For example, comparing fungi sold in markets in Yunnan Province, China, and Mexico, it is found that both markets shared 23 genera of fungi, which comprise 33.3 per cent and 62.2 per cent of the total of known genera in two markets respectively.

The application of molecular biology in taxonomic research has changed some traditional concepts and scopes of taxonomic groups. Splitting and merging has taken place in some taxa. Great changes have also occurred in understanding genetic

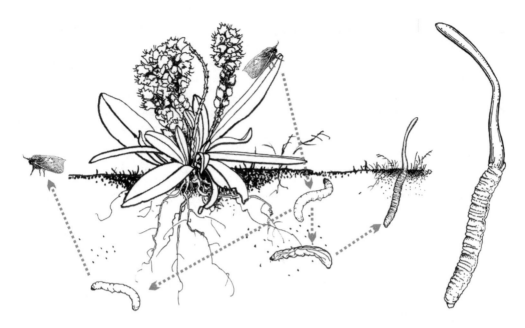

Figure 2.4   *The complex life-cycle of the entomophagous medicinal fungus,* Cordyceps sinensis

relationships among different taxonomic groups. Hawksworth (2005) discusses problems related to these changes.

Folk taxonomy

Local people have classified and named useful fungi for centuries and (as is discussed in Chapter 3), folk taxonomy is an important area for ethnomycological research. Local names are given for a range of reasons, with folk classification based on:

Morphological features of fruiting bodies

This is the most common basis for local names, based on:

- shape, e.g. species of *Ramaria* are called 'Sao Zou Jun' (Broom Fungus) (Wang Xianghua et al, 2004; Pérez-Moreno et al, 2008) in both China and Mexico;
- colour, e.g. a species of *Cantharellus* is called 'Ji You Jun' (chicken oil fungi) because the fruiting bodies are yellow, the colour of chicken oil;
- texture, e.g. species of *Boletus* are called 'deer liver' or 'liver fungi' in Mexico, while in China they are called 'NiuGan Jun' (ox liver fungi), which refers to the texture of the fruiting bodies.

Ecological factors

- Some species of the genus *Russula* are called 'Li Shu Qing' (oak green), indicating that they grow under plants of the family Fagaceae.

- The rare medicinal fungus *Taiwanofungus camphorates* is called 'Niu Zhang Zhi' since it grows on *Cinnamomum kanehirai* (Wu et al, 1997).
- Some species of the genus *Tricholoma* are called 'Song Mao Jun' in Yunnan province, China, meaning they grow under pine trees. The local names of Mexican *Hebeloma* species refer to pine needles.
- *Cordyceps sinensis* is called 'Chong Cao' (grass of insects), indicating that it grows on insect bodies.

How the fungi were found

In some areas of Sichuan Province, China, some species of *Tuber* are called 'Zhu Gong Jun' ('pig rooting fungi'). These are hypogeous fungi and their ascocarps grow underground, but they were discovered when pigs were rooting about for food.

Fruiting time

In Yunnan, species of *Lactarius sect. deliciosi* of the genus *Lactarius* fruit when rice is ready for harvest, so they are called 'GuShu Jun' ('rice ripe fungi'). Also in Yunnan, in the Jing Dong area, *Lyophyllum decastes* is called 'JiuYueGu' ('September mushroom') meaning it fruits in September (Liu P., 1993).

Relationships between formal scientific taxonomy and folk taxonomy

Folk taxonomy and Linnaean taxonomy share certain parallels, due to the fact that both systems are based on similarities in morphological features. Summarizing the relationships between the two can help us learn from previous experience of fungal resources used in daily life and better identify and use these fungi.

Although there are a lot of synonyms and homonyms in folk taxonomy and nomenclature, coincidences with scientific taxonomy can be found in classifications based on local names. A typical example is *Lactarius*. Species of this genus are often called 'Nai Jiang Jun', meaning in the fruiting bodies there is milk (*naijiang*). As this genus is one of the few groups of agarics that produce a milky liquid, the folk classification actually reflects the genetic relationship of these fungi. Interestingly, some species with little milk but also belonging to *Lactarius* such as *L. deliciosus* and *L. hatsudake* are called 'GuShu Jun' according to its fruiting time, the time when rice is ripe, in Yunnan, China. In scientific taxonomy, 'GuShu Jun' exactly tallies with the scope of *L. sect. deliciosi*. Another example is the classification and naming of boleti. In Yunnan, some species of *Boletus* are called 'JianShou Qing'. All of them are species of *B.* subsect. *Calopodes* and *B.* subsect. *luridi*. Those species of *B. sect. Boletus* whose fruiting bodies do not change colour when damaged are not called 'JianShou Qing'.

Besides providing valuable information of taxonomic characteristics, folk taxonomy can also provide information related to habitat. For example, *L. strigellus* of the genus *Lentinus* is called 'Zhu Gen Jun' ('Bamboo Root Fungus'), meaning it grows on bamboo seeds. Species of *Cortinarius tenuipes* are called 'Huang Li Wo' in the southern Yunnan, indicating they grow under trees of the family Fagaceae.

BOX 2.2 SYNONYMS AND HOMONYMS IN THE LOCAL NAMES OF EDIBLE FUNGI

Due to the fact that there are fewer local names than scientific names, some local names include species of several groups. Synonyms and homonyms are very common in the folk taxonomy of fungi in China. As a result, there are good opportunities for ethnomycological research on folk taxonomy using the methods described in Chapter 3.

A typical example for homonyms is *Ji Cong* (*Termitomyces albuminosus*). At least five genera of fungi are linked to this name:

- Ji Cong: Including all species of the genus *Termitomyces*, which are often further characterized by descriptive terms such as Huang Pi ('yellow skin') Ji Cong, DaGuo ('big fruit') Ji Cong, etc.
- (Lu) Shui ('dew') Ji Cong: This name refers to *Oudemansiella radicata* var. *furfuracea*. The base of the fruiting bodies of this species has rhizoids (small branching hyphae that anchor the fruiting body), similar to species of *Termitomyces albuminosus*. The cap is usually slimy, hence the reference to 'dew'.
- You ('oil') Ji Cong: Also refers to *Oudemansiella radicata* var. *furfuracea* because the slime on its cap looks oily.
- Cao ('grass') Ji Cong: There are two groups with this name. One includes *A. manginiana* and *A. pseudoporphyria* in the genus *Amanita*, which are both edible; *Cao Ji Cong* in markets mainly refers to these species. The second group is *I. fastigiata* and *I. flavobrunnea* in the genus *Inocybe*, also called *Cao Mao Jun* ('grass cap fungi') or *Ji Cong Hua* ('flower'). These are poisonous, but have been seen in markets in central Yunnan, China.
- Ma MuJi (Cong): This is *A. sinensis* of the genus *Amanita*, which can be seen in markets in Simao, Pu'er city, Yunnan, China.
- Bo Pi ('peeled') Ji Cong: This refers to *C. cf. variecolor* of the genus *Cortinarius*.

A typical example of a synonym is *T. indicum* of the genus *Tuber*. It is also called 'Song Mao Fu Ling', indicating that it grows in pine forests, in the Chuandian region, southwestern China. The name 'Wu NiangTeng' indicates that evidence of direct contact between its ascocarp and creatures around cannot be found. 'Zhu Gong Jun' is a specimen discovered when pigs are rooting about for food. 'Mei Hei' means the color of the ascocarp is black (Chen Juan, 2007).

CONCLUSION: THE FUTURE OF FUNGAL TAXONOMY

Professional fungal taxonomic research requires many years of experience. As discussed earlier, the characteristics of fresh specimens are important for taxonomy and identification. However, fungal taxonomists also need good field experience before the characteristics of fresh specimens are fully understood. Meanwhile, it is also necessary for those engaged in this field to be able to use microscopes expertly to make correct judgments, observation and analysis of different microscopic features. Only through long experience can one grasp what to focus on during recording, observation and analysis.

Compared with existing plant taxonomical research results, no matter in what scope or depth, world fungal taxonomy research still lags behind (Hawksworth, 2001). There are no global monographs on many taxonomic groups. In a lot of world regions, especially those tropical regions where fungal species are most plentiful and distinct, taxonomic research is limited (Hawksworth, 1998). When identifying the specimens in these regions, one would find that a lot of species have not been described, and often one could only adopt names of genetically-close species or even the wrong names for them. Among an estimated 1.5 million types of fungi, only between 12,000 and 74,000 have been described and, on average, only 1100 new species are described annually (Hawksworth, 2003). Although molecular biology has facilitated the development of fungal identification and classification, accurate knowledge on numerous and complex fungal species relies on long-term collaborations and the efforts of mycologists around the world (Hawksworth, 2003). For this reason, close networks of policy support for this process are essential (Chapter 9).

REFERENCES

Arora, D. (1986) *Mushrooms Demystified: A Comprehensive Guide to the Fleshy Fungi* (2nd edition), Ten Speed Press, Berkeley, CA

Baxter, A. P and van der Linde, E. (1999) *Collecting and preserving fungi: A manual for mycology*, SAFRINET/BioNet–International, National Collection of Fungi, Pretoria, South Africa, www.spc.int/pps/SAFRINET/fung-scr.pdf, accessed 10 June 2010

Bridson, D. and Forman, L. (1998) *The Herbarium Handbook*, Kew Gardens, Royal Botanic Gardens, London

Chen, J. (2006) 'Research on *Tuber* Species in China', Unpublished PhD thesis, Chinese Academy of Sciences

Chiu, W. F. (1948) 'The Boletes of Yunnan', *Mycologia*, vol 40, no 2, pp199–231

Corner, E. J. H. (1966) *A monograph of Cantharelloid Fungi*, New York, Oxford University Press

Courtecuesse, R. and Duhem, B. (1995) *Mushrooms and Toadstools of Britain and Europe*, Italy, Harper-Collins

Guzmán, G. (2008) 'Hallucinogenic mushrooms in Mexico: An overview', *Economic Botany*, vol 62, no 3, pp404–412

Hall, I., Stephenson, S. L., Buchanan, P. K., Wang, Y. and Cole, A. L. J. (2004) *Edible and Poisonous Mushrooms of the World*, New Zealand Institute for Crop and Food Research Limited, Christchurch

Hawksworth, D. L. (1998) 'Getting to grips with fungal biodiversity in the tropics', in C. H. Chou and K. T. Shao (eds) *Frontiers in Biology: The Challenges of Biodiversity, Biotechnology and Sustainable Agriculture*, Academia Sinica, Taipei

Hawksworth, D. L. (2001) 'The magnitude of fungal diversity: The 1.5 million species estimate revisited', *Mycol. Res.*, vol 105, no 12, pp1422–1432

Hawksworth, D. L. (2003) 'Monitoring and safeguarding fungal resources worldwide: The need for an international collaborative Mycoaction Plan', *Fungal Diversity* 13, pp29–45

Hawksworth, D. L. (2005) 'Reflections on changing names and related nomenclatural issues in edible and medicinal mushrooms', *International Journal of Medicinal Mushrooms*, vol 7, pp29–38

Hawksworth, D. L., Kirk, P. M., Sutton, B. C. and Pegler, D. N. (1995) Ainsworth & Bisby's dictionary of the fungi (8th edition) CAB International, Oxford

Hongo, T. (1957) *Notes on Japanese larger fungi(I)*, Osaka, Japan

Hongo, T. (1967) *Notes on Japanese larger fungi (II)*, Osaka, Japan

Hongo, T. and Izawa, M. (1994) *Yama-kei Field Books Fungi*, Yama-kei Publishers, Tokyo

Institute of Microbiology, Chinese Academy of Sciences (1979) *Poisonous Mushrooms* (2nd edition), Science Press, Beijing

Imazeki, R., Otani, Y. and Hongo, T. (1988) *Fungi of Japan*, Yama-kei Publishers, Tokyo

Jiang, Y. and Yao, Y. J. (2002) Names related to *Cordyceps sinensis* anamorph, *Mycotaxon* 84, pp245–254

Jones, E. B. G., Whalley, A. J. S. and Hywel-Jones, N. L. (1994) 'A fungus foray to Chiang Mai market in Northern Thailand', *Mycologist*, vol 8, no 2, pp87–90

Jordan, P. and Wheeler, S. (2005) *The practical mushroom encyclopedia*, Hermes House, London

Kirk, P. M., Cannon, P. F., David, J.C. and Stalpers, J. A. (2001) *Dictionary of the Fungi* (9th edition) CABI Publishing, Wallingford

Kornerup, A. and Wanscher, J. H. (1967) *Methuen handbook of colour*, Methuen, London

Læssøe, R. (2002) *Mushrooms*, DK Publishing, New York

Liu, J. (2004) *Biologically active substances from higher fungi*, University of Science and Technology of China Press, Beijing

Liu, P. (1993) 'Introduction of a Valuable edible fungi–Lyophyllumshimeji', *Edible Fungi of China*, vol 12, no 2, p29

Liu, Z., Liang, Z. and Xin, Z. (2003) *Microscopic re-observation of Cordyceps sinensis and study of its ascosporal development*, Guizhou Science 1–2, pp51–68

Maruyama, T., Kawahara, N., Yokoyama, K., Makino, Y., Fukiharu, T. and Goda, Y. (2006) 'Phylogenetic relationship of psychoactive fungi based on rRNA gene for a large subunit and their identification using the TaqMan assay (II)', *Forensic Science International*, vol 163, nos 1–2, pp51–58

Miller, O. K. and Miller, H. H. (2006) *North American Mushrooms*, Globe Pequot Press, Guilford

Moncalvo, J. M., Vilgalys, R., Redhead, S. A., Johnson, J. E., James, T. Y., Aime, M. C., Hofstetter, V., Verduin, S. J. W., Larsson, E., Baroni, T. J., Thorn, R. G., Jacobsson, S., Clemencon, H. and Miller, O. K. (2002) 'One hundred and seventeen clades of euagarics', *Mol. Phylogenet. Evol.* 23, pp357–400

Moser, M. (1983) *Keys to Agarics and Boleti*, Roger Phillips, London

Pérez-Moreno, J., Martínez-Reyes, M., Yescas-Pérez, A., Delgado-Alvarado, A. and Xoconostle-Cázares, B. (2008) 'Wild Mushroom Markets in Central Mexico and a Case Study at Ozumba', *Economic Botany*, vol 62, no 3, pp425–436

Petersen, R. H. and Zang, M. (1989) *Ramaria* Subgenera *Ramaria* and *Laeticolora* in Yunnan, *Act. Bot. Yunnanica*, vol 11, no 4, pp363–396

Phillips, R. (2006) *Mushrooms*, Pan Macmillan, London

Ridgway, R. (1912) *Color standards and color nomenclature*, Washington, DC

Ryman, S., Bergius, N. and Danell, E. (2000) 'Proposal to conserve the name *Armillaria matsutake* against *Armillaria nauseosa* (Fungi, Basidiomycotina, Tricholomataceae)', *Taxon* 49, pp555–556

Singer, R. (1986) *The Agaricales in Modern Taxonomy*, Hafner Publishing Co., New York

Stalpers, J. A. (1993) 'Keys to the species of the Thelephorales', *Studies in Mycology*, no 35

Sung, G. H., Sung, J. M., Hywel-Jones, N. L., Luangsa-ard, J. J., Shrestha, B. and Spatafora, J. W. (2007) 'Phylogenetic classification of *Cordyceps* and the clavicipitaceous fungi', *Studies in Mycology* 57, pp5–59

Wang, X. and Liu, P. (2002) 'Resources investigation and studies on the wild commercial fungi in Yunnan', *Biodiversity*, vol 10, no 3, pp318–325

Wang, X., Yu, F. and Liu, P. (2004) *Color Atlas of Wild Commercial Mushrooms in Yunnan*, Yunnan Science and Technology Publishing House, Kunming

Wu, S. H., Ryvarden, L. and Chang, T. T. (1997) '*Antrodia camphorata* ("niu-chang-chih"), a new combination of a medicinal fungus in Taiwan', *Bot. Bull. Acad. Sin.*, 38, pp273–275

Wu, S. H., Yu, Z. H., Dai, Y. C., Chen, C. T., Su, C. H., Chen, L. C., Hsu, W. C. and Hwang, G. Y. (2004) '*Taiwanofungus*, a polypore new genus', *Fung. Sci.*, vol 19, no 3–4, pp109–116

Yang, Z. (2005) 'Mycophyta of China', *27th Amanitaceae*. Science Press, Beijing

Ying, J., Zhao, J. and Mao, X. (1982) *Edible Mushrooms*, Science Press, Beijing

Ying, J., Mao, X., Ma, Q., Zong, Y. and Wen, H. (1987) *Chinese Medical Fungi*, Science Press, Beijing

Zang, M. and Su, Q. (1990) '*Ganoderma comphoratum*, a new taxon in genus *Ganoderma* from Taiwan, China', *Acta Bot Yunnan*, vol 12, no 4, pp395–396

Zhang, L. (2007) *International Code of Botanical Nomenclature – the 'Vienna Code'* [in Chinese] Science Press, Beijing

A Primer on Ethnobiological Methods for Ethnomycological Research: Studying Folk Biological Classification Systems

Egleé L. Zent and Stanford Zent

INTRODUCTION

Ethnomycology is part of a broader discipline, ethnobiology, which is dedicated to the study of the dynamic relationships among people, biota and environments. Yet the distinctive local knowledge systems, practices and uses of the fungi kingdom by human populations to date make up a tiny portion of the total subject matter of ethnobiological research performed worldwide. Fungi are fascinating bioforms that provoke diverse, and sometimes starkly opposed, reactions among different peoples. Viewpoints oscillate between use and avoidance, food and poison, mundane and ritual, divine and demonic, beautiful and hideous creatures. Considering the extreme variation in the types of material and in the symbolic interactions between human cultural groups and fungal taxa, it would seem that this subject offers a potentially rich and largely untapped opportunity for future scientific investigation. Furthermore, the proliferation of well-designed, in-depth studies of human–fungi relationships could make a substantial contribution, at both empirical and theoretical levels, to the continuing development of ethnobiology as a whole. It is suggested here that many field methods currently used in ethnobiology are relevant for ethnomycological research and the realization of this potential application could have an invigorating effect on the development of the subfield.

Ethnobiology may well be regarded as an interdisciplinary field, the unique development of which has been shaped by a creative mix of philosophies of knowledge, theoretical positions and research strategies borrowed from different scientific disciplines. The list of affiliated disciplines that have directly influenced lines of ethno-biological research includes cultural anthropology, archaeology, linguistics, cognitive psychology, geography, systematics, population biology, ecology, conservation biology, pharmacology, nutrition, economics and ethics. Therefore, becoming familiar with the basic concepts and methods of these disciplines is an important ingredient in preparation and planning for ethnobiological research. The proper selection of a specific methodological package depends upon individual research aims and priorities, whether cognitive, economic, religious, aesthetic, practice-oriented or otherwise. In this and the following chapter (Chapter 4) we suggest a broad variety of field methods derived mainly from ethnobiology and its affiliated disciplines, most of which have had little impact on ethnomycological research to date. One of our objectives is to stimulate prospective ethnomycological researchers to try out some of the methods described here in their future investigations of human–fungi interactions.

This chapter focuses on cognitive techniques for studying folk biological classification systems. Many of the methods discussed here were developed as part of the ethnoscientific approach to cultural description and were modified over the years to fit the circumstances of ethnobiological research. As a way of practising ethnography, ethnoscience puts an emphasis on the study of a given society's folk classifications – the particular ways of classifying its material and social universe – with the goal of representing accurately the native's point of view (Sturtevant, 1964). A hallmark of the ethnoscientific method is the use of explicit, systematic and replicable techniques for data collection and analysis (Metzger and Williams, 1966). While local language and terminological systems are treated as a primary source of data, this method also encompasses the documentation of physical objects and people's activities to the extent they shed light on classificatory behaviour (Kay, 1970; see also this chapter, section 'Two modes of inquiry: verbal and behavioural'). According to Warren (1997), the most recent phase of ethnoscience involves the study of indigenous knowledge systems, in particular the careful documentation of community-based classifications of natural resources and associated management practices, in support of facilitating sustainable approaches to development. In the following sections, we describe a number of concepts and procedures that have been developed to record and interpret different aspects of folk biological classification systems, including: (a) the local nomenclature; (b) the perceptual recognition of named entities; (c) the taxonomic classification of perceptually-distinguished groups of natural organisms; and (d) alternative forms of categorization. Before turning to specific methods, however, we discuss several general considerations about conducting fieldwork with people from another culture in general and ethnobiological research in particular.

GENERAL CONSIDERATIONS
OF A RESEARCH PROJECT

Concept and design

Before starting the research project, the researcher(s) must secure the free and informed consent of the people with whom the study will be carried out, as well as any legal permits required at local, provincial, national and international levels. The agreements made with the community can be accomplished in different ways, such as through consultation with community representatives (e.g. leaders) or public assemblies, written or oral – in line with local customs and protocols (Alexiades, 1996; Cunningham, 1996; Laird, 2002; Bannister and Barrett, 2004; Berlin and Berlin, 2004). Likewise, before initiating any systematic data collection it is a good idea to get to know some members of the community (Martin, 1995:103). Social contact and friendly dialogue are foundations for building a compatible long-term relationship. Ideally, local people should be consulted in regards to the concept and design of the research project, and encouraged to take an active part in data collection, processing and analysis. If any scientific or popular intellectual product, such as a written publication or audiovisual recording, arises, then proper credit or authorship must be given to the local participants. If the project is potentially capable of generating any kind of material benefits (e.g. royalties), the local community/ies, organizations and/or key informants must be included as beneficiaries in accordance with the wishes of the affected members.

Understanding contexts

Field research with human subjects has been characterized as a scientific activity that embraces two fundamental intellectual pursuits, the *sophy* and the *logos*. The first, *sophy*, 'discovers wisdom of human life, while the second, *logos* is aimed at logical structuring of knowledge' (Tinyakova, 2007:601). We qualify ethnographic fieldwork as an integrative endeavour that comprises a family of methods for relating scientific knowledge and extra-scientific forms of experience and practice. The so-called holistic approach to culture refers precisely to the investigation and integration of the different parts that make up the whole (Pelto and Pelto, 1978).

A holistic approach to analysing the interactions between people and fungi should begin with an understanding of the interwoven contexts. These multiple contexts can be grouped in two macro-levels:

Study site

Investigate as completely as possible the biocultural setting where the interactions take place. This includes:

- the biophysical habitat (climate, seasons, natural disasters, elevation, topography, geological substrate, soil classes, vegetation and fauna);
- the people (population size and distribution, language(s), ethnic affiliation(s), history of human occupation, migrations, settlement pattern, productive activities, trade, dietary habits, health situation, political system, socioeconomic composition, kinship and marriage, land tenure, magico-religious beliefs, ritual practices, moral dimensions);
- the human impact on the area (transportation infrastructure, man-made disasters, colonization, development projects, anthropogenic modification of habitat features, and conservation policies – such as the size and types of protected areas).

Research project

Understanding the multiple contexts should proceed in parallel with the data collection in the field. Contextualizing the research settings and dynamics is an ongoing and to some extent an endless task. Be aware of the particular position, background, motive and bias of the research team and how such 'cultural filters' can influence the research results. Factors such as nationality, gender, education, local language proficiency, age, political views, familiarity with the locality, etc. on the part of the data collector(s) may affect significantly the quantity and quality of the information provided by local people. Of particular importance in this regard is the academic training and experience of the researcher(s). One of the keys to success in ethnobiological research is being able to build transdisciplinary bridges in theory, methodology and epistemology. Thus collaboration with specialists outside one's primary field or team projects may be necessary.

In brief, contextualization is essential to adequately comprehend and interpret the complex interactions between humans and fungi from different perspectives: both synchronic (studies at one particular time, without considering the background history) and diachronic (studies over longer time periods).

TWO MODES OF INQUIRY: VERBAL AND BEHAVIOURAL

The interactions between people and members of the fungi kingdom can be understood through two kinds of data: verbal and behavioural. Words and actions (what people say and what people do) are different things and they imply the use of different methods. On one hand, vernacular vocabulary and verbal statements made by local people in the community being studied constitute the main data source for discovery of the emic (i.e. insider's) point of view. This data is elicited by means of interviews and casual conversations, followed by careful translation or semantic analysis. On the other hand, people's physical behaviours and movements, as well as the material effects and products of their activities, can be observed and recorded directly by the researcher. To the extent that such behaviours and objects are classified and interpreted according to the researcher's conceptual system, they provide the primary data used to construct an etic (i.e. outsider's) perspective. It is important to emphasize that these two levels of information are not opposed but rather complementary and therefore both kinds are crucial for grasping the full range of contacts with mushrooms. Eliciting verbal data is an indispensable method for tapping a large portion of local cognitions, perceptions, values, beliefs and attitudes. Such information is also crucial for the researcher who is initially unfamiliar with the local environment and the intricacies and motives of people's behaviour.

The recording of behavioural data is important because some aspects of knowledge are encoded behaviourally instead of linguistically and therefore learned through visual observation rather than verbal communication (e.g. practical skills). Furthermore 'a great deal of research has shown that about a third to a half of everything informants report about their behaviour is untrue' (Bernard, 1995:114). Verbal data can enhance comprehension of behavioural data and vice versa. The classic anthropological approach to fieldwork, which rests on the combined use of key informant interviewing and participant observation, sets the precedent for this integrated style of data collection (Pelto and Pelto, 1978). A good example of the creative combination of interview and observational methods in ethnomycological research is provided by Vasco-Palacios et al

Figure 3.1 *Ethnomycological knowledge can be surveyed among people of different ages and genders: A Jotï boy displaying fresh mushroom (Tricholomataceae, Agaricales); Jkayo Ijkuana, Amazonas, Venezuela*

Photograph: Stanford Zent

(2008). The researchers combined collection of specimens and intensive interviews of 29 elders wise in local mycology among three Amazonian groups (Andokes, Muinanes and Uitotos). The results were then contrasted with those obtained through random interviews with 97 people of different ages and genders (Figure 3.1). The results show a remarkable level and range of ethnomycological knowledge, including biological (substrates, habitats, associations, morphology), ecological (species associations such as coleoptera–plant–fungi, insects that eat fungi) and eco-cosmological (essential and spiritual notions of mushrooms with other bio-forms) information.

A diverse range of field and analytical methods which can be used to produce different kinds of ethnobiological data and information (verbal and behavioural, emic and etic, qualitative and quantitative) are described in this chapter as well as the following one (Chapter 4). The appropriateness of each method depends on the nature of the phenomena being studied. For instance, the documentation of highly specialized ethnomedicinal knowledge may be handled best by extended, open-ended interviews with a few expert healers in which the focus is on capturing qualitative details, whereas the topic of consumption patterns of seasonally available wild mushroom species will probably require the application of a structured dietary recall questionnaire administered to a sample of households over an annual cycle and then the results submitted to statistical analysis. Beyond trying to find the best approach for tackling the research problem at hand, the choice of method will have to be adjusted to a number of other factors, such as spatial scale and temporal duration of the study, social complexity of the target study population, number of researchers and their expertise, logistics of work and travel in the study area, and budgetary constraints.

The remaining part of this chapter is devoted to a discussion of specific methods that are relevant for exploring the cognitive dimensions of peoples' relationship to fungi, including the local naming systems, identification of real world natural organisms, folk taxonomies and several others.

METHODS FOR STUDYING COGNITION

The verbal interview is usually the core technique, but it is not the only one used to reveal how local people categorize and classify mushrooms and fungi. One of the primary tasks to undertake in any ethnobiological investigation is to determine the cognitive position of the biotic group in the conceptual universe of the people being studied: where does this group stand in relation to other groups of natural organisms recognized by the local people? (See Figure 3.2.)

The first question is whether there exists a segregated semantic domain, labelled or not, which includes all and only the bioforms belonging to the fungi kingdom. In other words, do fungi constitute a unique beginner category in the sense given by Brent Berlin (Berlin et al, 1973; see definition below)? To make this determination, one has to discover the inventory of biota that from the local point of view are recognized and grouped together as a natural class, and chart their relationships to one another. Next, one has to delineate the relationships of the class as a whole and/or the constituent class members individually to other biological groupings (such as plants or animals). In short, the proper demarcation of the domain will depend on mapping both the internal

Figure 3.2   *Mushrooms and indigenous people's conceptual universe: The authors conducting a detailed interview with Ijtö about ñamuliye yakino (the first mushroom that sprouted in the leg of the first woman-tree) and its role as entity in the myth of human creation (anthropogony). Kayamá, Venezuela, October 2005.*

Photograph: Yheicar Bernal

conceptual configuration as well as the external perceptual and cognitive boundaries from a local cultural perspective.

The taxonomic status of fungi as a separate ethnobiological domain, or unique beginner, is hinted at but nevertheless ambiguous in several folk classifications, and therefore the question of this status has drawn the attention of different researchers. Among the Gbëë Zapotec (Mexico), the category of mushroom can be considered 'as either an exceptionally large, heterogeneous folk generic taxon or a small life form' (Hunn, 2008:94), although after a linguistic analysis it is also conceivable to treat the mushroom category in Zapotec 'as an unaffiliated life form within a covert "superkingdom" of living things' (ibid, 95). Among the Ka'apor (Brazil) fungi cannot be easily classified as to life form and its affiliation with the plant domain 'remains unclear' (Balée 1994). A similar case of classificatory ambivalence appears among the Jotï (Venezuela). Some people consider mushrooms to be a separate life form but included within the plant kingdom, while most informants see them as separate from plants altogether (Zent et al, 2004). Similarly, based on linguistic and ecological data (mushrooms are highly seasonal, short-lived, fleeting, etc.), the Tzeltal Maya (Mexico) consider macro-fungi as a 'single, coherent domain that is separate and different from the domains of plants and animals' (Lampman, 2007:14–15). The Tzeltal category refers exclusively to species that are recognized as fungi in the Western scientific system (Shepard et al, 2008:450). Even in places where mushrooms are not very abundant or significant, in an ecological or in a cultural sense, such as the Nualulu of Seram (Indonesia), the use of a single term seems to support the reality of mushroom as a separate kingdom (Ellen, 2008:489).

At least three criteria can be used in the selection of informants: (1) community members who are exceptionally friendly, well-known or cooperative and therefore are highly trusted by the researcher to provide good reliable information; (2) community members who are recognized by their peers as being experts or having special knowledge of the domain being studied; and (3) a sample of different persons drawn from the study population in order to provide a more rounded view of the group as a whole. If the latter strategy is adopted, some care should be taken to select a representative sample (e.g. using random, systematic or stratified sampling). If the community is not too large, Bernard (1995) recommends a sample size of about 20 per cent of the total population. Keep in mind that a thorough population census and socioeconomic survey of all houses in the study community should be conducted, or previous censuses updated, prior to drawing the sample. If considerable socioeconomic variation is found, the sample should probably be stratified according to these variables.

According to Hunn (1975), the pre-scientific human apprehension of biodiversity in nature involves three primary cognitive processes or phases: nomenclature (linguistic labelling of classes and objects), identification (perceptual recognition of individuals, groups and key characters) and classification (conceptual categorization of groups of natural organisms and the organization of categories into taxonomic systems). Thus the understanding of how a local group conceptualizes fungi implies recording the different names assigned to different species of fungi or their fruiting bodies (mushrooms), as well as locating and collecting specimens that go with names. It is also important to explore the semantic contents of the inventory of terms that are included within the domain as well as the logical relationships (e.g. inclusion/contrast, focality/peripherality, transitive/nontransitive) among the different named and unnamed classes. An additional phase involves finding out the cultural and ecological significance and use value of the different recognized classes.

Specific methods pertinent to each of these facets are described and justified below.

Nomenclature

A good place to begin is by eliciting the lexemes (i.e. the fundamental unit of the lexicon of a language) that refer to the different segregates (i.e. terminologically-distinguished objects) comprising the domain of mushrooms as well as associated words or linguistic forms used to indicate their anatomical parts, growth habits, habitats and significances. Probably the fastest way to record the names is *free listing*, which consists of asking individuals to name all the kinds of X that they can recall. The question may be phrased in specific terms, such as 'Please name all the red/round/tree-sprouting/ edible/medicinal/etc. mushrooms that you know?' Individual lists can then be merged to produce a composite list. This collection of names provides the researcher with a handy checklist for purposes of organizing collection efforts and also conveys a rough idea of the size and complexity of the domain in terms of the number of taxa.

A second step is collecting secondary terms that denominate or hint at the taxonomic categories at lower and higher inclusive ranks. These data are usually recorded through structured interviews or controlled question-answer substitution frames. The structured interview format involves the same set of questions or response stimuli being administered to every informant in the sample and may take the form of a written questionnaire, for literate populations, or an oral interview schedule, for preliterate populations. The substitution frame involves formulating a standard query and plugging in different previously named taxa (e.g. 'What is the name of one/another kind of _____?'). Another query technique entails ostension (i.e. pointing out). For example, showing the informant a real specimen or pictorial representation and asking him or her 'What is this?' or 'How do you call it?'. Related questions could be: 'What other (related) kinds of it are there?'; 'Is there just one kind?'; or 'Does that name refer to something else or is it just a name?'. The formal interview procedures mentioned here are designed to control the linguistic context that is presented to the informant, using language that is appropriate and easy to understand. The objective is to ensure equal semantic values from source to receptor and thus stimulate consistent and comparable responses across different informants and different questions. The resulting list of terms elicited from a particular frame should be mutually exclusive, which is to say they form a contrast set. This data collection format has been referred to as 'white-room' to indicate that the context is homogenized and controlled. Besides controlling the linguistic context, the method also calls for the elimination of extraneous cultural noise and distracting influences, and is best administered to individuals or small focus groups. Some authors have argued that the concept of data elicitation frames should be broadened to include the wider social and behavioural contexts, facetiously called 'grass hut' ethnography, which involves carrying out conversational exchanges in more naturalistic and culturally realistic situations (cf. Frake, 1977).

Besides the structured interview, semi-structured and unstructured formats can also be used to collect terminological data. The semi-structured interview follows an interview guide, that is, a list of questions and topics to be covered, but actual administration of the interview is more flexible, allowing the respondent more freedom to answer in their own words and permitting the interviewer to follow up interesting lines of inquiry with spontaneous questions. The main advantage of this approach is that it can arise in potentially useful information that the informants consider worth mentioning but which was completely unanticipated by the researcher. The disadvantage is that the process of searching, extracting and analysing pertinent information from the response data is more complicated and time-consuming. Unstructured interviews and informal conversations may be invaluable to clarify gaps in the data, ambiguous categories, synonyms and polysemic terms (i.e. terms that have multiple meanings), non-transitive classes, focal vs. peripheral members or rare segregates, etc.

The names (lexemes) for ethnobiological taxa correspond to two basic types that are distinguished by linguistic, taxonomic and semantic properties: primary names and secondary names. The former can be either simple (mono-lexemic) or complex (two or more words or morphemes) and usually refer to taxa at the folk generic and life form ranks. The latter are always complex and invariably refer to sub-generic taxa. Complex primary names can be semantically productive or unproductive. Productive forms can be analysed (i.e. they make reference to some perceptual or functional attribute of the group of organisms) with the superordinate taxon as one of the lexemic constituents. Unproductive forms do not include the superordinate taxon and thus are usually arbitrary and cannot be analysed. Secondary names also include some mention of the superordinate category, in this case the folk generic, and thus may provide an easy lexical cue for determining membership in this class. The Jotï generic term for mushroom is *yakino* and some productive examples point to size (*jani yakino*, 'small mushroom'), colour (*kyabo yakino*, 'white mushroom'), texture (*jwaiño yakino*, 'soft mushroom'), animal associations (*uli jkwayo yakino*, 'spider monkey [*Ateles belzebuth*] fungus'), plant associations (*jkaile yakino*, 'tree [*Micropholis melinoniana* Pierre] fungus'), or spirit associations (*awëla yakino*, 'phantom fungus').

Identification

The main goal of this phase is to determine which real-world entities or attributes substantiate and structure the individual categorical constructs as well as the relationships among them. Berlin (1992) notes that the perceptual salience of plants and animals (we could perhaps add fungi here although he does not mention them) is determined by multiple attributes such as size, colouration, position, frequency of observation, cultural importance, biotaxonomic distance and morphological aberrancy.

The first step is to identify as completely as possible the biological genera and species that correspond to each named segregate. Scientific systematic biology constitutes the universal reference (both as a name and an object) or metalanguage in terms of which perceptible organisms and characters can be described and understood. The most reliable way of identifying the biosystematic content of folk biological taxa is by collecting voucher specimens (along with the local names) and then sending them to a specialist for taxonomic determination (see Chapter 2).

Another step involves specifying the perceptually salient phenotypic traits – morphological, behavioural and others – intrinsic to the organisms classified and which define membership in a particular class. There are two main category types that can be distinguished on the basis of perceptual processes: deductive (or monothetic), i.e. defined by abstract (widely applicable) features; and inductive (or polythetic), consisting of many concrete features which are perceived as a unitary configuration (also known as a 'gestalt image'). The former have been described as artificial and special-purpose classifications, imposed by practical considerations such as cultural uses, while the latter are considered to be natural and general-purpose concepts, based on the recognition of real perceptual gaps in nature (which in turn reflect phylogenetic relationships) (Hunn, 1982; Berlin, 1992). The task of the researcher during data analysis is to specify the necessary and sufficient features of class membership (e.g. colour, size, texture) in the first case and the relationships of similarity/difference (i.e. focal/peripheral members) in the second case.

Previously collected specimens or pictures (such as photographs or drawings) can be used as visual prompts for determining named or covert class membership and perceptual salience criteria (Berlin et al, 1981; Boster, 1987a). However, the appropriateness of such materials should first be tested because some groups or individuals may not be familiar with such media (Ross, 2002; Cruz García, 2006; Monteiro et al, 2006) or because some people may use other perceptual cues (colour, substrate, habitat, smell, taste) to identify the species (Jernigan 2006). Thus we recommend that the researcher adopt the 'walk in the woods' interview technique for eliciting mushroom names and distinguishing key characters, at least during the early phase of fieldwork. This method provides a more realistic and appropriate context for ethnobiological interviews as it features living individuals in their natural habitat (Zent, 2009:24). After the researcher has a basic grasp of the perceptual contours of the domain and its inhabitants, he or she can try out more controlled and experimental queries for exploring less obvious features (see Classification below).

Classification

According to the universalist theory of ethnobiological classification advanced by Berlin (1992), the semantic domains of living entities (plants, animals and mushrooms) are usually, if not universally, organized in the human mind as a taxonomy, which is to say a hierarchy of sets. However, the depth and elaboration of the hierarchy varies between different groups of people or between classes of organisms.

The objective of taxonomic analysis is to map the taxonomic structure. This is understood as encompassing two fundamental components: a finite set of categories or taxa that make up the entire domain; and a relational structure defined by the properties of progressive set inclusion (i.e. a set of contrasting taxa are included within a higher-level taxon which also belongs to a set of contrasting taxa which in turn are included within a still higher taxon, until reaching a single taxon which includes every other member of the entire domain) and partition (i.e. division of a set into subsets that places every member in exactly one subset) (Kay, 1971). Queries about domain organization are thus largely concerned with exploring the vertical relationships of inclusion or the horizontal relationships of contrast among different pairs or subsets out of the inventory of segregate categories. Direct forms of questioning about these might include the frames 'What is a kind of X?' and 'What is X a kind of?' respectively. Frake (1964) cautions that questions must be directed both upward and downward the taxonomic ladder in order to achieve classificatory precision.

Berlin (1976; 1992) argues further that the hierarchical structure of classification points to the existence of qualitatively separate ethnobiological ranks, which can be distinguished on the basis of nomenclatural, psychological, biological and taxonomic criteria. The theory stipulates that all systems of folk biological classification throughout the world display a minimum of three and a maximum of six such ranks. The 'universal' ethnobiological ranks are described as follows:

1   Unique beginner – the domain-defining or all-inclusive taxon, usually unnamed – in which case indicated by indirect linguistic and behavioural markers – or labelled by a single lexeme, corresponding to the kingdom level in western biosystematics.
2   Life form – preceded immediately by the unique beginner, includes a small number (one to ten) of very distinctive morphotypes based on the correlation of morphological features (size, shape, substance) and ecological adaptation (e.g. tree, vine, herb, fish, bird, snake, possibly mushroom?), usually broadly polytypic and containing the majority of lesser inclusive taxa, named by a single lexeme.

3   Intermediate – taxonomically fall between life forms and generics, group small numbers of generic taxa due to their perceived affinity, relatively rare and when found most commonly are not labelled overtly.

4   Generic – most (but not all) of these taxa are preceded immediately by life form taxa, the rank with by far the largest number of taxa, considered to be the backbone or nucleus of the entire classification system, the first segregates learned by children; perceived as a gestalt image, named by one or two words that are either productive or unproductive.

5   Specific – included within generic taxa, few in number, segregated by contrast sets defined by a few characters (e.g. colour, size, microhabitats), named by binomial expressions.

6   Varietal – lowest ranking and hence terminal category where found, rare or non-existent in foraging societies, more common in domesticated species, few in number, always part of a contrast set.

This taxonomic scheme corresponds to a general-purpose type of classification in the sense of being polythetic, which is to say its members possess many attributes in common, mainly morphological and behavioural attributes, as well as natural, meaning that it (somewhat) accurately represents phylogenetic diversity and relationships that actually exist in nature, hence it is valid in a variety of contexts. Other researchers criticize the natural taxonomic model of ethnobiological classification in general and the concept of rank in particular, and instead highlight the importance of other types of structural arrangements, such as fuzzy sets, coordination, cross-cutting associations, non-transitivity, residual categories, part-whole relationships, special-purpose classifications, and indexing of categorical meaning within social contexts (Ellen, 1975, 1986; Hunn, 1976, 1982; Randall, 1976; Maranhão, 1977; Hunn and French, 1984; Randall and Hunn, 1984). While we are not advocating one or the other theoretical position, the ethnomycological researcher should be aware that there may be different options for analysing the semantic content of categories as well as the structural relationships between them within a folk biological domain.

In this sense, it should also be kept in mind that certain methods are better suited for investigating different semantic-structural arrangements. For example, the basic elicitation frame involving the successive application of the query 'What are the names of all the kinds of X in Y?' is inherently designed to generate folk taxonomies of the hierarchical kind because it specifically refers to inclusive and contrastive relations while excluding other types of information (cf. Hunn, 1982). By contrast, special purpose classifications, such as utilitarian, ecological or gendered distinctions, may require additional lines of questioning or even participant observation to decipher properly (see next subsection below). Although such categories can be investigated by inserting the term referring to the target semantic feature into the same question frame mentioned above (e.g. 'edible/cultivated/female X') it is also important to limit such questioning to culturally valid categories. In this regard, Frake (1964) proposes a method of linked queries, in which the output responses of a question frame are used as input for new queries. The application of this method is demonstrated by presenting the case of the manufacture of beer by yeast spice (a fungi-activated process) among the Subanun of the Philippines. The cultural significance of plants as yeast spice ingredient is revealed by compiling categorical lists and tracing the inter-linkages among the botanical species selected for this purpose, the major plant types (i.e. life forms) in which these fall, the parts which are used, the habitats where the source plants grow, and the gastronomic properties (e.g. flavour) of the different species. Once all the relevant contrast sets are completed and the inter-linkages established, one can proceed with the componential analysis of the segregate set, which involves specifying all of the criterial attributes (i.e. distinctive features of meaning) for each and every segregate.

Besides direct verbal elicitation, there are several controlled experimental techniques, sometimes called cognitive exercises or games, which can be used to probe the underlying, often unconscious, perceptual or cognitive structure and content of selected cultural domains. These include: ranking exercises (Likerd scale), paired comparisons, triad tests and pile sorts (Bernard, 1995:237–255; Martin, 1995:117–135). The informant is asked to arrange categories along a scale (ranking), compare categories according to a given criterion (paired comparison) or organize categories into groups (triad tests, pile sorts) respectively. In some cases (e.g. triad tests), the informant is asked to explain the reasons for his or her choices. Pile sorts have been widely used to explore the non-obvious patterns of taxonomic knowledge of natural organisms, such as covert categories, and the intercultural correspondence of taxonomic knowledge (Berlin, et al 1968; Hays, 1976; Boster et al, 1986). These analytical tools are especially useful for exploring the internal structure of categories, such as absolute vs. graded class membership, identification of prototypical vs. marginal members of the class, relative salience of certain attributes and less vs. more valued taxa.

Utilitarian, ecological, spiritual and other cultural significances

As suggested in the preceding section, the ethnomycologist should probably anticipate that the people he or she works with will discriminate the fungal domain not only on the basis of morphological and behavioural attributes but also according to specialized cultural criteria, such as utility, habitat type and magico-religious significance, among others (cf. Shepard et al, 2008). For example, one of the key characteristics employed to partition the fungal domain across a wide range of cultures is the dichotomous feature of edible/inedible. A good example in the English language is the distinction between 'mushroom' and 'toadstool' (Shepard et al, 2008:454; see also Box 3.1).

Expanding Frame Analysis

In order to achieve a rounded understanding of this sort of special-purpose categorization, it may be necessary to augment the narrowly-focused, controlled elicitation procedures mentioned in the previous sections with more open-ended and flexible approaches to data collection. Possible options include: informal or spontaneous interviewing about fungi-related topics; participant observation of people's activities dealing with mushrooms; and even the study of other cultural behaviours and expressions that directly or indirectly might reveal insights into the semantic values attached to this biotaxonomic group and its members. In effect, we are suggesting attention to Frake's (1977) call for expanding frame analysis to encompass the wider social context that makes interpretation more meaningful and accurate. The complexity and variability of this context may well dictate methodological versatility and triangulation.

BOX 3.1 INDIGENOUS KNOWLEDGE AND USE OF FUNGI IN AUSTRALIA

Arpad Kalotas

Aboriginal people of Australia have a detailed knowledge of fungi, their uses and ecological relationships. Though the ethnomycological record is limited, many fungi are recorded as used for food, medicine and other purposes (Kalotas, 1996). Fungi are also incorporated into traditional beliefs and mythologies. In the late 19th century, for example, Spencer and Gillen (1899) recorded that 'Falling stars appear to be associated with the idea of evil magic in many tribes. The Arunta believe that mushrooms and toadstools are fallen stars, and look upon them as being endowed with *arungquiltha* (evil magic) and therefore will not eat them.' However, as I have suggested elsewhere (Kalotas, 1996), this belief does not apply to all fungi, for a number are eaten by Aboriginal people in Central Australia. Fungi are also the subject of contemporary Aboriginal art (Trappe et al, 2008).

Fungi used as food included species from a range of families and biogeographical regions:

- The native bread, the large sclerotium of *Laccocephalum mylittae*, is known from the temperate forests of southeastern and southwestern Australia. Aboriginal people could detect the presence of this vegetative mass that matures underground by the swelling of the ground (as the sclerotium grows) and the smell given off as it matures. Recent collections from Western Australia indicate that fire appears to play a part in stimulating the development of the sclerotium (Robinson, 2009).
- Species of edible large puffballs (*Pisolithus* spp) occur across the continent.
- Several truffle species are found in the arid zone of central Australia (Trappe et al, 2008). The truffles used as food by Aboriginal people predominantly occur in the arid zone. A recent revision of Australian species (ibid, 2008) indicates that: 'Seven truffle species (three of which are new to science) belonging to six genera (one being new to science) have been discovered' and continues:

> Desert truffles of the Australian Outback, once a cherished food resource for diverse Aboriginal ethnic groups, currently have little or no value for con-temporary Aboriginal communities either as a gathered food or as a saleable or even tradable commodity (Liddell, pers. observation). Likewise, no attempts have been made to commercially market Australian desert truffles in contrast to their African and Middle Eastern counterparts.

Interestingly, some other food species used by Australian Indigenous peoples include species that are the same or closely related to those recorded as food in other cultures. The beech orange (*Cyttaria gunnii*), which only grows on the myrtle (*Nothofagus cunninghamii*), was used for food in Tasmania. Other species of *Cyttaria* (also associated with *Nothofagus* spp) are known as food in Chile and in recent times have been sold in local markets there.

The fruiting body of beefsteak fungus (*Fistulina hepatica*, which is believed to have been used as a food source in south-western Australia) and various species of large puffballs (*Pisolithus* spp) are known as a food species in America and Europe.

Fungi also play a part in traditional medicine. The orange shelf fungus (*Pycnoporus coccineus*) was used as a disinfectant for children with sore lips and mouths, or thrush of the mouth, and the woody hoof fungi (*Phellinus* spp) were used in northern Australia for varying ailments including sores, coughs and fevers.

Miscellaneous uses of fungi include providing tinder and carrying fire, as is the case with the white punk (*Laetiporus portentosus*). This is not restricted to Australia, with records of other indigenous peoples using related fungi for the same use, such as the tinder fungus (*Fomes fomentarius*) used in Europe (Peintner et al, 1998). Some species such as the mature stalked puffball (*Podaxis pistillaris*) which produces a purplish-black spore mass, were used as decorative body paint, and by old men for cosmetic purposes, to darken grey hairs.

In addition to traditional Aboriginal uses of fungi, the ethnomycological record contains a rich assemblage of Indigenous names and beliefs, including those associated with the dreamtime and the exploits of ancestral beings. There is potential to continue the documentation of traditional use of fungi and to gain valuable ecological insights. Indigenous communities, and particularly Aboriginal language centres, are best placed to record this knowledge and undertake salvage ethnomycology. Trappe et al (2008) state in relation to truffles (although this can be applied to all useful species):

> *Traditional knowledge is increasingly endangered as the elders succumb one by one. A multidisciplinary collaboration between mycologists, ecologists, ethnobotanists, anthropologists, and linguists is urgently needed to document these remarkable truffles and their traditional place in the lives of Aboriginal peoples.*

Several specific methodological proposals for expanding the cultural and ecological scope of ethnobiological descriptions have been elaborated and will be mentioned briefly here.

Hunn's (1982) concept of *activity signature* is designed to systematically describe the practical significance of each taxonomic distinction from the native point of view. The method involves recording the total inventory of culturally valid affirmative or imperative sentences in which the taxon occurs as the object. The resulting series of statements amount to the taxon's activity signature, which can be considered 'recipes or instructions for action' within the life of the cultural group. This kind of practical classification can be used to discriminate the list of recorded taxa in terms of the sum total of how, when, where and who uses them. The activity signature method is conceptually consistent with Alcorn's (1995) thesis that ethno-ecological research should take the form of text analysis. She contends that efforts must be made to look into the interrelationships of biota and people 'embedded in dynamic ecosystems of natural and social context' (Alcorn, 1995:24). Given that such interrelationships are produced not just by immanent attributes of the species but also by the particular physical, ecological, social and historical milieus in which they are situated, the researcher must strive to elucidate the species' 'text' where the interactions are 'played out' (ibid).

A similarly holistic approach is found in Ellen's (1986) concept of *prehension*, referring to those processes which through various cultural and other constraints give rise to particular classifications, designations and representations of the species within unique ecological, social and cultural contexts. He advocates that an experientially realistic understanding of classificatory behaviour must begin by observing people assigning items to categories and using names in natural ethnographic settings. In this sense, knowledge and know-how are not independent; rather knowledge is socially distributed in terms of the know-how it may encode and also in terms of the value placed upon it.

A couple of examples of ethnomycological research that have used a multi-pronged approach to data collection can be mentioned here. Pieroni et al (2005) conducted individual and focus group interviews as well as specimen collections to record the edible wild mushrooms in Southern Italy. They found that mushrooms make up a prominent component of the local cuisine. Thirteen different species are gathered by men on a seasonal basis and are eaten either roasted or raw. Beyond their nutritional and gastronomic importance, the activities surrounding the procurement and consumption of this food type help to reinforce kinship and social networks (Pieroni et al, 2005:263). Aaron Lampman (2004, 2007) made use of specimen collections, semi-structured interviews and pile sort exercises (in which mounted photographs of the most frequently gathered species were used as stimuli) to elicit folk names, taxonomic categories and cultural uses of mushrooms in two municipalities of Tzetzal Maya in Chiapas, Mexico. The researcher recorded over 30 species of wild edible mushrooms gathered seasonally by Mayan families and some species used as medicine (2007:12). The data record shows that the Tzeltal possess a sophisticated understanding of 'mushroom ecology, substrate preferences, microhabitat tendencies, seasonality, edibility, and medical applications' (Lampman, 2007:14).

One of the most common and appropriate situations for collecting cultural information about folk taxa is precisely when making specimen collections. Two basic approaches have been described: (a) the artefact/interview, which consists of queries about what species a particular cultural artefact or product (e.g. edible dish, medicinal concoction, ornament) is made from, followed by collection of them; and (b) the inventory/interview, which involves the active collection of specimens in the field and the simultaneous or subsequent queries about the pertinent cultural information (Boom, 1989:81). It is a good idea to prepare a data sheet that should be filled out for each specimen or folk species collected. Besides the basic information such as date, location, habitat, collector's or informant's name and local name of the folk taxon, the following data should be recorded: phenology, spatial or habitat distribution, interactions with other species, life expectancy, seasonality, management techniques, specific uses or treatments, parts used, potential for domestication, salient attributes (odors, colours, shapes, etc.), physiological or psychological effects, rare uses and ideological notions.

Another constructive method for recording ethnomycological data is the life history interview, which involves asking an informant to narrate the key events in their life from early childhood to the present. In this case, the researcher prompts the subject to recall and recount their experiences and memories involving fungi, for example whether they collected and ate them when they were children and if they still do so. Since many mushroom species or genera produce strong psychobiological effects if consumed or even touched, it is not surprising to find their incorporation in myths, stories, ritual performances or magico-religious beliefs.

Figure 3.3 *Jotï children painting the arms of one of the authors (S. Zent) for a ritual celebration*

The admixture used to paint contains certain culturally meaningful mushrooms. Kayamá, Venezuela, December 2005.

Photograph: Egleé Zent

BOX 3.2 THE HUNTING MAGIC OF THE SPIDER MONKEY MUSHROOM

Egleé Zent

A melodious cry broke the stillness of the night. From a neighbouring shelter, Jkwiiaun ('Piping Guan's wife') answered the singing of her sister, Bölöaun ('Partridge's wife'), with her own alluring harmony. Their duet divulged the day's hunting plans to the game animals' guardian spirits. Towering trees swayed like restless guards keeping watch around the tiny encampment of three hasty lean-tos which housed twelve people. The intermingling of songs still embraced the hunters like the pre-dawn dampness that clung to their bodies as they slipped out of the camp. In a fleeting movement, the lead hunter veered briefly to snatch a soggy mushroom from a nearby log, stuffed it into his nostril and then sped off down the trail once again. A second man followed him into the forest after rubbing his nose with the same mushroom. A barrage of shooting darts was announced with the 'pop, pop, pop' of the blowgun some twenty minutes later. After a brief but frenetic chase, the fresh corpse of a spider monkey fell from the canopy just when the first daylight was breaking. An hour later, another prey of the same species crashed to the ground. At mid-morning, we headed back to the campsite with enough meat for two to three days. The snuff substance had been extracted from *ulijkwayoyakino*, a powerful mushroom named for the spider monkey (*Atelesbelzebuth*) and considered to be connected metaphysically to its guardian spirit. The Jotï believe that the act of inhaling the fungal essence is instrumental for securing the successful capture of this game species.

Accordingly, these venues offer possible fields of discourse for understanding the cultural significance of mushrooms in a particular group. It is not uncommon to find more than one version of the myths and legends and therefore it is advisable to record the text from more than one informant. Sometimes brief encounters with subtle ecological behaviours are more effective than words at opening up expansive doors for understanding people's eco-cosmological universe (see Box 3.2).

CONCLUSION

Mushrooms, like people, are cosmopolitan. In many places all over the world, during different historical periods, encounters with fungi have evoked a strong reaction in humans, ranging from fear to adoration. Rarely is the response one of indifference. In recognition of the conspicuous presence and significance of fungi among diverse cultural groups, we urge that ethnobiologists consider the need to expand their studies of this relationship. Mycophilic cultures have contributed to the increase of scientific knowledge on fungi precisely in areas where inventories of this biological group are poor (Fidalgo and Prance, 1976; Fidalgo and Hirata, 1979). Although there are certainly systematic and valuable studies in mycology (Alexopolus et al, 1996), some biologists believe that less than five per cent of the total estimated number of fungal species (~1.5 million) worldwide have been identified so far (Læssøe, 1998:6). The notion that there are species presently unknown to global science but recognized and used by folk people is more than a remote possibility, as some previous ethnographic field surveys indicate (Prance, 1984), and should prompt in-depth research that pays attention to both verbal and behavioural expressions of the relationship between people and fungi. We stress the benefits of a comprehensive approach to studying ethnobiological cognition, starting with description and explanation of the basic processes of nomenclature, identification and classification, but also potentially encompassing other cultural significances such as utilitarian, ecological and spiritual values. In a similar vein, we recommend that methods and epistemologies should be integrative in outlook, both qualitative (such as those described in this chapter) and quantitative (such as those described in Chapter 4).

REFERENCES

Alcorn, J. B. (1995) 'The scope and aims of ethnobotany in a developing world', in R. E. Schultes and S. von Reis (eds) *Ethnobotany: evolution of a discipline*, Chapman and Hall, London, pp23–39

Alexiades, M. N. (1996) 'Protocol for Conducting Ethnobotanical Research in the Tropics', in M. N. Alexiades (ed) 'Selected Guidelines for Ethnobotanical Research: A Field Manual', *Advances in Economic Botany* 10, pp5–18

Alexopoulos, C. J., Mims, C. W. and Blackwell, M. (1996) *Introductory Mycology* (4th edition) John Wiley, New York

Balée, W. (1994) *Footprints of the Forest: Ka'apor Ethnobotany – the Historical Ecology of Plant Utilization by an Amazonian People*, Columbia University Press, New York

Bannister, K. and Barrett, K. (2004) 'Weighing the Proverbial "Ounce of Prevention" Versus the "Pound of Cure" in a Biocultural Context: A Role for the Precautionary Principle in Ethnobiological Research', in T. Carlson and L. Maffi (eds) 'Ethnobotany and Conservation of Biocultural Diversity', *Advances in Economic Botany* 15, pp307–339

Berlin, B. (1976) 'The Concept of Rank in Ethnobiological Classification: Some Evidence from Aguaruna Folk Botany', *American Ethnologist* 3 (Special Issue on Folk Biology) pp381–399

Berlin, B. (1992) *Ethnobiological Classification: Principles of Categorization of Plants and Animals in Traditional Societies*, Princeton University Press, Princeton

Berlin, B., Breedlove, D. E. and Raven, P. H. (1968) 'Covert Categories and Folk Taxonomies', *American Anthropologist* 70, pp290–299

Berlin, B., Bredlove, D. E. and Raven, P. H. (1973) 'General Principles of Classification and Nomenclature in Folk Biology', *American Anthropologist*, vol 75, no 19, pp214–242

Berlin, E. A. and Berlin, B. (2004) 'Prior informed consent and bioprospecting in Chiapas', in M. Riley (ed) *Indigenous intellectual property rights*, AltaMira Press, Walnut Creek, CA, pp341–372

Berlin, B., Boster, J. and O'Neill, J. P. (1981) 'The Perceptual Bases of Ethnobiological Classification: Evidence from Aguaruna Folk Ornithology', *Journal of Ethnobiology*, vol 1, no 1, pp95–108

Bernard, H. R. (1995) *Research Methods in Cultural Anthropology*, Sage, Newbury Park, CA

Boom, B. (1989) 'Use of Plant Resources by the Chácobo', in D. Posey and W. Balée (eds) 'Resource Management in Amazonia: Indigenous and Folk Strategies', *Advances in Economic Botany* 7, pp79–96

Boster, J. S. (1987a) 'Agreement Between Biological Classification Systems is not Dependent on Cultural Transmission', *American Anthropologist*, vol 89, no 4, pp914–920

Boster, J. S., Berlin, B. and O'Neill, J. (1986) 'The Correspondence of Jivaroan to Scientific Ornithology', *American Anthropologist*, vol 88, no 3, pp569–583

Cruz García, G. S. (2006) 'The mother–child nexus. Knowledge and valuation of wild food plants in Wayanad, Western Ghats, India', *Journal of Ethnobiology and Ethnomedicine* 2(39)

Cunningham, A. B. (1996) 'Professional Ethics and Ethnobotanical Research', in M. N. Alexiades (ed) 'Selected Guidelines for Ethnobotanical Research: A Field Manual', *Advances in Economic Botany* 10, pp19–51

Ellen, R. F. (1975) 'Variable constructs in Nuaulu zoological classification', *Social Science Information*, vol 14 nos 3–4, pp201–228

Ellen, R. F. (1986) 'Ethnobiology, Cognition, and the Structure of Prehension: Some General Theoretical Notes', *Journal of Ethnobiology* 6, pp83–98

Ellen, R. F. (2008) 'Ethnomycology among the Nuaulu of the Moluccas: Putting Berlin's "General Principles" of Ethnobiological Classification to the Test', *Economic Botany*, vol 62, no 3, pp483–496

Fidalgo, O. and Hirata, J. M. (1979) 'Etnomicología Caiabi, Txicão e Txucarramãe', *Rickia* 8, pp1–5

Fidalgo, O. and Prance, G. (1976) 'The Ethnomycology of the Sanema Indians', *Mycologia*, vol LXVIII, no 1, pp201–210

Frake, C. (1964) 'Notes on Queries in Ethnography', *American Anthropologist*, vol 66, no 3, pp132–145

Frake, C. (1977) 'Plying Frames Can be Dangerous: Some Reflections on Methodology in Cognitive Anthropology', *The Quarterly Newsletter of the Institute for Comparative Human Development* (The Rockefeller University) vol 1, no 3, pp1–7

Hays, T. (1976) 'An empirical method for the identification of covert categories in Ethnobiology', *American Ethnologist*, vol 3, no 3, pp489–507

Hunn, E. (1975) 'Cognitive Processes in Folk Ornithology: The Identification of Gulls', *Working Paper* No. 42, Language-Behavior Research Laboratory, University of California, Berkeley

Hunn, E. (1976) 'Toward a Perceptual Model of Folk Biological Classification', *American Ethnologist* 3, pp508–524

Hunn, E. (1982) 'The Utilitarian Factor in Folk Biological Classification', *American Anthropologist* 84, 830–47

Hunn, E. (2008) *A Zapotec Natural History*, The University of Arizona Press, Tucson

Hunn, E. and French, D. (1984) 'Alternatives to Taxonomic Hierarchy: The Sahaptin Case', *Journal of Ethnobiology* 3, pp73–92

Jernigan, K. (2006) 'An Ethnobotanical Investigation of Tree Identification by the Aguaruna Jívaro of the Peruvian Amazon', *Journal of Ethnobiology*, vol 26, no 1, pp107–125

Kalotas, A. C. (1996) 'Aboriginal Knowledge and Use of Fungi', in K. Mallet and C. Grgurinovic (eds) *Fungi of Australia Vol. 1B, Introduction—Fungi in the Environment*, Australian Biological Resources Study, CSIRO Publishing, Canberra, Australia, pp269–295

Kay, P. (1970) 'Some theoretical implications of ethnographic semantics', in A. Fischer (ed) *Current Directions in Anthropology* (Bulletin of the American Anthropological Association) no 3, pt 2, pp19–31

Kay, P. (1971) Taxonomy and Semantic Contrast, *Language* 68, pp866–887

Læssøe, T. (1998) *Mushrooms*, Dorling Kindersley, London

Laird, S. (ed) (2002) *Biodiversity and Traditional Knowledge: Equitable Partnerships in Practice*, Earthscan, London

Lampman, A. M. (2004) 'Tzeltal ethnomycology: Naming, classification and use of mushrooms in the highlands of Chiapas, Mexico', PhD dissertation, University of Georgia, Athens

Lampman, A. M. (2007) 'General Principles of Ethnomycological Classification among the Tzeltal Maya of Chiapas, Mexico', *Journal of Ethnobiology* vol 27, no 1, pp11–27

Lepp, H. (2003) *Aboriginal use of fungi*, www.anbg.gov.au/fungi/aboriginal.html, accessed 31 July 2010

Maranhão, T. P. (1977) 'The Status of Taxonomies in Anthropology and Linguistics', *Anthropological Linguistics*, vol 19, no 3, pp111–122

Martin, G. (1995) *Ethnobotany: A methods manual*, Chapman and Hall, London

Metzger, D. and Williams, G. (1966) 'Some Procedures and Results in the Study of Native Categories: Tzeltal "Firewood"', *American Anthropologist*, 68, pp389–407

Monteiro, J. M., de Albuquerque, U. P., de Freitas Lins-Neto, E. M., de Araújo, E. L. and Cavalcanti de Amorim, E. L. (2006) 'Use patterns and knowledge of medicinal species among two rural communities in Brazil's semi-arid northeastern region', *Journal of Ethnopharmacology* 105, pp173–186

Peintner, U., Pöder, R. and Pümpel T. (1998) 'The iceman's fungi', *Mycological Research* 102, pp1153–1162

Pelto, P. J. and Pelto, G. H. (1978) *Anthropological Research. The Structure of Inquiry* (2nd edition) Cambridge University Press, Cambridge

Pieroni, A., Nebell, S., Santoro, R. F. and Heinrich, M. (2005) 'Food for two seasons: Culinary uses of non-cultivated local vegetables and mushrooms in a south Italian village', *International Journal of Food Sciences and Nutrition*, vol 56, no 4, pp245–272

Prance, G. (1984) 'The Use of Edible Fungi by Amazonian Indians', *Advances in Economic Botany* 1, pp127–139

Randall, R. (1976) 'How Tall Is a Taxonomic Tree? Some Evidence for Dwarfism', *American Ethnologist* 3, pp543–553

Randall, R. and Hunn, E. (1984) 'Do Life Forms Evolve or Do Uses for Life?' *American Ethnologist* 11, pp329–349

Robinson, R. (2009) 'Fire mosaics can enhance macrofungal biodiversity', Information Sheet 1/2009, Science Division, Department of Environment and Conservation, *www.dec.wa.gov.au/ component/option,com...1/gid.../task,doc_download/*

Ross, N. (2002) 'Cognitive aspects of intergenerational change: Mental models, cultural change, and environmental behavior among the Lacandon Maya of southern Mexico', *Human Organization* 61, pp125–138

Shepard, G., Arora, D. and Lampman, A. (2008) 'The Grace of the Flood: Classification and Use of Wild Mushrooms among the Highland Maya of Chiapas', *Economic Botany*, vol 62, no 3, pp437–470

Spencer, B. and Gillen, F. J. (1899) *The Native Tribes of Central Australia*, Macmillan, London

Sturtevant, W. C. (1964) 'Studies in Ethnoscience', *American Anthropologist*, vol 66, no 3, pp99–131

Tinyakova, E. (2007) 'Fieldwork: Man in the System of Nature and Priority of Natural Laws in Human Life', *Collegium Antropologicum*, vol 31, no 2, pp601–612

Trappe, J. M., Claridge, D. L., Claridge, A. W. and Liddle, L. (2008) 'Desert truffles of the Australian outback: Ecology, ethnomycology, and taxonomy', *Economic Botany*, vol 62, no 3, pp497–506

Vasco-Palacios, M., Suaza, S. C., Castaño-Betancur, M. and Franco-Molano, A. E. (2008) 'Conocimiento etnoecológico de los hongos entre los indígenas Uitoto, Muinane y Andoke de la Amazonía Colombiana', *Acta Amazónica*, vol 38, no 1, pp17–30

Warren, D. M. (1997) 'Ethnoscience', in T. Barfield (ed) *The Dictionary of Anthropology*, Blackwell, Oxford, pp165–166

Zent, E. L., Zent, S. and Ituriaga, T. (2004) 'Knowledge and Use of Fungi by a Mycophile Society from the Venezuelan Amazon', *Economic Botany*, vol 58, no 2, pp214–226

Zent, S. (2009) 'Final Report on Indicator No. 2: Methodology for Developing a Vitality Index of Traditional Environmental Knowledge (VITEK) for the Project "Global Indicators of the Status and Trends of Linguistic Diversity and Traditional Knowledge"', www.terralingua.org/ projects/vitek/ch5.htm, accessed 31 July 2010

CHAPTER 4

Ethnobiological Methods for Ethnomycological Research: Quantitative Approaches

Stanford Zent and Egleé L. Zent

INTRODUCTION

In the last 20 to 25 years there has been a growing trend of using quantitative methods and designs in ethnobiological research. The quantitative revolution in ethnobiology has helped to boost its appeal among students and budding researchers as well as its status within the greater scientific community. The benefits of a quantitative approach include: greater methodological rigour; explicit attention to sampling; more reliable data sets; enhanced analytical capabilities; and higher confidence in the research results and conclusions (cf. Phillips 1996; Höft et al, 1999). Moreover, this development has played a big role in expanding the investigative scope of ethnobiological research. In the past, most field studies in ethnobiology had a descriptive focus; they were occupied with compiling lists of locally known or used plants and animals, making collections of specimens and recording their cultural names, classifications, uses and manipulations (Phillips, 1996; Peters, 1996). By contrast, recent research has had a more analytical orientation, characterized by the careful measurement of selected bio-cultural variables, the statistical representation and analysis of data, the testing of hypotheses about relationships between variables, and occasionally the formulation of models depicting current states or trends of ethnobiological knowledge/behaviour and their causes or conditioning factors. This approach to research has not only advanced our understanding of the specific relationships and importance of the biological world for different cultural groups but also given us a better grasp of how these relationships are patterned or otherwise affected by the larger social and natural environments in which they are situated.

To date, quantitative methods have been employed mainly to study the cultural significance of different plants and animals, ethnomedical practices, agroecological management techniques, beliefs about animal–plant interactions, the economic importance of certain resources and habitats, or the ecological impacts of land and resource use. Another area of application relates to the social dimensions of ethnobiological knowledge systems, such as the distribution and exchange of knowledge within and across communities or societies, and the dynamics of persistence or change of knowledge over time. In some cases, the research findings have been directly used to support (or critique) resource management and conservation initiatives. This points to another important merit of quantitative ethnobiology: its applied significance for conservation and development policy issues.

Ethnomycological studies stand to benefit from the adoption of quantitative methods in the same general ways mentioned above and therefore the prospective researcher is encouraged to consider such methods for his/her own individual project. A major consideration in selecting which method(s) to use is to evaluate how relevant the data set will be in relation to the research problem or question(s) (Alexiades, 1996). If the focus of investigation is on the cultural perception and classification of fungi in a given society then perhaps a qualitative approach is more relevant (see Chapter 3) whereas a quantitative approach has excelled when the research is aimed at questions of process, such as the variation and/or change of knowledge/practices. In this chapter, we review a variety of methods that can be used to study different aspects or dimensions of the dynamic interactions between people and fungi. The chapter is divided into four sections: (1) valuation, a survey of different techniques for estimating the cultural significance or use value of biotaxa; (2) variation and change, dealing with measures of knowledge variation among individuals, social sub-groups and communities, and the inference of knowledge variation or transformation over time; (3) transmission, including methods for studying intergenerational and intercultural

Figure 4.1 *Training younger Jotï in the collection of ethnobiological data. Kayamá (Venezuela, December 2005)*

Photograph: Stanford Zent

knowledge transmission; and (4) behaviour, looking at the systematic observation of behavioural activities and their material consequences.

VALUATION

One of the primary applications of quantitative methods in ethnobiological research has been to compare and contrast the cultural value and significance of different folk taxa. It is not uncommon to find that rural (and some urban) societies around the world recognize and use hundreds of biological species in their daily lives. However, it is also true that not all plants/animals/fungi are treated equally by a given cultural group. Through a combination of formal interviewing and statistical analysis, ethnobiologists have been able to offer a more exact and detailed appreciation of the relative cultural importance value of each and every taxon, as measured by a single metric yet also based on the native point of view (Phillips and Gentry, 1993a, 1993b; Phillips, 1996). Moreover, the mathematical sense of value has been extended to encompass other biological units, such as families, life forms and ecosystem types (Phillips et al, 1994). This type of exercise has been instrumental for testing hypotheses about the relationships between eco-cultural characteristics (e.g. abundance, size, habitat, management, exotic/native species) and usefulness (Phillips et al, 1993a; La Torre-Cuadros and Islebe, 2003; Rocha Silva and Andrade, 2006). Alternatively, the biological content of different use categories has been analysed in terms of the richness of species diversity that fulfil this function (Figueiredo et al, 1997; Galeano, 2000). That a large number species are deemed useful for a particular use category is sometimes interpreted as evidence of the importance of that use category (Rossato et al, 1999; Galeano, 2000). Such measurements also have practical applications, such as identifying which species are more important from a cultural standpoint and thereby establishing conservation priorities or targets that are more relevant from a local perspective (Stoffle et al, 1990; Phillips and Gentry, 1993a, 1993b). Furthermore, it has proved to offer a valuable tool for assessing knowledge variation within and between communities as well as trends of knowledge change, as we describe in the section on Variation and Change.

Quantitative appraisals of the cultural importance value of folk taxa have generally relied on rather brief and simple structured interviews in which the key starting question is 'How do you use X?' or its semantic equivalent. The same standardized interview is conducted with a group of people from the study community, preferably a sample of systematic design (e.g. random, stratified or purposive; see Chapter 3). After the basic interview data have been recorded, the total sum of answers are tabulated and added up or otherwise converted into numerical form using a more complex procedure in order to rate and distinguish the use value of different taxa relative to one another. Quite a few different cultural importance/significance indices have been developed, which vary in terms of field methods, information incorporated and formulas of calculation (see Silva et al, 2006; Hoffman and Gallaher, 2007; Garibay-Orijel, et al 2007; Tardío and Pardo-de-Santayana, 2008 for selective reviews). Phillips (1996) categorizes these indices into three broad classes: uses totalled, researcher score and informant consensus.

The 'uses totalled' methodology

The 'uses totalled' methodology entails the simple addition of use citations per taxonomic category (e.g. Toledo et al, 1995). This operation can be carried out in two ways, which may be done separately or in combination:

- the total number of times that a particular use of the folk taxon is cited among the entire sample of respondents; and
- the total number of different uses that are attributed to the given taxon.

A variation of this approach has been employed to rate the usefulness of the forest by asking informants to state the uses of all plant species recorded in measured forest plots and then calculating the percentage of useful plants per unit area (Baleé, 1986, 1987; Boom, 1987, 1990; Bennett, 1992). This relative measure has in turn been utilized to compare the usefulness of local biodiversity across different cultural groups, subcultural groups or forest types (Prance et al, 1987; Caniago and Siebert, 1998; DeWalt et al, 1999; Galeano, 2000). The uses totalled method is easier and faster to carry out than the others but also yields less valuable information about the data set. For example, all use citations are counted equally and there is no recognition of relative differences in the degree of usage. Under this procedure, a rarely used species with more than one use could conceivably score higher than a frequently used species with only one use. Common species known and used by many people are automatically favoured over those species/uses which fall into the more restricted domain of specialist knowledge, regardless of how many people depend on and place value on the latter (cf. Silva et al 2006). In view of such distortions, simple counts are often made as a first step in the data analysis and then serve as input for more complex operations. Lawrence et al (2005) recommend conducting a rank order test of the relative importance of the inventory of taxa cited as being useful. The overall rank of each taxon per use category is calculated as the average ranking across the sample of informants.

The 'researcher score' method

In the 'researcher score' method the researcher assigns a score or quantitative value to the list of different folk taxa, which takes into account how extensively and intensively it is used. The precise method for calculating this score varies somewhat from study to study, from a simple distinction between major and minor uses to more elaborate formulas which encompass more variables. Prance et al (1987) used the former technique to quantify the cultural importance of forests for different Amazonian groups (see also Pinedo-Vasquez et al, 1990). They allowed a score of 1.0 for each major use and 0.5 for each minor use and added up the total for six general use categories (edible, construction, technology, remedy, commerce and other) per species and per family. Nancy Turner (1988) invented a Cultural Significance Index (CSI) of plants used by Salish groups (Canada), which is calculated as the product of three countable variables (quality, intensity, and exclusivity of use). Turner's CSI method has served subsequently as a model for other researchers who have elaborated on the original formula. Stoffle et al (1990) added the parts of a plant used for each purpose as well as the variable of 'contemporary use' into the CSI formula. Silva et al (2006) revised the list of constituent variables to species management, use preference and use frequency, changed the scale per variable to a binary scoring system, and incorporated a correction factor to the formula. The correction factor adjusts the score according to the informant consensus value (defined as the number of informants that cite a given species or the number of informants that cite the most cited species).

Pieroni (2001) developed a compound index, called the Cultural Food Significance Index (CFSI), for rating the variable importance of edible plants, which also included eight mushroom species in the analysis. This index aggregates a larger number (seven) of eco-cultural factors than any of the previous measures, and these refer specifically to this resource type: frequency of mention, perceived availability, frequency of use, taste score appreciation, plant parts used, multifunctional food use and food-medicinal role.

Garibay-Orijel et al (2007) adapted the CFSI specifically for the quantification of the cultural significance of edible mushrooms in their study of traditional mycological knowledge among the Ixtlan Zapotecs of Oaxaca (Mexico). Their index, labelled Edible Mushrooms Cultural Significance Index (EMCSI), incorporates eight scored variables: frequency of mention, perceived abundance, use frequency, taste, multifunctional food use, knowledge transmission, health and economy. The computations can be expressed in terms of each individual sub-index score or these can be added together to get the overall EMCSI. The results obtained for the different sub-indices were analysed by using multivariate ordination and grouping techniques (see section on Variation and Change) in order to reveal which variables combine and contrast to structure the Ixtlan Zapotecs' perceptions and behaviour with respect to different species of mushrooms. Garibay-Orijel et al (2007) consider that their index has several advantages. Firstly, the notion of cultural significance is divided into several domains, showing the relative position of species among a cultural significance gradient. Secondly, it is replicable yet flexible and can be used for cross-cultural comparison (ibid:16). The main criticism of these approaches is that they are subjective and biased toward the criteria imposed by the researcher, and therefore may not reflect accurately cultural insiders' notions of significance (Phillips, 1996; Hoffman and Gallaher, 2007).

Informant consensus

Informant consensus-based scoring techniques were explicitly designed to overcome researcher-biased measures of cultural importance. This approach relies on measuring the pattern of group consensus (i.e. level and distribution of agreement or disagreement across informants) in regards to a given data set. Different methods and formulas for calculating consensus were applied to investigate the medical efficacy of herbal remedies in different cultural contexts (Adu-Tutu et al, 1979; Friedman et al, 1986; Trotter and Logan, 1986; Johns et al, 1990; Varghese et al, 1993).

Trotter and Logan (1986) measured consensus by way of an Informant Agreement Ratio (IAR), formulated as the total number of cases of an ailment in a sample minus the number of separate remedies cited for the ailment, divided by the total cases of the ailment minus 1. Friedman et al (1986) computed efficacy as a function of rank order priority (ROP), calculated as the product of fidelity level (FL = ratio between the number of informants who gave the use of a species for the same treatment and the total number of informants who mentioned the plant for any use) and relative popularity level (RPL = ratio of the number of diseases treated by a particular plant and the number of informants). Johns et al (1990) used a log-linear model to calculate the interaction effect for each remedy cited in a sample as a measure of its degree of confirmation.

Probably the most well-known and influential consensus-based method used to quantify cultural importance or use value in ethnobiological research is the informant-indexing technique pioneered by Phillips and Gentry (1993a; 1993b; Phillips 1996). This method determines the use value (UV) of a species as a function of the overall average frequencies with which a group of informants state particular uses of particular species throughout a series of walking interviews in natural settings. Interviews may be repeated with the same informants in order to distinguish between consistent and inconsistent information, major and minor uses, and mistakes and true answers at the individual level. The use value of each species (s) for each informant (i), UV_{is}, is calculated as the sum of the number of uses mentioned in each interview event by the informant divided by the number of such events for species (s) with informant (i). The total use value for each species, UV_s, is the sum of all UV_{is} divided by the number of informants interviewed for species. The informant-indexing use-value measure has subsequently been utilized or adapted by a large number of ethnobotanical researchers (Figueiredo et al, 1993, 1997; Kvist et al, 1995; Kremen et al, 1998; Rossato et al, 1999; Galeano, 2000; Luoga et al, 2000; Byg and Balslev, 2001, 2004; Gomez-Beloz, 2002; Kristensen and Lykke, 2003; La Torre-Cuadros and Islebe, 2003; Lykke et al, 2004; Gazzaneo et al, 2005; Monteiro et al, 2006).

Although informant-based techniques strive to be more objective and to better reflect the study population's general knowledge and use of biological species, a valid criticism of this approach is that the major use categories themselves still tend to be defined by the researcher (Zent, 2009). Furthermore, the operation of assigning continuous quantitative values (by the researcher) to what are in fact discrete qualitative judgments of value (by the local people), no matter how rigorous or sophisticated these mathematical procedures may look, nonetheless represents a grave distortion of the folk point of view. Thus the numerical values that are produced in any given case should be looked upon as very approximate and relative measures at best.

VARIATION AND CHANGE

The assessment of variation and change in traditional ecological knowledge/practices is another prominent theme of recent ethnobiological research in which the use of quantitative research methods has made a crucial difference. The focus on intra-cultural variation takes into account the fact that cultural knowledge is unevenly distributed within a given community and is patterned by age, gender, kinship, marriage, residence, education, occupation, socioeconomic class, ethnic affiliation, trade, religion and other social statuses (Boster, 1987; see Figure 4.2).

These variables constrain and determine people's customary activities, spatial mobility, and access and control of resources; thus they directly affect people's contact and familiarity with environmental components (Pfeiffer and Butz, 2005). Moreover,

Figure 4.2 *Training Jotï boys in the collection of ethno-ecological data and taking GPS readings (Kayama, Venezuela, June 2003)*

Photograph: Yheicar Bernal

social relationships constitute channels for the exchange and flow of information between individuals and groups. Hence the pattern of social distribution of knowledge within a community closely reflects the pattern of knowledge transmission (Boster, 1987). Intra-cultural variation of knowledge is closely associated with the dynamic process of culture change over time just as genetic variation within a population is the source of biological evolution (Pelto and Pelto, 1975). Through diffusion and experimentation, new forms of knowledge – such as local names, cognitive categories, use values, recipes and skills – are constantly being introduced. Old and new forms coexist and compete with each other and eventually those which confer adaptive advantage are propagated at the expense of others. Thus synchronic variation can be used to infer ongoing processes of change over time, including ontogenetic development (i.e. life-cycle of the individual to maturity) as well as phylogenetic development (i.e. evolutionary transition of the society/tribe) (Zent and Zent, 2000).

A focus on the distributive and dynamic properties of knowledge dictates a shift of the analytical locus from the group to the individual. The characterization of individual knowledge variation depends essentially on two basic operations: the inter-subjective sampling of individual knowledge, and the measurement of inter-informant patterns of similarity and difference. The sampling of knowledge in an individual sense means that interviews or observations are conducted with one person at a time and their responses are recorded separately and independently of those recorded from other individuals. Furthermore, the goal of assessing cognitive variation requires that the recorded data are directly comparable across individuals. This criterion is usually achieved by adopting a standardized data collection method. Most studies of ethnobiological variation and change rely on structured interviews or questionnaires because these are relatively easy to code and the results are directly comparable (i.e. do not require interpretation). After the raw data is collected and coded, it must be submitted to an appropriate statistical analysis of variance for the purpose of producing precise measurements of the patterns of similarity/difference of responses among the sample of persons interviewed.

A wide variety of statistical procedures can be used to quantify individual knowledge and to analyse patterns of variation within a sample population. The optimum choice of method will depend on the field methods used, the type(s) of data collected and the research questions being asked.

'Matching and scoring' methods

The most elegant and extensively used measures are simple counts or percentage comparisons between different subgroups (based on age, gender, occupation, etc.) as determined by the average number of biotaxa named in free-listing interviews or the average proportion of known vs. unknown elements in identification tasks (Chipeniuk, 1995; Katz, 1989; Nabhan, 1998, 2001). One of the hidden assumptions of this method is that the researcher has already has an idea of what constitutes a true vs. false answer. In many cases, all answers supplied by one's informants are simply accepted as valid without further evaluation. One alternative is the 'matching with expert' test. This entails preliminary elicitation of response items from one or more locally recognized experts. Individual scores are then determined by proportional agreement with the expert(s) over a structured set of questions (Albuquerque, 2006; Caniago and Siebert, 1998; Zent, 2009). The 'matching with science' procedure has a similar test design but uses published scientific information as the answer key against which local respondent's answers are scored (Godoy et al, 1998; Reyes-García et al, 2006). These methods have been questioned on the grounds that the knowledge of average persons should not be expected to match the knowledge of so-called experts (especially given the distributional culture concept stated in the introduction to this section) just as the knowledge of folk peoples will probably not coincide perfectly with that of scientists.

Consensus analysis

An alternative approach to quantifying knowledge differentials at the individual level is by carrying out group consensus analysis. The cultural consensus model (CCM) developed by Kimball Romney and associates (Romney et al, 1986, 1987) is one of the most popular forms of quantitative consensus analysis used in social science research in recent years and it has also been employed previously in several important studies of ethnobiological variation and change (Atran, 1999, 2001; Atran and Medin, 1997; Boster, 1986; Zent, 1999, 2001, Zent and Zent, 2004). CCM is a mathematical technique, based on factor analysis, designed to measure patterns of inter-informant agreement (or levels of disagreement) about selected culturally shared domains. The method requires obtaining a single factor solution (expressed by a first eigenvalue at least three times greater than the second eigenvalue), which indicates that a group consensus model exists. Having established that consensus configures the domain, it permits: (a) determination of the correct answers when such answers are unknown beforehand and (b) rating of the individual knowledge levels, expressed in terms of estimated competence scores. According to the computational formulas used, correct answers are usually the most popular answers but greater weight is given to individuals who display greater competence and lesser weight is given to individuals who display lower competence. The individual competence scores are essentially measured as a function of the degree to which an individual's answers concord or agree with the 'correct' answers derived from the group. Phillips and Gentry (1993b) adapted their informant-indexing technique for measuring the cultural use value of different plant species (a plant-centric measure; see the Valuation section of this chapter) to the analysis of botanical knowledge differences by age in their study population (an anthropocentric measure). The overall plant use knowledge for each informant was measured as the standardized ratio between the total use value recorded for him/her and the total use value recorded for the entire group of informants. This technique amounts to a kind of inter-informant consensus analysis in the sense that the average number of plant uses known by an individual is compared to the average number of plant uses expressed by the population.

Classification and ordination

Classification and ordination represent another set of techniques that can be used to represent and measure the variation of knowledge within a given community or cultural group.

Classification, also known as cluster analysis, is an exploratory mathematical technique which has the aim of sorting an array of heterogeneous objects into a smaller number of homogeneously defined groups or clusters. Applied to the analysis of interpersonal differences of cultural knowledge, it can be used to identify subgroups in a population based on the calculation of degrees of shared understandings among individuals. Hierarchical cluster analysis provides an idea of the stepwise distance of these groupings in relation to one another through divisive (i.e., progressive splitting) or agglomerative (i.e. progressive merging) graphic displays (Höft et al, 1999).

Ordination is a statistical method that orders objects characterized by values on multiple variables (i.e. multivariate objects) along gradients so that similar objects are near each other and dissimilar objects are further apart. These relationships between the objects, on each of several axes (one for each variable), are then characterized numerically and/or graphically. While ordination has been used mainly for studying community ecology (e.g. floristic composition in relation to environmental gradients), it can also be applied to ethnobiological research by incorporating people as one of the object variables (for example, a People × Species data matrix). Höft et al (1999) propose that the applications of ordination for examining human-biotic relationships include the following: (a) revealing whether certain groups of people value the same species in the same ways, (b) spotting individuals who respond differently from the majority, and (c) grouping species according to the use values assigned by people.

The main types of ordination applied to ethnobiological data thus far are principal components analysis (PCA) and non-metrical multidimensional scaling (NMDS). In addition to segmenting and ordering the social universe according to patterns of shared (or non-shared) knowledge or behaviour, these techniques also afford insight into how knowledge is structured and distributed within a community. Different from consensus-based measures, which rate an individual's knowledge in reference to a single linear scale determined by the average collective response (i.e. one-to-all comparisons), classification and ordination produce aggregate measures of the degree of conformity of an individual to all other individuals in the sample (i.e. one-to-one comparisons).

Variation over time

The observed pattern(s) of ethnobiological variation in space can be used as input for inferring the processes of change of the ethnobiological system over time. This requires some additional analytical steps such as considering how different groups and subgroups are affected by surrounding changes in the socioeconomic or biophysical environment. Beyond simply measuring the historical shifts or trends, this body of work also addresses the major questions of why knowledge changes or persists and what are the main environmental factors driving this process. There are two basic approaches for documenting cultural knowledge change/continuity through time: longitudinal studies and cross-sectional studies.

The longitudinal study

The most simple, straightforward and accurate way to measure change is by carrying out a longitudinal study. This entails the collection and comparison of time-series data – i.e. similar type of data, using similar methods, at the same site(s) at two or more different time periods. A variation of this approach is the community restudy, which involves going back to a community that was studied sometime in the past, usually by somebody else. The observed changes in ethnobiological knowledge and practices can then be related to more general socio-cultural and ecological changes that also took place during this interval to get some idea of the causal factors and mechanisms involved. The requirements of this approach are that reliable and comparable baseline data are available or that data collection can be sustained over a relatively long time span. Due to the difficulty of meeting these conditions, it is not surprising that there are few precedents of this kind in ethnobiological research (Zarger and Stepp, 2004; van Etten, 2006). Thus for most researchers, the only option is to rely on indirect methods for inferring the transmission process.

The cross-sectional study

Cross-sectional (or transversal) studies refer to data collecting operations at one point in time. However, several creative techniques have been devised for inferring diachronic processes of ethnobiological loss, change or persistence from synchronic data. After the patterns of variation within and between study groups are measured, the next step is to examine the correlations of such variations with other social and environmental variables which are indexed to time (thus permitting an explanation of past events) or are themselves relevant indicator variables of change in a more general sense. A third step is to interpret the observed relationships by reference to the larger historical-ecological context. The overwhelming majority of empirical studies of ethnobiological knowledge change and process conform to this type.

People's age stands out as the social variable most commonly used to chart the slope of knowledge change in dynamic contexts, probably because it is universal and directly indexed to time. In studies of the ontogenetic development of knowledge acquisition, the array of individually recorded and scored knowledge types and amounts are ordered according to the person's age and the resulting knowledge-by-age trend lines are read as site-specific models of the age-dependent learning process (e.g. Stross, 1973; Dougherty, 1979; Hunn, 2002; Zarger, 2002; Hatano and Inagaki, 1999; Keil et al, 1999; Ki-fong Au, 1999; Coley, 2000) Age-on-knowledge curves are also frequently employed to infer the diachronic evolution of TEK amount and content in groups over time (Hewlett and Cavalli-Sforza, 1986; Ohmagari and Berkes, 1997; Rosenberg, 1998; Zent, 1999, 2001; Lizarralde, 2001, 2004; Heckler, 2002; Byg and Balslev, 2004; Zent and Zent, 2004). In that case, the difference(s) between older versus younger people's knowledge levels is measured and thought to approximate the degree of change (whether loss or increase) that has occurred in that time interval. Some researchers have pointed out that the knowledge-on-age trend-line in a stable (i.e. 'non-erosional') situation where knowledge is not being lost, should reflect gradual increments of change, whereas trend-lines displaying sharp breaks or noticeable tips are indicative of irreversible change (e.g. erosion of local knowledge) over time (Ross, 2002; Voeks and Leony, 2004; Florey, 2009). An alternative approach is to confine the sample population to adults beginning with the age level at which intellectual maturity is thought to be reached. Accordingly, the difference between knowledge levels of younger versus older generation adults is represented as an approximate measure of the direction and rate of knowledge change (Voeks and Leony, 2004; Caniago and Siebert, 1998; Lee et al, 2001).

Besides age, we were able to observe a number of other social variables that are treated as proxies or indicators of acculturation. Some of these are obviously direct markers of modernization and are easily measured on an individual basis, like years of school education completed, literacy, fluency in the national language, amount of income obtained from cash copping or wage labor, material possessions and travel experience (Wester and Yongvanit, 1995; Godoy et al, 1998; Zent, 1999, 2001; Sternberg et al, 2001; Byg and Balslev, 2004; Voeks and Leony, 2004; Reyes-García et al, 2005a, 2007). Others are more indirect or qualitatively described change indicators that are assumed to affect entire communities: availability of modern services (e.g. schools, health clinics, communications and transportation, nontraditional housing, indoor plumbing); changes in settlement pattern; introduction of exogenous technology, economic orientation (e.g. commercial vs. subsistence activity); proximity to roads or urban areas; contact with outsiders; habitat degradation; and non-traditional beliefs and values (Caniago and Siebert, 1998; Benz et al, 2000; Ross, 2002; Ghimire et al, 2004; Shanley and Rosa, 2004; Zarger and Stepp, 2004; Lawrence et al, 2005; Reyes-García et al, 2005a, 2005b; Ross and Medin, 2005; Cruz-García, 2006). In addition to measuring the co-variation between ethnobiological variables and the socioecological change indicator variables mentioned above, it may be necessary to take into consideration qualitative aspects of the socio-historical context, not only at the local level but also at regional, national and international scales (Lawrence et al, 2005).

TRANSMISSION

The transmission of knowledge represents another dynamic property or dimension of ethnobiological systems that has begun to attract more attention from researchers in recent years. The study of patterns of transmission can shed considerable light on how and why changes take place, including not only the erosion of traditional knowledge but also the acquisition of new forms. For example, Zent (2009) examined the impact of intercultural contact and missionary activities on the trans-generational continuity (or change) of ethnobotanical knowledge among the Jotï people of Venezuela. Several important social and economic transformations associated with the missionary process were identified as having a detrimental impact on the acquisition of such knowledge among younger people:

- more sedentary settlement patterns;
- substitution of traditional with nontraditional activities;
- more time spent in agricultural tasks as opposed to foraging;
- decreased amount of time that children and adults spend together;
- diminished consumption and use of wild natural resources;
- positive valuation of allotochtonous knowledge (derived from outside influences) over autochtonous (locally derived) knowledge.

By contrast, Campos and Ehringhaus (2003) observed that 20 to 30 per cent of the particular uses of palms by indigenous groups of southwestern Amazonia (Brazil) were non-traditional uses adopted from their non-indigenous neighbours. The two cases mentioned here illustrate two main types of transmission: from generation to generation and from group to group.

Inter-generational, or vertical, transmission is extremely important: this is how a society's traditional knowledge and practices are reproduced and perpetuated over time. The transmission process can be analysed in terms of a few key elements:

- Social channels: the social relationships of individuals (e.g. parent-child, older sibling-younger sibling, expert-novice) between whom knowledge is passed.
- Situational contexts: the combination of physical, social, symbolic and intentional elements that frame the dynamic learning events.
- Learning/teaching strategies: to the modes of communication and psycho-behavioural operations used to convey/capture information.

Different data collecting styles have been used to explore these phenomena.

One style relies on the traditional anthropological methods of participant observation and in-depth, informal interviewing of key informants. This group of studies is characterized by normative, anecdotal and qualitative ethnographies of how young people are socialized in different ethno-ecological domains (e.g. plant uses, food procurement tasks, phytotherapies), with culturally sensitive descriptions of the routine acquisition mechanisms (e.g. peripheral participation, observation, imitation, informal instruction, supervised practice) and the key social relationships (e.g. grandmother–granddaughter, father–son, grandfather–grandson, female co-residents) (Messer, 1975; Ruddle and Chesterfield, 1977; Katz, 1986, 1989; Lave and Wenger, 1991; Murphy, 1992; Wilbert, 2002).

A second approach to data collecting makes use of structured questionnaires or interviews administered to a sample of respondents and statistical analysis of the results. The interview schedule consists of questions about whether the person knows or performs certain traditional practices (e.g. wild plant gathering, craft-making, bush skills), their age when first learned, the person who taught it and their relationship to the respondent, and in some cases where and how learned. This exercise produces a descriptive statistical profile of the knowledge transmission process, specifying according to the category of knowledge: average age (range) when acquired, most common personal sources, and typical locations and methods of acquisition (Hewlitt and Cavalli-Sforza, 1986; Ohmagari and Berkes, 1997; Lozada et al, 2006).

A third approach to studying ethnoecological knowledge transmission can be identified as social network analysis. The specific method used for this type of analysis by Scott Atran in his study of Mayan and Ladino groups in the Petén region of Guatemala involves two basic steps of data collection: (a) elicitation of ranked lists of socially significant others, of most frequent interlocutors about forest matters, and of recognized forest experts, and (b) follow-up interviews with the highest and lowest ranked individuals appearing in the aforementioned lists, eliciting their respective social interaction and forest expert networks. The results of this exercise are then added up and projected graphically to model the density, diffuseness and directionality of putative knowledge exchanges within the social group (Atran, 1999, 2001; Atran et al, 2002).

The investigation of intercultural knowledge transmission helps to bring out the creative, adaptive and historical aspects of ethnobiological systems. One way in which this topic can be investigated is by means of controlled comparisons of resource inventories and their use values across two or more cultural groups who occupy a contiguous space or are in direct contact with each other, especially where at least one of these groups is indigenous and another is immigrant (Campos and Ehringhaus, 2003; Byg and Balslev, 2004). The sharing of cognate names for the same species by ethnolinguistically-distinct groups, particularly when their languages are not genetically related, is a telling indication of ethnobiological contact and diffusion in the past (Austerlitz, 1968; Svanberg, 2009). Atran (1999, 2001), in the study mentioned above, extends network analysis to investigate the flow of ethnoecological information between distinct ethnic communities inhabiting the same region. Although we are not aware of any research which specifically deals with the question of ethnomycological knowledge transmission, given the rapidly shifting nature of fungi use as food, medicinal and commercial resource in many places around the world, this appears to offer a particularly apt domain for investigating transmission issues.

Figure 4.3 *Training Jotï research participants in the collection of ethno-ecological data (Kayama, Venezuela, June 2003)*

Photograph: Stanford Zent

BEHAVIOUR

Observational studies of human behaviour can open another window onto people's relationship to fungi and therefore provide a necessary complement to cognitive research (see Figure 4.3 and Chapter 3). Informant statements and recollections about cultural practices tend to present a normative picture and gloss over the exceptions, whereas a focus on the behaviour of different individuals helps to capture more diversity and complexity. People do not always do what they say they do. Actually observing what they do provides a corrective control on their statements (Zent, 1996). Moreover, people do not always say everything they do. Paying attention to the latter is useful for filling in missing information and obtaining further details. Some forms of knowledge are embodied in behaviour (physical movements) and not necessarily conscious or verbalized. Our ability to detect and apprehend such knowledge, often referred to as skills or 'know-how', may depend entirely on the opportunity to witness it in live action. The listing of folk taxonomies, perceptual properties and use categories by way of standardized elicitation formats tends to convey fragmented and formalized representations of cultural knowledge removed from their normal natural and social contexts (Ellen, 1986). A broadly conceived method that integrates both cognitive and behavioural data is able to provide a more holistic grasp of the knowledge system. Participant observation involves not simply taking up residence in the study community but also taking an active part in the social and economic activities that make up community life. Going along on foraging or trading expeditions, helping out in the kitchen, sharing the meals and participation in other activities is a good way to build rapport and familiarity with local people, and also gives the researcher first-hand experience of the subject.

Many different methods have been developed for recording people's social and ecological behaviour in natural settings, including qualitative as well as quantitative approaches. The choice of method used depends on the research topic and specific questions being studied. If the goal is a detailed ethnographic description, then participant observation of the full range of activities involving mushrooms – from collecting to processing, consuming and marketing – is a standard technique. Observational ability, style and language will vary from person to person, but it is recommended that field notes are taken as soon as possible and at the lowest level of abstraction (Pelto and Pelto, 1978). Attention should be given to both the ecological and social context of the activity. Besides the description of the focal activity itself, records of behavioural events often include relevant information about the date and time, the actors and their respective roles, the social relationships between participants, the sequence of constituent activities that make up the entire event, the timing of these sequences, the tools and/or materials used, the place or habitat, weather, and material outcome of the activity (Johnson, 1978). The full meaning and significance of an activity often goes beyond what meets the eye at one moment in time and therefore the researcher might have to conduct follow-up inquiries or relate the observed event to other types of data (Pelto and Pelto, 1978). In order to avoid bias and unreliability in behavioural data collection, a reasonable sampling strategy should be developed with the aim of distributing observational events among different people, locations and seasons. This ideal of maximizing data representativity is valid whether the study has a qualitative or quantitative orientation.

The study of behaviour through field observation lends itself easily to quantitative data collection and analysis (cf. Altmann, 1974). As a general research strategy, quantitative measurement has several advantages: increased reliability, comparability, theoretical precision and statistical power (Johnson, 1978:43–45). At the same time, the quantitative study of behaviour must confront several methodological challenges: (a) sampling design, (b) coding of behaviour, and (c) currency type or counting units. The sample design should seek to maximize coverage of the socioeconomic diversity of the study population, the range of different activities and seasonal variations while at the same time minimize the time and cost for the researcher as well as the intrusiveness and disruption for the study group. The recording of different behaviours should be done according to an explicitly defined code that is somewhat compatible and thus comparable with the categories used in other studies. Units of measurement depend on what dimension of behaviour is being looked at, but the main rule of thumb is to use the most universal measure possible – such as the time spent in different behavioural categories (in minutes or hours) or the gross weight of particular products (in grams or kilograms) – to allow for convertibility to other derived measures (such as market values) if the need arises.

Ethnomycological researchers may want to consider the potential applications of quantitative data for examining certain aspects of the procurement or allocation process. For example, the measurement of time or energy inputs and production outputs would be crucial components of a micro-economic cost-benefit analysis (Montoya et al, 2008). This in turn would permit the inferential exploration of decision-making processes such as why to pursue one resource strategy versus another. Other topics that require a quantitative approach include: the significance of mushroom hunting as a part of the total activity budget, the proportional contribution of this resource type to the local diet, the comparison of harvest amounts across different sites or time periods, and the impact of cash cropping on local subsistence habits. A quantitative approach permits the statistical integration and comparison of different data sets, leading to more sophisticated analysis and hypothesis testing. For example, a comparative analysis of mushroom production levels, market prices and export figures over time could provide information for exploring the relationships between the mushroom trade, ecological pressures and social impacts (cf. Winkler, 2008; Yang et al, 2008).

Useful field methods for producing quantitative descriptions of ethnoecological behaviour can be conveniently grouped into three primary dimensions: spatial relationships, human activities and resource production (Zent, 1996), which are discussed below.

Spatial relationships

The spatial dimension encompasses measurements of geographic data and information. Relevant information includes the mapping of resource distributions, foraging routes and exchange circuits, which in turn can be used to calculate land areas exploited or distances travelled. At a local scale, this type of data can be recorded easily and efficiently by using a portable GPS (Global Positioning System), which computes the precise geographic coordinates of resource or activity locations (Figure 4.4).

The productivity of a species in a given area can also be extrapolated by taking sample measurements of yield per unit of land area and then multiplying by the total resource catchment area. Samils et al (2008) analysed yield in spatial terms (kg/ha per year) in combination with market price (EUR/kg) to compare income generation from truffle plantations with income earned from cereal production in rural Spain. They found that truffle cultivation was far superior in economic potential and therefore offers a more profitable land use option for farmers. Further discussion on economic valuation methods is given in Chapter 5.

Human activity

Activities are usually measured in terms of time units although energy expenditure or monetary value could also be used according to the nature of the research problem. The sampling of activity patterns can be divided into two main techniques: (1) continuous observation, observing an activity, or sequence of activities, over a specified time frame; and (2) state observation, recording the activity which occurs at a single moment in time (Hames, 1992). The former, sometimes called time-motion study, entails recording the time it takes to carry out a specified cultural activity. The time of the activity is

Figure 4.4 *Ara taking a GPS reading while collecting ethnoecological data (Jkalo Ijkuana, Venezuela, May 2002)*

Photograph: Stanford Zent

sometimes measured in relation to a second variable, such as the amount of resource harvested or area worked, in order to calculate the efficiency or time cost per unit of product output. Although the timing operation is usually performed by the researcher who participates or follows along in the activity, it is also feasible to train the local actors to do this work themselves. Another alternative for timing organized activities outside the home is to record exit and arrival times. Depending on the activity type and the analytical objectives, it may be necessary to delineate and time separately the different key operations or phases of the total activity sequence. For example, in order to test hypotheses under optimal foraging theory, it may be necessary to separate search time, pursuit/handling time per resource type and transport time for all resources (see Hill and Kaplan, 1992). The spot check or instantaneous scan sampling methods are the most common types of state observations used in human behavioural research. The basic technique consists of recording the activities of a sample of different individuals of the study population at randomly or systematically selected time points. The repeated application of this method over a reasonable time period (e.g. one year, in order to capture seasonal variations) produces a frequency distribution of the number of observed events per activity category, which in turn allows the researcher to calculate the proportional allocation of time to different types of behaviour, such as work vs. leisure, collecting vs. marketing (Johnson, 1975).

Another important dimension has to do with person-number, distinguishing individual vs. group observations. Observations on focal individuals involve closely following and recording the movements and actions of chosen individuals even in the context of group activities. Such focal person observations can be carried out in a continuous fashion – timing the start and finish times of different behaviours – or using a point sampling method – noting the person's behaviour at set intervals (every 5, 10, 30, etc. minutes). Similar focal observations of (sub)groups can also be done but obviously it is more difficult to effectively monitor several individuals at the same time especially if the activities imply physical separations beyond immediate view.

Resource production

Resource production (or consumption) can be estimated by measuring sampled quantities over a specified temporal or spatial frame and then extrapolating the results according to the parameter and scale most pertinent to the research objective (e.g. per hour, day, week, year, person, household, village, region, person–day). This kind of measure is very useful for assessing economic productivity, consumption habits and ecological impact. Although resources can be counted by way of different currencies, Johnson (1978) recommends that the quantity of the raw product itself is the most versatile measurement and can easily be converted into other currencies (e.g. local market value). Many different sampling procedures have been used and only a few examples can be mentioned here. The best method would be to count and weigh all the resources that are brought back to the house or village during the entire research period. But since it is extremely difficult to achieve complete coverage, more accurate results may actually be obtained by sampling certain days and/or certain households/ producers. In our own research, we have trained and hired local people to do this job, with reasonably good results. Alternatively, people can be asked to recall all of the resource items and approximate amounts (according to their own measuring units) they collect or harvest during the day; the reported amounts can then be converted into estimated weights based on a sample of actual weighing events per resource item. One technique used in consumption studies is to count or weigh all the resources of a certain class at the start of the study period, all amounts introduced during the period and the amounts remaining at the end, in order to calculate how much was actually consumed. The same basic method can be adapted to studying product exchange in a market setting. If the researcher wants a more detailed picture of exchange, then the focus of observation may be on the transactions themselves, noting the content (e.g. species type) and frequency or volume of the transactions as well as relevant variables of the vendor and consumer populations (e.g. sex, ethnic background, education, occupation). For example, Montoya et al (2008) made weekly visits to a mushroom dealer's store in central Mexico over a four month period and recorded the species sold, price per kilo paid, amount of each species bought in the store that day, the number of people who came to sell mushrooms and the criteria used by the dealer for choosing which mushrooms to buy.

CONCLUSION

Although the main focus in this chapter has been on quantitative ethnobiological techniques, we should also emphasize that these are meant to complement, rather than substitute, qualitative methods of data collection and analysis (see Chapter 3). It is quite possible that some sort of qualitative assessment of cultural categories, meanings and behaviours will have to be undertaken before any counting can even begin. For example, it doesn't make much sense to tally up use value citations mentioned in individual interviews if you haven't accurately translated the emically-valid use categories. In our opinion, the most interesting case studies are those that manage to integrate different types of data and methods. In any case, it is worthwhile to recognize the special value of quantitative data and mathematical analysis, especially in regard to revealing the distributive and dynamic parameters of human–fungi relationships. How important is a particular species for a cultural group? Which sub-groups or individuals know about it and which ones don't? Is this knowledge being retained, lost or transformed from one generation to the next? How is this knowledge or skill set being passed on? Are traditional forms of learning/teaching being affected by formal schooling and other socio-cultural changes? How much of a particular resource is actually being harvested or consumed or sold? Are species being harvested at a sustainable level? These are just a few of the questions that are best answered by way of supporting mathematical data and evidence. They are also questions with deep implications for ecological or cultural management problems. Quantitative data collection and analysis are not always easy to do but the benefits clearly outweigh the costs.

REFERENCES

Adu-Tutu, M., Afful, Y., Asante-Appiah, K., Lieberman, D., Hall, J. B. and Elvin-Weis, M. (1979) 'Chewing stick usage in southern Ghana', *Economic Botany* 33, pp320–328

Albuquerque, U. P. (2006) 'Re-examining hypotheses concerning the use and knowledge of medicinal plants: a study in the Caatinga vegetation of NE Brazil', *Journal of Ethnobiology and Ethnomedicine* 2(30)

Alexiades, M. N. (1996) 'Introduction to Quantitative Methods in Ethnobotanical Fieldwork', in M. N. Alexiades (ed) *Selected Guidelines for Ethnobotanical Research: A Field Manual*, Advances in Economic Botany, vol 10. The New York Botanical Garden, New York, pp167–169

Altmann, J. (1974) 'The observational study of behavior', *Behavior* 48, pp1–41

Atran, S. (1999) 'Managing the Maya Commons: The Value of Local Knowledge', in V. D. Nazarea (ed) *Ethnoecology: Situated Knowledge/Located Lives*, University of Arizona Press, Tucson, pp190–214

Atran, S. (2001) 'The Vanishing Landscape of the Peten Maya Lowlands', in L. Maffi (ed) *On Biocultural Diversity: Linking Language, Knowledge, and the Environment*, Smithsonian Institution Press, Washington, D.C., pp157–174

Atran, S. and Medin, D. (1997) 'Knowledge and Action: Cultural Models of Nature and Resource Management in Mesoamerica', in M. H. Bazerman, D. M. Messick, A. E. Tenbrunsel and K. A. Wade-Benzoni (eds) *Environment, Ethics, and Behavior: The psychology of environmental valuation and degradation*, The New Lexington Press, San Francisco, pp171–208

Atran, S., Medin, D., Ross, N., Lynch, E., Vapnarsky, V., Ucan Ek', E., Coley, J., Timura, C. and Baran, M. (2002) 'Folkecology, cultural epidemiology, and the spirit of the commons', *Current Anthropology* 43, pp421–450

Austerlitz, R. (1968) 'Native Seal Nomenclatures in South-Sahalin', in J. K. Yamagiwa (ed) *Papers of the CIC Far Eastern Language Institute*, Panel on Far Eastern Language Institutes of the Committee on Institutional Cooperation, Ann Arbor, MI, pp133–141

Baleé, W. (1986) 'Análise preliminar de inventário florestal e a etnobotânica Kaápor (Maranhão)', *Boletim do Museu Paraense Emílio Goeldi*, vol 2, no 2, pp141–167

Baleé, W. (1987) 'A etnobotânica quantitativa dos índios Tembé (Rio Gurupi, Pará)', *Boletim do Museu Paraense Emílio Goeldi, Botânica*, vol 3, no 1, pp29–50

Bennett, B. C. (1992) 'Plants and People of the Amazonian Rainforests', *BioScience* 42, pp599–607

Benz, B. F., Cevallos E. J., Santana M. F., Jesus Rosales A., and Graf, S. (2000) 'Losing knowledge about plant use in the Sierra de Manantlan Biosphere Reserve, Mexico', *Economic Botany* 54, pp183–191

Boom, B. (1987) 'Ethnobotany of the Chacobó Indians, Beni, Bolivia', *Advances in Economic Botany* 4, pp1–68

Boom, B. (1990) 'Useful plants of the Panare Indians of the Venezuelan Guayana', *Advances in Economic Botany* 8, pp57–76

Boster, J. S. (1986) 'Exchange of Varieties and Information Between Aguaruna Manioc Cultivators', *American Anthropologist*, vol 88, no 2, pp428–436

Boster, J. S. (1987) 'Introduction', *Behavioral Scientist*, vol 31, no 2, pp150–162

Byg, A. and Balslev, H. (2001) 'Diversity and use of palms in Zahamena, eastern Madagascar', *Biodiversity and Conservation* 10, pp951–970

Byg, A. and Balslev, H. (2004) 'Factors affecting local knowledge of palms in Nangaritza Valley, southeastern Ecuador', *Journal of Ethnobiology*, vol 24, no 2, pp255–278

Campos, M. T. and Ehringhaus, C. (2003) 'Plant Virtues are in the Eyes of the Beholders: A comparison of known palm uses among indigenous and folk communities of Southwestern Amazonia', *Economic Botany*, vol 57, no 3, pp324–344

Caniago, I. and Siebert, S. F. (1998) 'Medicinal plant economy, knowledge and conservation in Kalimantan, Indonesia', *Economic Botany* 52, pp229–250

Chipeniuk, R. (1995) 'Childhood Foraging as a Means of Acquiring Competent Human Cognition about Biodiversity', *Environment and Behavior*, vol 27, no 4, pp490–512

Coley, J. D. (2000) 'On the Importance of Comparative Research: The Case of Folkbiology', *Child Development*, vol 71, no 1, pp82–90

Cruz García, G. S. (2006) 'The mother–child nexus. Knowledge and valuation of wild food plants in Wayanad, Western Ghats, India', *Journal of Ethnobiology and Ethnomedicine* 2, pp39.

DeWalt, S., Bourdy, G., Chavez de Michel, L. R. and Quenevo, C. (1999) 'Ethnobotany of the Tacana: Quantitative inventories of two permanent plots of Northwestern Bolivia', *Economic Botany* 53, pp237–260

Dougherty, J. W. D. (1979) 'Learning Names for Plants and Plants for Names', *Anthropological Linguistics* 21, pp298–315

Ellen, R. F. (1986) 'Ethnobiology, Cognition, and the Structure of Prehension: Some General Theoretical Notes', *Journal of Ethnobiology* 6, pp83–98

Figueiredo, G. M., Leitão-Filho, H. F. and Begossi, A. (1993) 'Ethnobotany of Atlantic forest coastal communities: diversity of plant uses in Gamboa (Itacuruça Island, Brazil)', *Human Ecology* 21, pp419–430

Figueiredo, G. M., Leitão-Filho, H. F. and Begossi, A. (1997) 'Ethnobotany of Atlantic forest coastal communities: II. Diversity of plant uses at Sepetiba Bay (Brazil)', *Human Ecology*, vol 25, no 2, pp353–360

Florey, M. (2009) 'Sustaining indigenous languages and indigenous knowledge: developing community training approaches for the 21st century', in P. Bates, M. Chiba, S. Kube and D. Nakashima (eds) *Learning and Knowing in Indigenous Societies Today*, UNESCO, Paris, pp25–37

Friedman, J., Yaniv, Z., Dafni, A. and Palewitch, D. (1986) 'A Preliminary Classification of the Healing Potential of Medicinal Plants, Based on a Rational Analysis of an Ethnopharmacological Field Survey among Bedouins in the Negev Desert, Israel', *Journal of Ethnopharmacology* 16, pp275–287

Galeano, G. (2000) 'Forest use at the Pacific coast of Chocó, Colombia: a quantitative approach', *Economic Botany* 54, pp358–376

Garibay-Orijel, R., Caballero, J., Estrada-Torres, A. and Cifuentes, J. (2007) 'Understanding cultural significance, the edible mushrooms case', *Journal of Ethnobiology and Ethnomedicine*, vol 3, no 4, pp1–18

Gazzaneo, L. R., Lucena, R. F. P. and Albuquerque, U.P. (2005) 'Knowledge and use of medicinal plants by local specialists in a region of Atlantic Forest in the state of Pernambuco (Northeastern Brazil)', *Journal of Ethnobiology and Ethnomedicine*, vol 1, no 9

Ghimire, S. K., McKey, D. and Aumeeruddy Thomas, Y. (2004) 'Heterogeneity in Ethnoecological Knowledge and Management of Medicinal Plants in the Himalayas of Nepal: Implications for Conservation', *Ecology and Society*, vol 9, no 3, art 6

Godoy, R., Brokaw, N., Wilkie, D., Colón, D., Palermo, A., Lye, S. and Wei, S. (1998) 'On trade and cognition: Markets and the loss of folk knowledge among the Tawahka Indians', *Journal of Anthropological Research*, 54, pp219–233

Gomez-Beloz, A. (2002) 'Plant Use Knowledge of the Winikina Warao: The Case for Questionnaires in Ethnobotany', *Economic Botany*, vol 56, no 3, pp231–241

Hames, R. B. (1992) 'Time Allocation', in E. Smith and B. Winterhalder (eds) *Evolutionary Ecology and Human Behavior*, Aldine de Gruyter, New York, pp203–235

Hatano, G. and Inagaki, K. (1999) 'A Developmental Perspective on Informal Biology', in D. Medin and S. Atran (eds) *Folkbiology*, MIT Press, Cambridge, MA, pp321–354

Heckler, S. (2002) 'Traditional Ethnobotanical Knowledge Loss and Gender among the Piaroa', in J. R. Stepp, F. S. Wyndham and R. K. Zarger (eds) *Ethnobiology and Biocultural Diversity: Proceedings of the Seventh International Congress of Ethnobiology*. International Society of Ethnobiology. University of Georgia Press, Athens, GA, pp532–548

Hewlett, B. S. and Cavalli-Sforza, L. L. (1986) 'Cultural transmission among Aka Pygmies', *American Anthropologist*, vol 88, no 4, pp922–934

Hill, K. and Kaplan, H. (1992) 'Food Acquisition', in E. A. Smith and B. Winterhalder (eds) *Evolutionary Ecology and Human Behavior*, Aldine de Gruyter, New York

Hoffman, B. and Gallaher, T. (2007) 'Relative Cultural Importance Indices in Quantitative Ethnobotany', *Ethnobotany Research and Applications*, vol 5, no 1, pp185–199

Höft, M., Barik, S. and Lykke, A. (1999) 'Quantitative Ethnobotany: Applications of Multivariate and Statistical Analyses in Ethnobotany', *People and Plants Working Paper* 6, UNESCO, Paris

Hunn, E. (2002) 'Evidence for the Precocious Acquisition of Plant Knowledge by Zapotec Children', in J. R. Stepp, F. S. Wyndham and R. K. Zarger (eds) *Ethnobiology and Biocultural Diversity: Proceedings of the Seventh International Congress of Ethnobiology*. International Society of Ethnobiology. University of Georgia Press, Athens, GA, pp604–613

Johns, T., Kokwaro, J. O. and Kimanani, E. K. (1990) 'Herbal Remedies of the Luo of Siaya District, Kenya: Establishing Quantitative Criteria for Consensus', *Economic Botany*, vol 44, no 3, pp369–381

Johnson, A. W. (1975) 'Time Allocation in a Machiguenga Community', *Ethnology*, vol 14, no 3, pp301–310

Johnson, A. W. (1978) *Quantification in Cultural Anthropology. An Introduction to Research Design.* Stanford University Press, Stanford

Katz, C. (1986) 'Children and the Environment: Work, Play and Learning in Rural Sudan', *Children's Environments Quarterly*, vol 3, no 4, pp43–51

Katz, C. (1989) 'Herders, gatherers and foragers: The emerging botanies of children in rural Sudan', *Children's Environments Quarterly*, vol 6, no 1, pp46–53

Keil, F. C., Levin, D. T., Richman, B.A. and Gutheil, G. (1999) 'Mechanism and Explanation in the Development of Biological Thought: The Case of Disease', in D. Medin and S. Atran (eds) *Folkbiology*, MIT Press, Cambridge, MA, p285–320

Ki-fong Au, T. and Romo, L. F. (1999) 'Mechanical Causality in Children's "Folkbiology"', in D. Medin and S. Atran (eds) *Folkbiology*, MIT Press, Cambridge, MA, pp355–401

Kremen, C., Raymond, I. and Lance, K. (1998) 'An Interdisciplinary Tool for Monitoring Conservation Impacts in Madagascar', *Conservation Biology* 12, pp549–563

Kristensen, M. and Lykke, A. M. (2003) 'Informant-based valuation of use and conservation preferences of savanna trees in Burkina Faso', *Economic Botany* 57, pp203–217

Kvist, L. P., Andersen, M. K., Hesselsoe, M. and Vanclay, J. K. (1995) 'Estimating use-values and relative importance of Amazonian flood plain trees and forests to local inhabitants', *Commonwealth Forestry Review* 74, pp293–300

La Torre-Cuadros, M. A. and Islebe, G. A. (2003) 'Traditional ecological knowledge and use of vegetation in southeastern Mexico: A case study from Solferino, Quintana Roo', *Biodiversity and Conservation* 12, pp2455–2476

Lave, J. and Wenger, E. (1991) *Situated Learning: Legitimate peripheral participation*, Cambridge University Press, Cambridge

Lawrence, A., Phillips, O. L., Ismodes, A. R., López, M., Rose, S., Word, D. and Farfan, J. (2005) 'Local values for harvested forest plants in Madre de Dios, Peru: Towards a more contextualised interpretation of quantitative ethnobotanical data', *Biodiversity and Conservation* 14, pp45–79

Lee, R. A., Balick, M. J., Lee Ling, D., Sohl, F., Brosi, B. J. and Raynor, W. (2001) 'Cultural Dynamism and Change – An Example from the Federated States of Micronesia', *Economic Botany*, vol 55, no 1, pp9–13

Lizarralde, M. (2001) 'Biodiversity and loss of indigenous languages and knowledge in South America', in L. Maffi (ed) *On Biocultural Diversity: Linking Language, Knowledge, and the Environment*, Smithsonian Institution Press, pp265–281

Lizarralde, M. (2004) 'Indigenous Knowledge and Conservation of the Rain Forest: Ethnobotany of the Barí of Venezuela', in T. Carlson and L. Maffi (ed) 'Ethnobotany and Conservation of Biocultural Diversity', *Advances in Economic Botany* 15, pp113–131

Lozada, M., Ladio, A. and Weigandt, M. (2006) 'Cultural Transmission of Ethnobotanical Knowledge in a Rural Community of Northwestern Patagonia, Argentina', *Economic Botany*, vol 60, no 4, pp374–385

Luoga, E. J., Witkowski, E. T. F. and Balkwill, K. (2000) 'Differential utilization and ethnobotany of trees in Kitulanghalo Forest Reserve and surrounding communal lands, eastern Tanzania', *Economic Botany* 54, pp328–343

Lykke, A. M., Kristensen, M. K. and Ganaba, S. (2004) 'Valuation of local use and dynamics of 56 woody species in the Sahel', *Biodiversity and Conservation* 13, 1961–1990

Messer, E. (1975) 'Zapotec Plant Knowledge: Classification, Uses, and Communication about Plants in Mitla, Oaxaca, Mexico', PhD Dissertation, University of Michigan, Ann Arbor

Monteiro, J. M., de Albuquerque, U. P., de Freitas Lins-Neto, E. M., de Araújo, E. L. and de Amorim, E. L. C. (2006) 'Use patterns and knowledge of medicinal species among two rural communities in Brazil's semi-arid northeastern region', *Journal of Ethnopharmacology* 105, pp173–186

Montoya, A., Hernández, N., Mapes, C., Kong, A. and Estrada-Torres, A. (2008) 'The Collection and Sale of Wild Mushrooms in a Community of Tlaxcala, Mexico', *Economic Botany*, vol 62, no 3, pp413–424

Murphy, I. I. (1992) '"And I, in my turn, will pass it on": Indigenous education among the Kayapó Amerindians of central Brazil', PhD dissertation, University of Pittsburgh.

Nabhan, G. (1998) 'Passing on a Sense of Place and Traditional Ecological Knowledge between Generations: A Primer for Native American Museum Educators and Community-Based Cultural Education Projects', *People and Plants Handbook* 4, pp30–33

Nabhan, G. (2001) 'Cultural Perceptions of Ecological Interactions: An "Endangered People's" Contribution to the Conservation of Biological and Linguistic Diversity', in L. Maffi (ed) *On Biocultural Diversity: Linking Language, Knowledge, and the Environment*, Smithsonian Institution Press, Washington, DC, pp145–156.

Ohmagari, K. and Berkes, F. (1997) 'Transmission of Indigenous Knowledge and Bush Skills Among the Western James Bay Cree Women of Subarctic Canada', *Human Ecology*, vol 25, no 2, pp197–222

Pelto, P. J. and Pelto, G. H. (1975) 'Intra-cultural diversity: some theoretical issues', *American Ethnologist* 2, pp1–18

Pelto, P. J. and Pelto, G. H. (1978) *Anthropological Research. The Structure of Inquiry* (2nd edition) Cambridge University Press, Cambridge

Peters, C. M. (1996) 'Beyond Nomenclature and Use: A Review of Ecological Methods for Ethnobotanists', in M. N. Alexiades (ed) *Selected Guidelines for Ethnobotanical Research: A Field Manual*, Advances in Economic Botany, vol. 10. The New York Botanical Garden, New York, pp241–276

Pfeiffer, J. M. and Butz, R. J. (2005) 'Assessing Cultural and Ecological Variation in Ethnobiological Research: The Importance of Gender', *Journal of Ethnobiology*, vol 25, no 2, pp240–278

Phillips, O. (1996) 'Some Quantitative Methods for Analyzing Ethnobotanical Knowledge', in M. N. Alexiades (ed) *Selected Guidelines for Ethnobotanical Research: A Field Manual*, Advances in Economic Botany, vol 10, The New York Botanical Garden, New York, pp171–197

Phillips, O. and Gentry, A. H. (1993a) 'The Useful Plants of Tambopata, Peru: I. Statistical Hypothesis Tests with a New Quantitative Technique', *Economic Botany*, vol 47, no 1, pp15–32

Phillips, O. and Gentry, A. H. (1993b) 'The Useful Plants of Tambopata, Peru: II. Additional Hypothesis Testing in Quantitative Ethnobotany', *Economic Botany*, vol 47, no 1, pp33–43

Phillips, O., Gentry, A. H., Reynel, C., Wilkin, P. and Gálvez-Durand, C. (1994) 'Quantitative Ethnobotany and Amazonian Conservation', *Conservation Biology* 8, pp225–248

Pieroni, A. (2001) 'Evaluation of the cultural significance of wild food botanicals traditionally consumed in Northwestern Tuscany, Italy', *Journal of Ethnobiology*, vol 21, no 1, pp89–104

Pinedo-Vasquez, M., Zarin, D., Zipp, P. and Chota-Inuma, J. (1990) 'Use Values of Tree Species in a communal forest reserve in Northeast Peru', *Conservation Biology* 4, pp405–416

Prance, G., Baleé, W., Boom, B. and Carneiro, R. (1987) 'Quantitative Ethnobotany and the Case for Conservation in Amazonia', *Conservation Biology*, vol 1, no 4, pp296–310

Reyes-García, V., Vadez, V., Byron, E., Apaza, L., Leonard, W. R., Pérez, E. and Wilkie, D. (2005a) 'Market Economy and the Loss of Folk Knowledge of Plant Uses: Estimates from the Tsimane of the Bolivian Amazon', *Current Anthropology*, vol 46, no 4, pp651–656

Reyes-García, V., Vadez, V., Huanca, T., Leonard, W.R. and Wilkie, D. (2005b) 'Knowledge and consumption of wild plants: A comparative study in two Tsimane' villages in the Bolivian Amazon', *Ethnobotanical Research Applications* 3, pp201–207

Reyes-García, V., Vadez, V., Tanner, S., McDade, T., Huanca, T. and Leonard, W. R. (2006) Evaluating indices of traditional ecological knowledges: A methodological contribution, *Journal of Ethnobiology and Ethnomedicine* 2, p21

Reyes-García, V., Vadez, V., Huanca, T., Leonard, W. R. and McDade, T. (2007) 'Economic Development and Local Ecological Knowledge: A Deadlock? Quantitative Research from a Native Amazonian Society', *Human Ecology*, vol 35, no 3, pp371–377

Rocha Silva, A. J. and Cavalcante Andrade, L. H. (2006) 'Cultural Significance of Plants in Communities Located in the Coastal Forest Zone of the State of Pernambuco, Brazil', *Human Ecology*, vol 34, no 3, pp447–465

Romney, A. K., Weller, S. C. and Batchelder, W. H. (1986) 'Culture as Consensus: A Theory of Culture and Informant Accuracy', *American Anthropologist*, vol 88, no 2, pp313–318

Romney, A. K., Batchelder, W. H. and Weller, S. C. (1987) 'Recent Applications of Cultural Consensus Theory', *American Behavioral Scientist*, vol 31, no 2, pp163–177

Rosenberg, J. (1998) 'Documenting and Revitalizing Traditional Ecological Knowledge: Seri Survey', *People and Plants Handbook* 4, pp34–35

Ross, N. (2002) 'Cognitive aspects of intergenerational change: Mental models, cultural change, and environmental behavior among the Lacandon Maya of southern Mexico', *Human Organization* 61, pp125–138

Ross, N. and Medin, D. L. (2005) 'Ethnography and Experiments: Cultural Models and Expertise Effects Elicited with Experimental Research Techniques', *Field Methods*, vol 17, no 2

Rossato, S. C., Leitão-Filho, H. D. F. and Begossi, A. (1999) 'Ethnobotany of Caiçaras of the Atlantic forest coast (Brazil)', *Economic Botany* 53, pp387–395

Ruddle, K. and Chesterfield, R. (1977) *Education for Traditional Food Procurement in the Orinoco Delta*, Ibero-Americana 53, University of California Press, Berkeley

Samils, N., Olivera, A., Danell, E., Alexander, S. J., Fischer, C. and Colinas, C. (2008) 'The Socioeconomic Impact of Truffle Cultivation in Rural Spain', *Economic Botany*, vol 62, no 3, pp331–342

Shanley, P. and Rosa, N. A. (2004) 'Eroding knowledge: An ethnobotanical inventory in Eastern Amazonia's logging frontier', *Economic Botany* 58, pp135–160

Silva, V. A., Cavalcante Andrade L. H. and Albuquerque, U. P. (2006) 'Revising the Cultural Significance Index: The Case of the Fulni-ô in Northeastern Brazil', *Field Methods*, vol 18, no 1, pp98–108

Sternberg, R. J., Nokes, C., P. Wenzel Geissler, Prince, R., Okatcha, F., Bundy, D .A. and Grigorenko, E. L. (2001) 'The relationship between academic and practical intelligence: a case study in Kenya', *Intelligence* 29, pp401–418

Stoffle, R. W., Halmo, D. B., Evans, M. J. and Olmsted, J. E. (1990) 'Calculating the Cultural Significance of American Indian Plants: Paiute and Shoshone Ethnobotany at Yucca Mountain, Nevada', *American Anthropologist* 92, pp416–432

Stross, B. (1973) 'Acquisition of Botanical Terminology by Tzeltal Children', in M. S. Edmonson (ed) *Meaning in Mayan Languages*, Mouton, The Hague, pp107–141

Svanberg, I. (2009) 'Plant Knowledge as Indicator of Historical Cultural Contacts', in A. Pieroni and I. Vendebroek (eds) *Traveling Cultures and Plants: The Ethnobiology and Ethnopharmacy of Human Migrations*, Studies in Environmental Anthropology and Ethnobiology, vol 7 (paperback edition) Berghahn Books, New York, pp227–244

Tardío, J. and Pardo-de-Santayana, M. (2008) 'Cultural Importance Indices: A Comparative Analysis Based on the Useful Wild Plants of Southern Cantabria (Northern Spain)', *Economic Botany*, vol 62, no 1, pp24–39

Toledo, V. M., Batis, A. I., Bacerra, R., Martinez, E. and Ramos, C. (1995) 'La selva util: etnobotánica cuantitativa de los grupos indígenas del trópico húmedo de México', *Interciencia* 20, pp177–187

Trotter, R. T. and Logan, M. H. (1986) 'Informant Consensus: A New Approach for Identifying Potentially Effective Medicinal Plants', in N. L. Etkin (ed) *Plants in Indigenous Medicine & Diet: Biobehavioral Aproaches*, Redgrave Publishing Co., New York, pp91–112

Turner, N. J. (1988) '"The Importance of a Rose": Evaluating the Cultural Significance of Plants in Thompson and Lillooet Interior Salish', *American Anthropologist* 90, pp272–290

Van Etten, J. (2006) 'Changes in farmers' knowledge of maize diversity in highland Guatemala, 1927/37–2004', *Journal of Ethnobiology and Ethnomedicine* 2 (29)

Varghese, E., Jain, S. K., and Bose, N. (1993) 'A quantitative approach to establish efficacy of herbal remedies: A case study on the Carias', *Ethnobotany* 5, pp149–154

Voeks, R. A. and Leony, A. (2004) 'Forgetting the Forest: Assessing Medicinal Plant Erosion in Eastern Brazil', *Economic Botany* 58 (Supplement) S294–S306

Wester, L. and Yongvanit, S. (1995) 'Biological diversity and community lore in northeastern Thailand', *Journal of Ethnobiology* 15, pp71–87

Wilbert, W. (2002) 'The Transfer of Phytomedical Knowledge among the Warao', in J. R. Stepp, F. S. Wyndham and R. K. Zarger (eds) *Ethnobiology and Biocultural Diversity: Proceedings of the*

Seventh International Congress of Ethnobiology, International Society of Ethnobiology, University of Georgia Press, Athens, GA, pp336–350

Winkler, D. (2008) 'Yartsa Gunba (*Cordyceps sinensis*) and the Fungal Commodification of Tibet's Rural Economy', *Economic Botany*, vol 62, no 3, pp291–305

Yang, X., He, J., Li, C., Ma, J., Yang, Y. and Xu, J. (2008) 'Matsuke Trade in Yunnan Province, China: An Overview', *Economic Botany*, vol 62, no 3, pp269–277

Zarger, R. (2002) 'Acquisition and Transmission of Subsistence Knowledge by Q'eqchi' Maya in Belize', in J. R. Stepp, F. S. Wyndham and R. K. Zarger (eds) *Ethnobiology and Biocultural Diversity: Proceedings of the Seventh International Congress of Ethnobiology*, University of Georgia Press, Athens, GA, pp593–603

Zarger, R. K. and Stepp, J. R. (2004) 'Persistence of botanical knowledge among Tzeltal Maya children', *Current Anthropology*, vol 45, no 3, pp413–418

Zent, S. (1996) 'Behavioral Orientations toward Ethnobotanical Quantification', in M. N. Alexiades (ed) *Selected Guidelines for Ethnobotanical Research: A Field Manual*, Advances in Economic Botany, vol 10. The New York Botanical Garden, New York, pp199–239

Zent, S. (1999) 'The Quandary of Conserving Ethnobotanical Knowledge: A Piaroa Example', in T. Gragson and B. Blount (eds) *Ethnoecology: Knowledge, Resources, Rights*, University of Georgia Press, Athens, GA, pp90–124

Zent, S. (2001) 'Acculturation and Ethnobotanical Knowledge Loss among the Piaroa of Venezuela: Demonstration of a Quantitative Method for the Empirical Study of TEK Change', in L. Maffi (ed) *On Biocultural Diversity: Linking Language, Knowledge, and the Environment*, Smithsonian Institution Press, Washington, DC, pp190–211

Zent, S. (2009) *Final Report on Indicator No. 2: Methodology for Developing a Vitality Index of Traditional Environmental Knowledge (VITEK) for the Project 'Global Indicators of the Status and Trends of Linguistic Diversity and Traditional Knowledge'*, www.terralingua.org/projects/vitek/ch5.htm

Zent, S. and Zent, E. L. (2000) 'Inferring Processes of Ethnobotanical Knowledge Acquisition from Patterns of Knowledge Acquisition', Paper presented at the VII International Congress of Ethnobiology, Athens, GA, 23–27 October 2000

Zent, S. and Zent, E. L. (2004) 'Ethnobotanical Convergence, Divergence, and Change Among the Hoti', in T. Carlson and L. Maffi (ed) *Ethnobotany and Conservation of Biocultural Diversity*, Advances in Economic Botany, vol 15, The New York Botanical Garden, New York, pp37–78

CHAPTER 5

Challenges and Approaches to Assessing the Market Value of Wild Fungi

Susan J. Alexander, Rebecca J. Mclain,
Eric T. Jones and Sonja N. Oswalt

INTRODUCTION

Commercial trade in fungi harvested from wild, wild-simulated or cultivated populations in forests is a significant source of income for diverse people worldwide. Hundreds of species are harvested and sold for food, medicine and other purposes. For example, Jones and Lynch (2007) list 35 species of mushrooms and truffles commercially harvested in the Pacific Northwest region of the US; Pérez-Moreno et al (2008) recorded 90 species of wild edible mushrooms in 12 markets in central Mexico; and Guissou et al (2008) identified 88 species of wild mushrooms being sold in markets and at roadside stands in central and western Burkina Faso. Italy's Ministry of Health regulations include 60 mushroom species on its list of species that are traded nationally, with an additional 90 species that are traded regionally (Sitta and Floriani, 2008). Sales of *Cordyceps sinensis*, a medicinal fungus, accounted for 40 per cent of rural cash income in the Tibet Autonomous Region in 2004 (Winkler, 2008).

Determining the economic value of these harvests is usually difficult and economic valuation methods are in their infancy. Traditional commodity tracking systems, such as national trade databases, list few if any wild fungi species and on-the-ground tracking systems are typically insufficient where they exist at all. One notable example is the trade data from the Japan External Trade Organization for matsutake (*Tricholoma* spp) imports to Japan. Furthermore, harvesting practices and market networks are often deeply rooted in cultural values, indigenous knowledge systems and stewardship practices. Commercial, recreational and subsistence activities may be interconnected and/or operating alongside each other. These concurrent gatherings make isolating market values difficult and potentially create misleading descriptions that omit the real economic values of fungi harvests. Yet, despite the lack of reliable statistics, the commercial fungi trade is an important part of many local economies. The evidence for commercial importance is exemplified by the existence of field buying stations where harvesters sell mushrooms and the presence of fresh and value-added products in village markets, grocery stores, airport specialty shops, in restaurants and on internet marketing sites. Additionally, the economic potential for commercialized wild fungi is unknown, because limited active management of wild fungi on a commercial scale occurs in native forests or in forests managed for industrial timber production.

Countries in North America, Latin America, Central and Eastern Europe, the Middle East and Asia export large quantities of wild edible and medicinal fungi (Boa, 2004 and Chapter 1). For example, exports of *Tricholoma matsutake* from Korea (mostly North Korea until 2006 trade sanctions were put in place) to Japan were estimated at US$24 to US$103 million (in US$ 2007) per year in the late 1990s (Koo and Bilek, 1998). The province of Yunnan, China alone exported matsutake (*Tricholoma* spp) valued at US$44 million in 2005 (Yang et al, 2008). In 2003, Italy recorded 69.5 metric tons of fresh truffles (*Tuber* spp), exports worth €13.5 million (Sitta and Floriani, 2008). In many countries, including China, Finland, France, Japan, Korea, Italy, Mexico, Russia, South Africa and Tanzania, domestic wild fungi markets also provide important income earning opportunities (Boa, 2004 and Chapter 1). Significant declines in the production of certain economically important wild fungi in some parts of the world, such as Périgord truffles in France and matsutake in Japan, have occurred over the past century (Hall and Yun, 2000). Declines in wild fungi populations have been variously attributed to habitat loss from changes in land use, air pollution, use of pesticides and herbicides, competition from introduced species of fungi and global warming (Hall and Yun, 2000).

In many parts of the world, land managers and conservationists have voiced concern that commercial harvesting negatively affects wild mushroom populations. For example, in the 1990s large areas of the northwest US were declared off-limits to commercial wild fungi harvesting owing largely to pressure from conservationists (McLain et al, 1998; McLain, 2008). Similarly, international environmental organizations succeeded in listing wild matsutake (*Tricholoma* spp) as a second class protected species under the CITES (Convention on International Trade in Endangered Species) Authority of China (Menzies and Li, 2010). In neither case, however, did scientific studies support contentions that the populations of wild fungi being 'protected' were declining. Indeed, research in Europe and the US indicates that most standard harvesting practices do not significantly affect wild fungi productivity or populations (Egli, 2006; Luoma et al, 2006; Pilz et al, 2003). Moreover, recent studies suggest that some wild fungi populations (including the Périgord truffles and matsutake mentioned above) have co-evolved with humans and their expansion is positively linked to specific kinds of woodland habitats created by humans (Arora and Shephard, 2008; Buyck, 2008; Saito and Mitsumata, 2008).

Declines in local supplies of preferred fungi species in Japan and Western Europe have created strong demand for alternate foreign sources or product substitutes from other regions or countries during the past several decades. For example, *Tricholoma magnivelare* from North America has been exported to Japan as an imperfect substitute for *Tricholoma matsutake* since the mid-1980s (Hosford et al, 1997). *Cantharellus* and *Morchella* species are now shipped from many parts of the world to Western Europe (Boa, 2004). And while Italy continues to export significant quantities of dried porcini (*Boletus edulis* and related species), most of that trade is now based on product sourced from China or Eastern Europe and processed and re-packaged in Italy for export (Sitta and Floriani, 2008).

In some parts of the world, such as the US and Canada, weakly defined property rights over wild fungi have contributed to temporary resource supply shortages when demand has risen sharply over relatively short periods. However, irrespective of the type of property rights, wild fungi appear to follow the economic cycle characteristic of many non-timber forest products (NTFPs) (Homma, 1992). This cycle involves an expansion phase characterized by growth in demand, followed by a stabilization phase, when supply and demand reach equilibrium. If demand continues to grow, however, prices rise, supply shortages develop and increasing pressure is exerted on wild fungi populations. As the cost of harvesting rises and the resource base shrinks, incentives arise for domestication or substitution, and also for the development of some form of property rights.

Weigand (2000:41) warns that 'viewing wild mushrooms crops as out in the woods and free for the taking undermines notions of sustainability and stewardship of a resource that can bring [...] a new source of income.' However, land managers need to recognize that informal and traditional claims often exist over what appear at first-glance to be open access resources (Arora, 2008). Managers must be careful to ground policies aimed at encouraging sustainable harvesting practices in an understanding of these already-existing practices so as to avoid inadvertently undermining cultural systems, including inter-generational knowledge production and stewardship practices that have evolved to mitigate negative impacts of harvesting, whether these impacts are perceived or real (Jones and Lynch, 2007).

No reliable estimates exist of the number of individuals, households and firms engaged in the commercial wild fungi sector worldwide. National accounting systems are notoriously poor at identifying the firms and individuals employed in the NTFPs sector (Vantomme, 2003). For example, in 2006, the US Bureau of Census reported only 231 firms with a total of 2098 employees as active in the 'forest nurseries and gathering of forest products' sector for the entire nation. Yet a decade earlier, Schlosser and Blatner (1995) estimated that 10,400 individuals participated in the commercial wild mushroom harvest in just three states (Washington, Oregon and Idaho), with an additional 520 individuals employed in processing activities. Since the wild fungi industry is not mechanized and demand for wild mushrooms has increased over time, the number of workers in the wild mushroom industry has probably remained stable or increased. The US Census probably vastly underestimates economic activity related to wild fungi (and other NTFPs) because it is not structured to account for very small businesses operating partly in the informal sector, workers who participate intermittently or seasonally, and harvesters who lack legal authorization to work in the US (McLain et al, 2008).

The convoluted web of issues surrounding commercial trade of wild edible fungi, from ecological and sustainability issues (such as decreasing productivity of key species) to the underlying economic and social drivers of markets and trade, make the assessment of the economic importance of fungi difficult, complex and fascinating. We set the stage for this chapter by providing an overview of the concept of total national economies, in which informal and formal economic activity are viewed as forming one integrated national economy. We then briefly describe three common concepts – distribution analysis, economic impact analysis and efficiency analysis – that economists use to value goods and actions. We follow this with an overview of the key market structure characteristics that affect how economic costs and benefits associated with wild fungi harvesting, processing and trade are distributed. We end the chapter with a description of several common approaches to non-market valuation and discuss their applicability for wild fungi.

TOTAL NATIONAL ECONOMIES: FORMAL AND INFORMAL ECONOMIC ACTIVITIES

Arriving at reasonable estimates for the economic value of wild fungi in total national economies requires looking at the value of activities taking place in both the formal and informal sectors. The NTFP sector has two reporting components within the informal sector, the household subsistence unpaid sector and the paid informal market sector. However, current systems of national economic accounting do not incorporate either of these significant kinds of economic activities associated with wild fungi. The reason for this lies in the almost unrecognized statistical revolution that took place during the last half-century in the development of Systems of National Accounts, which provide summary measures of national economic performance (Ironmonger, 2001). Measures of Gross Domestic Product (GDP) and Gross National Product (GNP) are at the heart of these national accounting measures, and have been elevated internationally as major tools of economic and social policy through the International Labour Office, the International Monetary Fund and the World Bank. These national statistics, with few exceptions, do not account for the value of unpaid labour and economic output contributed through household production. Ironmonger (2001:8) argues that as a result, 'discussion of public issues such as gender equality, labour market policies, and wages and income policies [...] is statistically uninformed'. Such activities *could* be included in national accounts, as evidenced by national income estimates in Denmark, Norway and Sweden prior to the Second World War, which did include estimates of household production. However, these countries discontinued this practice in 1950 with the adoption of United Nations recommendations. Not until forty years later did the UN Statistical Commission acknowledge the importance of informal economic activity. This change in views was reflected in recommendations issued by the Commission in 1993 that 'satellite' accounts should be prepared to show household economic production and use of natural resources. Ironmonger (2001:12) states:

> *Proper recognition of the household economy will have arrived when national house-hold accounts are published each quarter alongside national accounts for the market economy. These data will enable greater scientific research on the organization of household production, the interactions with the market economy, the role of households in building human capital, on the effects of household technology and alternative social and economic policies on gender divisions of labor and on family welfare.*

In a recent review of literature on the informal economy for the US and Canada, McLain et al (2008:1) found that informal economic activity is most often defined as 'economic activity that takes place outside of nation-state regulatory and reporting systems'. Some authors consider the informal economy to be synonymous with household economy; others see it as encompassing a much larger variety of economic activities, legal and illegal. Importantly, however, many NTFPs sectors remain in the informal economy or at the interface of the informal and market (formal) economies, even in developed countries where many other natural resource activities (e.g. wood products extraction, mining, fishing) have moved largely into the formal economy. As a result, it is impossible to assess the total contributions of wild fungi and other non-timber resources to local, regional and national economies without incorporating approaches that measure the value of activity that takes place in the informal sector. Chapter 4 describes in detail some of the methods used to measure the value of many types of activities taking place in the informal sector. This chapter therefore focuses on methods for estimating the economic contribution of wild fungi activity based on data available through nation-state regulatory and reporting systems.

Measuring the economic value of fungi

Efforts to compare the economic value of NTFPs in different parts of the world are fraught with challenges. Neumann and Hirsch (2000) assessed studies focusing on valuations of standing forests, in which the goal was to assess alternative forest uses, and identify conservation and development options based on extraction. They caution us to take care when drawing conclusions from estimates of potential value, due to differences in methodology, or lack of clarity as to what is being valued. They did find that the significance of non-timber resource income, particularly to rural households, is well documented. Chopra (1993) identified two primary issues in valuing non-timber resources. The first is the definition of value. 'Value' may mean exchange value, use value, option value and even existence value. These measures are generally not additive. Forests also provide positive externalities, such as clean water. A key question is whether these externalities should be included in assessments of forest resource value. The second issue Chopra (1993) identified is how to measure value. Market price, labour cost and tradeoff costs can all be used to approximate value. However, since many products that are used are not marketed, the relationship between value and price is problematic.

Alexander et al (2002a) outline three general concepts – distribution, economic impact, and efficiency analyses – used to value goods or actions. Each of the three approaches has distinct uses depending on whether one needs to analyse distribution and equity, assess and measure economic impacts or develop basic efficiency measures.

Distribution analysis

Distribution analysis focuses on issues about the rights to, and distribution of, goods, services, and property. For the wild fungi industry, distribution analyses have tended to focus on how access to wild fungi harvesting sites is allocated (Alexander and Fight, 2003; Arora, 2008; Dyke and Emery, 2010; Menzies and Li, 2010; McLain 2008; Saito and Mitsumata, 2008; Winkler, 2008; Yang et al, 2008). Recently scientists have begun to describe wild fungi value chain structures as well (Edoaurd et al, 2006; Montoya et al, 2008; Pérez-Moreno et al, 2008; Winkler, 2008; Yang et al, 2008). Jensen's (2009) value chain analysis for agarwood (*Aquilaria crassna* Pierre ex H. Lec) in the Lao People's Democratic Republic illustrates both the feasibility and utility of gathering detailed quantitative data at multiple points along a product value chain. However, similarly detailed documentation of how benefits are distributed at different points along fungi value chains has not yet been done for fungi product chains.

Economic impact analysis

Economic impact analysis examines the flow of money through a region or an economy, and assesses the impacts of that flow. Studies of employment or trade fall into this category. Several studies of economic impacts of NTFP markets in North America assess total economic contributions at regional levels (e.g. Allen, 1950; Cronemiller et al, 1950; Schlosser et al, 1991; Schlosser and Blatner, 1995). Other North American impact analysis type studies have reported on wages and employment in NTFP industries (Schlosser et al, 1991; Tedder et al, 2000). Researchers in Scandinavia and Central and Eastern Europe have developed estimates of the total economic value of NTFP resources, including wild fungi, by multiplying estimated quantities harvested (for both commercial and domestic use) by the average price per unit harvested (Olmos, 1999). Sisak (1998) used this method to estimate the average yearly value of wild fungi in the Czech Republic for the period 1994 to 1996. He estimated the average yearly value at US$27 million, which amounted to 10 per cent of the value of timber sold in Czech markets for the same time period. Using a similar technique in Tibet, Winkler (2008) found that the *yartsa gunbu* harvest (*Cordyceps sinensis*) contributed US$225 million to the Tibetan GDP (roughly eight per cent), and accounted for an average of 40 per cent of rural cash income in Tibet's counties.

Efficiency analysis

The third concept, efficiency analysis, is used to compare prices of two goods at the same level of production. Efficiency analysis is useful at smaller scales such as stands or forests, but does not address questions of employment or equity. Little work exists on the value of any NTFP, including wild edible fungi, on a per-hectare or per-acre basis (an efficiency type analysis), as the biology is not generally understood well enough to create yield functions.

Three studies in western North America address the values of wild edible fungi production in forests. Pilz et al (1998) assessed the value of *Cantharellus* species and timber in western Washington State. The discounted present net value in perpetuity was calculated for productive Douglas fir (*Pseudotsuga menziesii* (Mirb.) Franco) forests using 50 and 80 year timber harvest rotations, and three levels of Chanterelle (*Cantherellus* sp.) productivity. The value of the timber was considerably more than the value of the mushrooms in every scenario. Both can be produced at the same time from the same landscape, although not at the same time in any given stand of trees.

Pilz et al (1999) examined the relative value of timber and American matsutake (*Tricholoma magnivelare*) in south-central Oregon. The discounted present net value for a 90-year period was calculated for three timber management scenarios, one with timber harvest to enhance American matsutake, one with timber harvest assumed not to affect current mushroom productivity and one with no timber harvest. Since mushroom harvester costs are unknown, two assumptions about harvester costs were analysed. If harvester costs are about half of the mushroom sales value at the buying sheds, the mushroom values were slightly less than or greater than the value of the timber in the timber harvest scenarios. The combined value of trees and mushrooms is the highest when the forest is managed to produce mushrooms.

Alexander et al (2002a) outline necessary assumptions in assessing joint production and value of trees and wild fungi in US Pacific Northwest forests, in several stand-level efficiency analyses of the value of land (soil expectation value) that produces both trees and wild fungi. This study built on and modified Pilz et al (1998) and Pilz et al (1999) and added morels (*Morchella* spp) in eastern Oregon in a managed forest within a grand fir/big huckleberry (*Abies grandis/Vaccinium membranaceum*) plant association. In every study, the value for the fungi and the timber were site- and species-specific. Any assessment of the value of fungi and other resources in the forest depends on assumptions about biological productivity, prices, forest management actions and their associated costs, and mushroom harvester behaviour and costs. Such analyses are a snapshot of possibilities, but are by no means inclusive of all the values of the forest or of all the options for forest management and joint production of forest resources.

In a similar vein, Bonet et al (2008) recently developed a predictive model for estimating wild mushroom production in even-aged Scots pine (*Pinus sylvestris* L.) forests in the Central Pyrenees. Their study found that timber and wild fungi exist in a complementary rather than competitive relationship, with the greatest fungal productivity occurring when wood volume growth is greatest. They point to the need for incorporating monitoring of fruiting body production and additional site variables and site types for the development of more broadly applicable predictive models.

Determining market values

Market values for wild fungi are important to know for many kinds of economic analyses. Prices paid for wild fungi to harvesters, to intermediate buyers, and prices paid by consumers are all critical in determining who produces and sells wild fungi, where they are harvested and sold, and even what kinds of wild fungi will be available at any one time where wild fungi are sold to consumers. The interaction of supply and demand determines price, and prices for wild fungi can fluctuate daily at an international scale. High prices signal demand is high or inventories are low, so producers rush to supply what they can. As more wild fungi enter the market, price shifts down. Or perhaps a particular species of wild fungi is consumed more at certain times of the year, and price will respond to the seasonal fluctuation in demand.

Price determines whether wild fungi harvested in North America are sold to markets in Europe, or whether demand in Europe for morels or other fungal species will be satisfied by supplies from other countries, such as China or Eastern Europe (Pilz et al, 2006). Price can determine if the wild fungi buyer will ship product fresh or dry it for later sale. Price competition in international markets can drive producers to develop domestic markets for wild fungi they might be having trouble selling into export markets. Average annual prices for wild fungi fluctuate from year to year depending on many factors, including annual production, changes in taste and preferences, and the amount of disposable income consumers have to spend on food.

Crops and markets within countries and around the world determine local wild fungi prices and trade is very competitive. Large amounts of wild fungi are harvested in countries such as China, India, Pakistan and Turkey. Wage expectations are lower in these countries than in Canada and the US, where large quantities of wild fungi are also harvested. Countries in Eastern and Central Europe, which also produce large quantities of wild fungi, may have shipping cost advantages for end markets in Europe, while China and Korea may have advantages for shipping product to Japan.

Markets for wild fungi are well-established worldwide. However, other than international trade data, formal and publicly accessible information on wild fungi prices and sales are rarely collected. Even international trade data is often a combination of many species, both wild-harvested and agriculturally produced (Vantomme, 2003). The vast majority of price studies are state-wide, province-wide, or regional economic impact assessments of prices or market size, such as Blatner and Alexander's (1998) work on wild fungi prices in the US Pacific Northwest or Yang et al's (2008) study of matsutake markets in Yunnan, China. Winkler's (2008) research on the *yartsa gunbu* market in Tibet is a rare example of a detailed national-level wild fungi economic impact assessment.

In the US, the only annual national price data available for wild fungi, other than export prices in US export data and import prices from other countries importing wild edible fungi from the US (such as Japanese import data), is from contracts and permits sold by Federal land management agencies. An example of an economic impact analysis estimating national values for wild fungi is given in Box 5.1. The information presented is derived from annual contract and permit data from the US Forest Service (Automated Timber Sale Accounting database) and Bureau of Land Management (Timber Sale Information System).

BOX 5.1 COMMERCIAL PRODUCTION AND VALUE: A US EXAMPLE

Although regularly collected national information on the collection and sale of wild edible fungi in the US is not available, permits and contracts sold on Federal lands in the US give an indication of the size of wild edible fungi markets in North America. These data can be used to roughly estimate total national wholesale value for wild edible fungi harvested in the US. The first step is to assume that the value per pound the Federal agencies receive of all wild edible fungi harvested on federal lands is 10 per cent of the price paid at first point of sales (i.e. where harvesters sell their mushrooms), a common appraisal policy with US Federal agencies for these types of products. Next, we assume the Forest Service (FS) and Bureau of Land Management (BLM) provide 12 per cent of total national production based on the proportion of forest land each agency constitutes. The last step is to assume first point of sales values are 40 per cent of wholesale values. First point of sales value is comparable to 'farm values'. Farm values commonly run at about 40 per cent of wholesale value.

The resulting estimate for 2007 for national wholesale value of wild edible fungi harvested in the US is about US$43 million (Table 5.1). The value of wild edible fungi has fluctuated between about US$35 million and US$57 million from 1998 to 2007.

By using a similar adjustment to quantities sold by Federal agencies and comparing the estimate of national quantities of wild edible fungi to export data, we see the expanded estimates of national wild edible fungi harvests are often less than estimated total export quantities (Table 5.2). This illustrates the difficulty in estimating wild edible fungi production due to lack of data. To calculate total national production, we assume permit and contract

Table 5.1 *Estimated wholesale value of wild-harvested fungi in the US, 1998–2007 (million adjusted 2007 US$)*

Year	1998	1999	2000	2001	2002	2003	2004	2005	2006	2007
National Value	52.41	36.74	40.75	54.67	43.32	47.12	57.32	45.46	35.47	42.72

sales by the FS and BLM are 22 per cent of total US quantities harvested, based on forest land area proportions. The estimate of national quantities of wild edible fungi harvests combines domestic and international markets. Dried mushrooms and truffles are about one-seventh the weight of fresh fungi. The total estimated fresh weight of exports constitutes a large proportion of national production, or even exceeds it, as would be expected. US mushroom trade data since 2002 has split out common domesticated mushrooms, including *Agaricus*, *Auricularia* and *Tremella* species. Mushroom trade data in Table 5.2 after 2001 does not include these species, and can be assumed to be highly influenced by wild-harvested fungi such as *Morchella* and *Cantharellus* species, *Tricholoma magnivelare* and various truffle species. In the earlier years shown in Table 5.2, most harvest of wild edible fungi was undocumented, so estimated national harvest figures probably vastly underestimate actual harvests.

Table 5.2 *Quantities of US wild-harvested mushrooms and truffles and US exports of selected species, 1998–2007 (metric tons)*

	1998	1999	2000	2001	2002	2003	2004	2005	2006	2007
Wild Edible Fungi sold on US Federal lands	313	186	1976	361	302	308	4618	3908	3718	578
Estimated national Wild Edible Fungi harvest	1424	845	896	1639	1373	1400	2098	1773	1687	2626
Fresh mushroom exports	4908	7144	6,623	5435	477	663	617	416	221	712
Fresh truffle exports	3	6	1	10	36	6	6	22	10	7
Dried and preserved truffle and mushroom exports	184	405	462	486	330	375	477	206	187	433
Estimated total fresh weight of fungal exports	6199	9985	9858	8847	2823	3294	3956	1880	1540	3750

Note: US trade code definition changed in 2002

Market structure and the distribution of economic costs and benefits

Wild edible fungi are harvested worldwide for commercial sale to both domestic and foreign markets. Commercial brokers of wild fungi sell fungi to the market that gives them the best price, whether that market is a local restaurant buying fresh *Boletus* or a foreign buyer purchasing dried *Morchella*. No country's trade position is assured (Weigand, 2000; Alexander et al, 2002b) and understanding how markets for wild fungi work is key for commercial success and management of wild fungi habitats and harvesters. Weigand (2000) used econometrics, the statistical study of patterns of behaviour, to understand how different wild fungi markets in North America operate. In his economic impact analysis, he found that conventional income and price relations do not always fully explain amounts of wild fungi exported from one country to another.

One important reason is that all *Cantharellus* and *Tricholoma* in export markets are not equal. For example, Japanese consumers prefer *Tricholoma* from Korea over the same genus from Canada or China. In truly competitive markets, consumer taste and preferences, labour costs, transportation cost and other market factors assure that the best products in terms of both quality and price will be successful, regardless of where they originated. However, markets for wild fungi are often oligopolies (i.e. a state in which the market is not be competitive, as a limited number of sellers have the power to affect supply and prices). Yang et al's (2008) study of wild matsutake markets in Yunnan, China, identified four market levels (sporadic village-level markets, small-scale local or village markets, regional markets and export markets). They found that information flow about prices was poor at the village level but improved noticeably as one moved up the market chain. Social networks and increasing market control by fewer and fewer players along commodity chains also affect trade (Alexander, 2002b). For example, the *Cordyceps sinensis* market in most parts of Tibet is controlled by 15 large brokers, most of whom are Hui Muslims (Winkler, 2008).

Value chain analysis (commodity chains)

Commodity chain analysis describes how a product moves from harvest and production, through various stages of wholesale and retail, to the end consumer. Looking at commodity chains is a way to step back and see how all the ideas in this chapter interact to bring mushrooms from the field to the consumer. Fungal commodity chains illustrate how neoclassical concepts of market competition can be integrated with ideas of national economies, the distribution of costs and benefits, formal and informal economic behaviour and social relations in markets.

In neoclassical economic theory, markets range from being perfectly competitive to being monopolies. As Alexander et al (2000b:116) state:

> *An imperfect market is one in which any one of the following conditions, necessary for a perfect market, do not hold true: a homogeneous product; a large number of buyers and sellers; freedom of entry and exit for buyers and sellers; all buyers and sellers have perfect information and foresight with respect to the current and future array of prices; the sales or purchase of each market agent are insignificant with respect to the current and future array of prices; the sales or purchases of each market agent are*

insignificant in relation to the aggregate volume of transactions; there is no collusion among buyers and sellers; consumers maximize total utility and sellers maximize total profit; and the commodity is transferable.

Of course, markets vary considerably with respect to these conditions (Pearce, 1992). The degree to which a market, or node on the commodity chain, meets these conditions for a 'perfect market' reveals a great deal about how that node functions. Hopkins and Wallerstein (1994) state that monopoly (or monopsony) power and competition are keys to understanding the distribution of wealth along the nodes of a commodity chain. Profitability shifts from node to node in global commodity chains according to competitive pressures. A global commodity chain approach highlights the need to look at linkages between raw material suppliers, factories, traders and retailers, in order to understand sources of stability and change. For example, many – if not all – NTFPs exported from the US enter buyer-driven commodity chains where large retailers, merchandisers and trading companies set up decentralized production networks in a variety of countries.

Wild edible fungi markets in the US provide insight as to how concepts of informal economies and commodity chains interact. From the 1980s through much of the 1990s, demand for fungi from Japan and Europe for species that are not easily domesticated, such as *Cantharellus* and *Tricholoma*, increased. The US part of the market was characterized by a network of informal and formal activities, mostly in very small businesses. At the harvesting and primary processing levels, wild edible fungal markets have many of the characteristics of peripheral nodes along a commodity chain, which are vulnerable to shifts in labour availability, transportation costs and social structural change.

Global economic and social structural change hit the US wild edible fungi markets hard in the 1990s. The depression in Asian economies during the 1990s reduced Japanese demand and prices paid to harvesters for *Tricholoma magnivelare* harvested in North America decreased substantially. In addition, countries near Japan were able to offer the preferred *Tricholoma matsutake* with lower transportation and labour costs. At about the same time, opening of trade with Eastern European countries gave the European Union access to *Cantharellus* species that were closer, with lower transportation and wage costs than US supplies. In response, US producers worked hard to expand domestic markets, create product differentiation, and take advantage of seasonal gaps in Asian and European markets when other suppliers could not keep up with demand.

Importance of social relations in markets

Alexander et al (2002b) note that NTFP firms at the edge of the informal economy tend to rely predominantly on social networks. The reliance of many wild fungi businesses in North America on relationships or networks of workers, buyers, producers and distributors is well known. Non-timber businesses reflect the greater societies in which they function, in that there is no clear-cut distinction between the formal and informal sectors, but instead a network of complex interactions and relationships. Social relations can determine the success or failure of businesses at every stage of local, domestic and even global commodity chains.

Non-market valuation (environmental goods and services)

Non-market valuation estimates the willingness of consumers to pay for specific goods or services under defined conditions. Non-market values are not directly comparable to market-based exchange values. Estimates of non-market values of recreation and personal uses of forest resources can be important information for land managers in trade-off analysis and planning, particularly when other information on values is lacking.

There have been some discussions of how non-market values for NTFPs could be estimated (e.g. Adepoju and Salau, 2007; Neumann and Hirsch, 2000). However, studies that assess the non-market value of recreational or personal use gathering of specific NTFP are rare. Two studies in the US use the travel cost method to assess non-market values; one study on Christmas trees and another on berry and mushroom picking, both in the western US. Markstrom and Donnelly (1998) used the travel cost method to derive value estimates for Christmas tree cutting in Colorado (US). They estimated an average value of US$9.37 per standing tree, with an average consumer surplus of US$4.37. Starbuck et al (2004) used a two-step travel cost model to assess the value of berry and mushroom picking on the Gifford Pinchot National Forest in Washington State (US). A recreation visitor day (RVD) of harvesting berries and mushrooms was valued at US$30.02 (in 1996 US$). Comparing this value with other US Pacific West forest recreation demand studies, this estimate of RVD value is in line with the mean value for camping of US$86.96 (1996 US$, with four observations) and the mean value for picnicking at US$53.52 (1996 US$, with four studies) reported by Rosenberger and Loomis (2001). The term 'recreation visitor day' is used in the US to put different non-market values on an equal footing, i.e. the value of a specific activity for one day. This way, various activities can be compared on the same terms. The activity may have elements of subsistence, such as berry and mushroom gathering.

The travel cost method is one way to evaluate non-market values for fungi. The method is based on actual behaviour. Starbuck et al (2004) used information about how far people travelled to pick berries and mushrooms, how much they harvested, how much time they spent and so on. There are numerous methods to assess non-market values, some based on actual behaviour (e.g. travel cost and random utility), some based on a hypothetical situation (such as contingent valuation) and some based on comparing goods sold in markets where all characteristics of the product are the same except the one characteristic of interest (e.g. hedonics). Contingent valuation requires that the hypothetical product or service being analysed must be defined clearly, so different people will visualize the same thing. For example, if people are asked about their willingness to pay a fee or tax to protect a section of a river which they can visualize or are familiar with, the value calculated will be more robust. If the willingness to pay question is about something harder to conceptualize, such as a sustainable ecosystem, the questions must be very carefully formed so that the calculated non-market value has meaning. It would be possible to develop a study to assess the value of wild fungi using contingent valuation, but so far it has not been done.

John Loomis (2009) suggests two possible contingent valuation studies of willingness-to-pay values for wild edible fungi. One possibility would be to survey current collectors on-site and ask their additional willingness to pay to do the collecting. For example, ask respondents if the cost of this most recent trip to collect the fungi had been $X higher, would you have made this trip, yes or no? As the question is a dichotomous choice, the $X would vary over the sample. A contingent valuation study could also be done as a household survey in rural communities or villages. In this case you could, for example, ask respondents if they would be willing to pay $X into a trust fund to protect a collection area from incompatible development that would result in a loss of fungi there. Analysis of the survey results would yield a willingness to pay value for the particular area and fungi in question.

Hedonic valuation has been used to assess, for example, how wildfires affect home prices (Loomis et al, 2009). Repeated wildfires reduce home prices, according to the authors. This study compared house prices of homes in areas without repeated wildfires to similar homes in areas with repeated wildfires to assess how wildfires affect home prices. Hedonic valuation has not been used to assess values for NTFPs, but it is a possibility for calculating the value of certain ecosystem services, such as a forested view versus no view. The hedonic method probably would not work well for valuing wild edible fungi.

CONCLUSION

Communities, individuals, and households around the globe rely on commercial trade in NTFPs, including wild-harvested edible fungi, as a source of income. Though the need for quantification and valuation of wild fungi harvest and trade at multiple scales is apparent, both metrics are difficult to obtain. Other than international trade data, few countries collect information on wild fungi prices and sales. Differing definitions and concepts of what constitutes 'value' make attempts to summarize the resource in global markets complicated. Even international trade data may be misleading, as they often combine wild and domestically produced fungi. Non-market (e.g. services) values are not often estimated, but may be modeled in some scenarios. If and when they are, they are not directly comparable to market-based values. Nonetheless, it is important to consider non-market values, and they should not be excluded in overall valuations of wild fungi. Understanding the economic contribution of wild fungi also requires taking into account those activities taking place in the informal economy or at the interface between the informal and formal sectors. Market structure plays an important role in the commercial success of wild fungi, as well as in how the economic benefits of wild fungi are distributed.

Although wild fungi are economically important around the world, quantification and valuation of their contributions to the global marketplace are far from complete. Such information, however, is important not only to better understand the significance of wild fungi to rural communities and global trade, but also to permit the development of economic and resource tenure policies that promote social equity and sustainability of human uses of wild fungi.

BOX 5.2 UNCOVERING MATSUTAKE (*TRICHOLOMA MATSUTAKE*) HARVESTER LIVELIHOOD PREFERENCES IN YUNNAN, CHINA

Cheryl Geslani

The commodification of natural resources affects how we interact in a global society, with our neighbours and with the land. Japanese consumption of matsutake mushroom has exceeded the supply from domestic forests to the point where more is now imported than produced. For this study 126 matsutake harvesters in Yunnan, China completed Conjoint Choice Experiment surveys that were used to indirectly uncover how matsutake harvesting livelihood priorities were relatively valued. Conjoint Choice Experiment is a methodology used in business to design products based on various attributes and the preferences of a targeted survey (Orme, 2006). This methodology has been adapted to value the environment (Hanley et al, 1998). For the purpose of this survey four attributes of the matsutake harvesting livelihood were surveyed in order to determine how village policy makers can regulate the forest and the livelihood of matsutake harvesting. The surveyed attributes were: 1) Available Tree Species (biodiversity), 2) Regulation Scheme, 3) Market Price (per kg) and 4) Seasonal (Annual) Income. These livelihood priority attributes were represented with levels (see Table 5.3 for attributes and associated levels); in the end the levels as well as the attributes preferred by the harvesters were identified.

Table 5.3 *Livelihood priority attributes and level used in Conjoint Choice Experiment*

Livelihood Priorities	Levels				
Available Tree Species	*Pinus yunnanensis*	*Pinus yunnanensis* *Quercus guayavae-folia*	*Pinus yunnanensis* *Quercus guayavae-folia* *Pinus armandi*		
Market Price per Kilogram	¥100	¥300	¥500	¥700	¥1000
Annual Matsutake Income	¥500	¥3000	¥5000	¥10,000	
Regulation Scheme	Open Access	Effective Private Land Division	Yearly Fallow Area	One Rest Day Per Week	Rotating Group Harvests

Note: ¥ represents Chinese Yen, at ¥700 to US$100 (2009 average exchange rate)

Table 5.4 *Two out of eight sample questions from Conjoint Choice Experiment*

	A	B	C
Matsutake Harvesting Livelihood Priorities			
Available Tree Species	1) *Pinus yunnanensis* 2) *Quercus guayavaefolia*	1) *Pinus yunnanensis*	Last Season's Conditions (None)
Regulation Scheme	Yearly Fallow Area	Open Access	
Market Price	¥300/kg	¥100/kg	
Annual Matsutake Income	¥10,000/year	¥1000/year	

	A	B	C
Matsutake Harvesting Livelihood Priorities			
Available Tree Species	1) *Pinus yunnanensis* 2) *Quercus guayavaefolia*	1) *Pinus yunnanensis* 2) *Quercus guayavaefolia* 3) *Pinus armandi*	Last Season's Conditions (None)
Yearly Fallow Area	Rotating Group Harvest	One Rest Day Per Week	
Market Price	¥500/kg	¥1000	
Annual Matsutake Income	¥5000/year	¥3000/year	

Note: ¥ represents Chinese Yen, at ¥700 to US$100 (2009 average exchange rate)

Table 5.5 *Summary of Latent Class Analysis Results*

	Class 1	Four-Class Solution Class 2	Class 3	Class 4
126 respondents:	32.97%	31.53%	22.41%	13.08%
Livelihood Attribute				
Regulation*** Scheme		+ Open access**	− Open access*	
		− Private management** −Yearly fallow area**	+ Private management**	+ Private management**
	− One rest day**	+ One rest day*		− One rest day*
		− Rotating group**	+ Rotating group**	
Annual Matsutake Income***	+ Chose scenarios with Higher Income**	− Chose scenarios with Lower Income*	− Chose scenarios with Lower Income**	+ Chose scenarios with Higher Income**
Biodiversity	Insignificant across all classes			
Market Price	Insignificant across all classes			
Status Quo (None)***	− Did not choose**	− (Did not choose)**		+ (Chose)**
Demographic Characteristic				
Years of Education				− (Less)**
Prefecture*		+ Di Qing ** (Open Access) − Chu Xiong **	− Di Qing * + Chu Xiong * (Rotating Group Harvests)	

Notes: (a) Numbers in parentheses are z statistics; (b) The parameters or attributes marked with asterisks (*/**/***) are significantly different from 0 at the 0.10, 0.05 and 0.01 levels respectively; (c) + indicates a preference for livelihood attribute or association with demographic characteristic; (d) − indicates opposition to livelihood attribute or disassociation from demographic characteristic.

The survey data was analysed using Latent Class Analysis which uncovers groups of respondents based on the similarity of their answers (Boxall and Adamowicz, 2002). Four classes of harvesters were identified. Three of the four classes selected preferences similar to their current conditions. When choosing between four different matsutake harvesting livelihood priorities harvesters did not consider biodiversity or market selling price to be important factors. Instead they were concerned about annual income from matsutake and harvesting regulation schemes. These results indicate that harvesters are more concerned about long-term income earning opportunities than they are about short-term fluctuations in price. Additionally harvesters exhibited a strong preference for the regulatory scheme currently used in their villages, which may indicate that most harvesters are either unaware of alternative options or feel it is too cumbersome to change current regulations for their benefit.

REFERENCES

Adepoju, A. A. and Salau, A. S. (2007) *Economic valuation of non-timber forest products (NTFPs)*, Munich Personal RePEc Archive Paper No. 2689, posted 7 November 2007, http://mpra.ub.uni-muenchen.de/2689/, accessed 13 May 2009

Alexander, S. J., Pilz, D., Weber, N. S., Brown, E. and Rockwell, V. A. (2002a) 'Mushrooms, trees and money: Value estimates of commercial mushrooms and timber in the Pacific Northwest', *Environmental Management*, vol 30, no 1, pp129–141

Alexander, S. J., Weigand, J. F. and Blatner, K. A. (2002b) 'Nontimber forest products commerce', in E. T. Jones, R. J. McLain and J. F. Weigand (eds) *Nontimber Forest Products in the United States*, University Press of Kansas, Lawrence, pp115–150

Alexander, S. J. and Fight, R. (2003) 'Managing access to nontimber forest products', in R. A. Monserud, R. W. Haynes, and A. C. Johnson (eds) *Compatible Forest Management*, Kluwer Academic Publishers, pp383–400

Allen, J. W. (1950) *Marketing woodlot products in the State of Washington*, Bulletin 1, Washington Department of Conservation and Development, Institute of Forest Products, Olympia, Washington

Arora, D. (2008) 'California *porcini*: Three new taxa, observations on their harvest, and the tragedy of no commons', *Economic Botany*, vol 62, no 3, pp356–375

Arora, D. and Shepard, G. H. Jr. (2008) 'Mushrooms and economic botany', *Economic Botany*, vol 62, no 3, pp207–212

Blatner, K. A. and Alexander, S. (1998) 'Recent price trends for non-timber forest products in the Pacific Northwest', *Forest Products Journal*, vol 48, no 1, pp28–34

Boa, E. (2004) *Wild edible fungi: A global overview of their use and importance to people*, Non-Wood Forest Products, vol 17, Food and Agricultural Organization of the United Nations, Rome

Bonet, J. A., Pukkala, T., Fischer, C. R., Palahí, M., de Aragón, J. M. and Colinas, C. (2008) 'Empirical models for predicting the production of wild mushrooms in Scots pine (*Pinus sylvestris* L.) forests in the central Pyrenees', *Annuals of Forest Science*, vol 65, no 206, pp1–9

Boxall, P. C. and Adamowicz, W. L. (2002) 'Understanding heterogeneous preferences in random utility models: a latent class approach', *Environmental and Resource Economics* 23, pp421–446

Buyck, B. (2008) 'The edible mushrooms of Madagascar: An evolving enigma', *Economic Botany*, vol 62, no 3, pp509–520

Chopra, K. (1993) 'The value of non-timber forest products: An estimation for tropical deciduous forest in India', *Economic Botany*, vol 47 no 3, pp251–257

Cronemiller, L. F., Woods, J. B. Jr., Ladd, C. H., Parker, A., Hanneman, E. D., Sasser A. H., Maus, C. W. and Phelps, W. S. (1950) *Secret treasures in the forest*, Bull. 14, Oregon State Board of Forestry, Salem, Oregon

Dyke, A. and Emery, M. (2010) 'Non-timber forest products in Scotland: Changing attitudes to access rights in a reforesting land', in S. Laird, R. McLain and R. Wynberg (eds) *Wild Product Governance: Finding Policies that Work for Non-Timber Forest Products*, Earthscan, London

Edouard, F., Quéro, R. and Marshall, E. (2006) 'Wild mushrooms: *Boletus edulis, Cantharellus cibarius, Amanita caesarea, Tricholoma magnivelare* (Basidiomycetes): Fresh, dried and exported mushrooms: community business and entrepreneurs', in E. Marshall, K. Schreckenberg and A. C. Newton (eds), *Commercialization of non-timber forest products: Factors influencing success. Lessons learned from Mexico and Bolivia and policy implications for decision-makers*, United Nations Environmental Programme, World Conservation Monitoring Center, Cambridge, UK, pp49–52

Egli, S., Peter, M., Buser, C., Stahel, W. and Ayer, F. (2006) 'Picking does not impair future harvests – results of a long-term study in Switzerland', *Biological Conservation*, vol 1292, pp271–276

Guissou, K. M. L., Lykke, A. M., Sankara, P. and Guinko, S. (2008) 'Declining mushroom recognition and usage in Burkina Faso', *Economic Botany*, vol 62, no 3, pp530–539

Hall, I. R., Buchanan, P., Wang, Y. and Cole, A. L. J. (1998) *Edible and poisonous mushrooms: an introduction*, New Zealand Institute for Crop and Food Research, Christchurch, New Zealand

Hall, I. R. and Wang, Y. (2000) 'Edible mushrooms as secondary crops in forests', *Quarterly Journal of Forestry*, vol 94, no 4, pp299–304

Hanley, N., Wright, R. and Adamowicz, V. (1998) 'Using Choice Experiments to Value the Environment', *Environmental & Resource Economics* 11, pp413–428

Hopkins, T. K. and Wallerstein, I. (1994) 'Commodity chains: Construct and research', in G. Gereffi and M. Korzeniewicz (eds) *Commodity Chains and Global Capitalism*, Greenwood Press, Westport, CT, pp17–34

Hosford, D., Pilz, D., Molina, R. and Amaranthus, M. (1997) *Ecology and management of the commercially harvested American matsutake mushroom*, Pacific Northwest General Technical Report 412, US Department of Agriculture, Forest Service, Pacific Northwest Research Station, Portland, OR

Ironmonger, D. (2001) 'Household production and the household economy', University of Melbourne Department of Economics Research Paper, Parkville, Melbourne, www.economics. unimelb.edu.au/downloads/wpapers-00-01/759.pdf, accessed 13 May 2009

Jensen, A. (2009) 'Valuation of non-timber forest products value chains', *Forest Policy and Economics*, vol 11, pp34–41

Jones, E. T. and Lynch, K. A. (2007) 'Biodiversity conservation and nontimber forest products', *Forest Ecology and Management*, vol 246, no 1, pp29–37

Koo, C. and Bilek, E. M. (1998) 'Financial analysis of vegetation control for sustainable production of Songyi (*Tricholoma matsutake*) in Korea', *Journal of Korean Forestry Society*, vol 87, no 4, pp519–527

Loomis, J. B., Mueller, J. and González-Caban, A. (2009) 'Do repeated wildfires change homebuyers' demand for homes in high-risk areas? A hedonic analysis of the short and long-term effects of repeated wildfires on house prices in southern California', *Journal of Real Estate Finance and Economics*, vol 38, no 2, pp155–172

Loomis, J., Email communication (with Susan J. Alexander), 3 March 2009

Luoma, D. L., Eberhar, J. L., Abbott, R., Moore, A., Amaranthus, M. P. and Pilz, D. (2006) 'Effects of mushroom harvest technique on subsequent American matsutake production', *Forest Ecology and Management*, vol 236, pp65–75

Markstrom, D. C. and Donnelly, D. M. (1998) 'Christmas tree cutting: demand and value as determined by the travel cost method', *Western Journal of Applied Forestry*, vol 3, pp83–86

McLain, R. (2008) 'Constructing a wild mushroom panopticon: The extension of nation-state control over the forest understory in Oregon, USA', *Economic Botany*, vol 62, no 3, pp343–355

McLain, R., Alexander, S. J. and Jones, E. T. (2008) *Incorporating understanding of informal economic activity in natural resource and economic development policy*, Pacific Northwest General Technical Report, PNW-GTR-755, U.S. Department of Agriculture, Forest Service, Pacific Northwest Research Station, Portland, OR

McLain, R. J., Christiansen, H., and Shannon, M. A. (1998) 'When amateurs are the experts: Amateur mycologists and wild mushroom politics in the Pacific Northwest, USA', *Society and Natural Resources*, vol 116, pp615–626

Menzies, N. and Li, C. (2010) 'One eye on the forest, one eye on the market: Multi-tier regulation of matsutake harvesting, conservation, and trade in northwestern Yunnan province', in S. Laird, R. McLain and R. Wynberg (eds) *Wild Product Governance: Finding Policies that Work for Non-Timber Forest Products*, Earthscan, London

Montoya, A., Hernández, N., Mapes, C., Kong, A. and Estrada-Torres, A. (2008) 'The collection and sale of wild mushroooms in a community of Tlaxcala, Mexico', *Economic Botany*, vol 62, no 3, pp413–424

Neumann, R. P. and Hirsch, E. (2000) *Commercialization of non-timber forest products: review and analysis of research*, Centre for International Forestry Research, Bogor, Indonesia, www.cifor.cgiar.org/publications/ntfpsite/pdf/MgNTFP3.pdf, accessed 13 May 2009

Olmo, S. (1999) 'Non-wood forest products: utilization and income generation in the Czech Republic, Finland and Lithuania', *Unasylva*, vol 50, no 198, pp27–33

Orme, B. (2006) *Getting Started with Conjoint Analysis: Strategies for Product Design and Pricing Research*, Research Publishers, LLC, Madison, WI

Pearce, D. W. (ed) (1992) *The MIT dictionary of modern economics* (4th edition) MIT Press, Cambridge, MA

Pérez-Moreno, J., Martínez-Reyes, M., Yescas-Pérez, A., Delgado-Alvarado, A. and Xoconostle-Cázares, B. (2008) 'Wild mushroom markets in central Mexico and a case study at Ozumba', *Economic Botany*, vol 62, no 3, pp425–436

Pilz, D., Brodie, F. D., Alexander, S. and Molina, R. (1998) 'Relative value of chanterelles and timber as commercial forest products', *Ambio*, Special Report no 9, pp14–16

Pilz, D., Smith, J., Amaranthus, M. P., Alexander, S., Molina, R. and Luoma, D. (1999) 'Mushrooms and timber: Managing commercial harvesting in the Oregon Cascades', *Journal of Forestry*, vol 97, no 3, pp4–11

Pilz, D., Norvell, L., Danell, E. and Molina, R. (2003) *Ecology and management of commercially harvested chanterelle mushrooms*, Pacific Northwest General Technical Report PNW-GTR-576, US Department of Agriculture, Forest Service, Pacific Northwest Research Station, Portland, OR

Pilz, D., McLain, R., Alexander, S., Villarreal-Ruiz, L, Berch, S., Wurtz, T. L., Parks, C. G., McFarlane, E., Baker, B., Molina, R. and Smith, J. E. (2007) *Ecology and management of morels harvested from the forests of western North America*, Pacific Northwest General Technical Report PNW-GTR-710, US Department of Agriculture, Forest Service, Pacific Northwest Research Station, Portland, OR

Rosenberger, R. S. and Loomis, J. (2001) *Benefit transfer of outdoor recreation use values: A technical document supporting the forest service strategic plan*, Rocky Mountain Research Station General Technical Report, RMRS-GTR-72, US Department of Agriculture, Forest Service, Rocky Mountain Research Station, Fort Collins, CO

Saito, H. and Misumata, G. (2008) 'Bidding customs and habitat improvement for matsutake (*Tricholoma matsutake*) in Japan', *Economic Botany*, vol 62, no 3, pp257–268

Schlosser, W., Blatner, K. and Chapman, R. (1991) 'Economic and marketing implications of special forest products harvest in the coastal Pacific Northwest', *Western Journal of Applied Forestry*, vol 6, no 3, pp67–72

Schlosser, W. and Blatner, K. (1995) 'The wild mushroom industry of Washington, Oregon and Idaho: a 1992 survey of processors', *Journal of Forestry*, vol 93, no 3, pp31–36

Sisak, L. (1998) 'Importance of main non-wood forest products in the Czech Republic', in H. G. Lund, B. Pajari and M. Korhonen (eds) *Sustainable development of non-wood goods and benefits from boreal and cold temperate forests*, Proceedings of the International Workshop held in Joensuu, Finland, 18-22 January 1998, European Forest Institute Proceedings no 23, pp79-85

Sitta, N. and Floriani, M (2008) 'Nationalization and globalization trends in the wild mushroom commerce of Italy with emphasis on porcini (*Boletus edulis* and allied species)', *Economic Botany*, vol 62, no 3, pp307–322

Starbuck, C. M., Alexander, S. J., Berrens, R. P. and Bohara, A. K. (2004) 'Valuing special forest products harvesting: a two-step travel cost recreation demand analysis', *Journal of Forest Economics*, vol 10, no 1, pp37–53

Tedder, S., Mitchell, D. and Farran, R. (2000) *Seeing the forest beneath the trees: The social and economic potential of non-timber forest products and services in the Queen Charlotte Islands/Haida Gwaii*, Mitchell Consulting and the British Columiba Ministry of Forests, Victoria, British Columbia

Vantomme, P. (2003) 'Compiling statistics on non-wood forest products as policy and decision-making tools at the national level', *International Forestry Review*, vol 5, no 2, pp156–160

Weigand, J. F. (2000) 'Wild edible mushroom harvests in North America: Market econometric analysis', in J. A. Fortin and Y. Piché (eds) *Les champignons forestiers: récolte, commercialisation et conservation de la ressource*, Centre de recherche en biologie forestière, Université Laval, Québec, 22–23 February 1999, pp35–43

Winkler, D. (2008) '*Yartsa Gunbu* (*Cordyceps sinensis*) and the fungal commodification of Tibet's rural economy', *Economic Botany*, vol 62, no 3, pp291–305

Yang, X., He, J., Li, C., Ma, J., Yang, Y. and Xu, J. 2008 'Matsutake trade in Yunnan province, China: An overview', *Economic Botany*, vol 62, no 3, pp269–277

Yun, W. and Hall, I. R. (2004) 'Edible ectomycorrhizal mushrooms: challenges and achievements', *Canadian Journal of Botany*, vol 82, pp1063–1073

CHAPTER 6

Hidden World, Crucial Role: The Ecology of Fungi and Mushrooms

Cathy Sharp

INTRODUCTION

Some aspects of the ecology of fungi in woodlands and forests are covered in Chapters 1 and 7. This chapter discusses the ecological role of fungi in more detail. After the introduction, the second part of this chapter discusses fungi in particular habitat types. As the following deals with harvesting of fungi by people, the third part of this chapter goes beyond people's uses and discusses links between fungi, animals and conservation. Fourthly, the roles of fungi in carbon and nutrient cycling are described, followed by a fifth section dealing with human impacts on habitat, the many hidden effects on fungal communities and attempts at ecological restoration. In the last section, the concept of using functional traits of fungi as ecological tools is raised as an interesting challenge. The final part of this chapter concludes with a section on future research and the rapid development in molecular research that provides an important tool in understanding the crucial environmental role of fungi.

The ecological role of fungi has a very long history, and it is likely that mycorrhizal symbiosis contributed to plant adaptation to life on land 400 million years ago through facilitating uptake of mineral nutrients in exchange for photosynthetically derived sugars (Simon et al, 1993).

Fungi are important in terrestrial food chains, involving a range from minute invertebrates to larger vertebrates, including humans. Tiny invertebrates in the genus *Collembola*, commonly known as 'springtails', are a good example. Collembolans are known to be fungivores, consuming both mycelia and spores of fungi, and therefore often contribute to the control of pathogenic fungi (Sabatini and Innocenti, 2001). A collembolan fossil *Rhyniella praecursor* is estimated to date back 400 million years and is the 'oldest' terrestrial arthropod found in Scotland (Haaramo, 2008). Would it be too audacious to think that all those years ago, these tiny creatures may also have been involved in the adaption of plants to a life on land, together with mycorrhizal fungi?

Attine leaf-cutting ants are another essential part of food chains in Central and South America. The larvae of these ants are totally dependent on the fungus as their only source of food while the fungus benefits in having a protected substrate and is assured of dispersal as the ants move to new colonies taking along mycelium as inoculum for the new nests. The fungus rarely produces fruiting bodies in the wild but has been grown in culture and has been identified as *Leucoagaricus gonglyophorus* (Spooner and Roberts, 2005).

Humans have long been part of the mushroom food chain, collecting edible mushrooms for home use and, in more modern times, for commercial purposes (see chapters by Eric Boa (Chapter 1) and David Pilz (Chapter 7)). The nomadic San people in the Kalahari have traditionally collected the edible desert truffle, *Kalaharituber pfeilli* (=*Terfezia pfeilii*) for centuries. They look out for cracks in the ground that give away the presence of this underground fungus, and today the people of Ghanzi in Botswana are involved in the commercial collection of this fungus (Pole Evans, 1918; Boa, 2004; Trappe et al, 2008). In Zimbabwe it has long been known that different mushrooms grow under different trees and those fungal communities have been allocated separate vernacular names in order to differentiate them (Piearce and Sharp, 2000). Similarly, it is traditionally understood that mushrooms growing under exotic plantations are viewed with distrust and therefore avoided. No doubt this suspicion has arisen from poisonings by the cosmopolitan mycorrhizal *Amanita* species that were imported along with their inoculated host trees, *Pinus* and *Eucalyptus*. Sadly, fatal poisonings have occurred due to a lack of appreciation that underground mycorrhizal networks may extend well into adjacent indigenous woodland and produce their exotic, toxic species alongside edible indigenous mushrooms. This has led to confusion between the toxic *A. pantherina* and an edible *A. rubescens* 'look-alike' that remains undetermined (Harris, 1981; Gelfand and Harris, 1982).

Modern technology has opened a whole new field of research that sheds more light on the hidden world of fungi. Until now, the cryptic nature of many fungi has limited ecological and socio-mycological studies. It is accepted that the appearance of a mushroom on the forest floor is by no means the whole story because there is so much more going on below-ground (Horton and Bruns, 2001). The interconnected system of underground rhizomorphs (root-like strands) of *Armillaria bulbosa* has been found to be genetically the same individual (a clone or 'genet'), which makes one 'humongous fungus among us' (Gould, 1992). This enormous underground organism covers an area of over thirty acres (12ha) in Michigan, USA, and its estimated collective potential weight (including the mass of fine hyphae emanating from the rhizomorphs into the surrounding soil and wood) is near 100 tons (Smith et al, 1992). This equates to the weight of an adult blue whale! If the rate of vegetative growth of hyphae is extrapolated it is suggested that this 'individual' fungus ranges from 1500 to 10,000 years old but is more likely to be closer to the 10,000 year mark. This is quite a revelation considering that scattered appearance of mushrooms was previously thought to indicate a scattered population of individuals.

Many molecular techniques have been developed and are currently available to fungal ecologists. Establishing the structure of a fungal community is now possible as are methods of its quantification. A 'molecular fungal species' is one in which there is a variation in DNA sequences and this often correlates well with what the species looks like in the field (Peay et al, 2008). The erratic fruiting of mushrooms on the surface can now be linked to what is happening (or not happening) below-ground and it is very likely that species richness in a community will turn out be far greater than previously imagined. The availability of molecular tools has encouraged advances in other aspects of fungal community research e.g. population dynamics, food webs and evolutionary ecology.

The full picture of biodiversity in the fungal kingdom is poorly known. The global estimate has been increased from 1.5 million species (using the ratio 6 fungi:1 plant), (Hawksworth, 1991) to possibly more than 5.1 million species of fungi (Hawksworth, 2001). However, in a forest ecosystem one tree may be associated with several hundred species of fungi so it follows that the total number of fungal species must surely exceed the 5 million stated above and will certainly exceed the number of plants. There are 2000 tree species alone in the lowland rain forests of Borneo so although a vast number of fungi is expected to exist in this habitat, only one in ten species of mushroom can be recognized by name (Pegler, 1997).

Attempts have been made to estimate the global numbers of macro-fungi (those visible to the naked eye) and a figure of over 56,000 species has been suggested in an area that excludes most of southeastern Europe, Africa, Western Asia and tropical East Asia from which little or no data has been collected (Mueller et al, 2007). Combining this figure with estimates of un-discovered species and then using the plant:macro-fungus ratio of 2:1 in temperate zones and 5:1 for the tropics, a range of 53,000 to 110,000 species of macro-fungi is suggested. This is approaching the estimate of 140,000 species postulated by Hawksworth (2001) and interestingly, this means that to date, only 16 to 41 per cent of all macro-fungi have been described.

HABITAT TYPES AND FUNGI

Although this chapter is focused on forests and woodlands, a mention of fungal communities in other habitats and within particular groups of plants (such as orchids that have a close relationship with fungi) will give emphasis to the ecological importance of fungi on a global scale.

Grasslands

Grasslands are extremely diverse, determined by soil factors and climate and are maintained directly (e.g. mowing, grazing by livestock) or indirectly (e.g. rampant wildfires in Africa, Australia and California) by human activities. Mosses are often an important component of grasslands and the number of macro-fungi in grassland has been positively correlated with a well-developed moss layer (Arnolds, 1981). Waxcaps (*Hygrocybe*) are particular to mossy areas and it is possible that they are actually woodland fungi that have extended their habitat range into grasslands (Spooner and Roberts, 2005). The more exposed nature of grasslands results in a greater variability in the microclimate which in turn influences fungal communities. However, pioneering studies on ecology of grassland fungi in Britain found that soil type had the greatest impact on species composition in grassland (Wilkins and Patrick, 1939; 1940).

Heathland

Heathland is a well-defined but fragile habitat characterized by ericaceous ('heather-like'), dwarf shrubs growing on poor, acid soils. It is generally accepted that this habitat is man-made and has become established over a time span of 1,500 years following extensive clearing of the original forests for sheep grazing (Spooner and Roberts, 2005). It is a unique habitat for fungi but, more recently, these areas have been encroached by pine and birch which shade out species of *Erica* and *Calluna*. These plant species have an ericoid type of mycorrhizal relationship that enables them to colonize acidic heathland soils which lack nitrogen and phosphorus. Together with their fungi these plants are highly evolved in their capability in extracting elemental nutrients from their organic substrate of peat (Allen, 1991). Ericoid mycorrhizas further benefit their plant partners by providing resistance to heavy metals (e.g. copper, zinc and arsenic). An even more ingenious trait of ericoid mycorrhizas is their ability to prevent invasion of spruce trees by suppressing development of their particular ectomycorrhizas assisted by the production of anti-fungal substances in *Calluna* roots (Spooner and Roberts, 2005). However, ericoid mycorrhizas seem to actually stimulate growth of *Pleurotus involutus* and *Suillus grevillei*, both ectomycorrhizal fungi, and this may explain the ease with which pine and birch colonize heathlands compared to the 'rejection' of spruce. The most important heathland macro-fungi are *Mycena* and *Galerina* although these are also common in other habitats. Equally important is the parasitic fungus *Marasmius androsaceus* that invades the branches of *Calluna* and *Erica* and causes die-back. Extensive areas of heather in Scotland have been infected and controlled burning programmes have been successful in controlling the fungus, along with a beetle pest that also causes damage to this habitat (Spooner and Roberts, 2005).

Plant tissue

There is an interesting hidden community of fungi that exist inside living plants. These fungi are called 'endophytes' and colonize healthy tissue of plants, often without showing any outward sign of their presence. Leaves from two tree species in forests of Panama were found to have 418 species of endophytic fungi living within them (Arnold et al, 2000) illustrating the significance of this unusual habitat. Different assemblages of fungi are present in different tissues (e.g. roots, stems, leaves and seeds) and the fungi may vary from season to season. Both partners benefit from nutrient cycling, the fungus is assured of survival within the plant, the plant itself is protected from pathogenic diseases and also protected from foraging invertebrates by production of toxic compounds. The amount of toxin in the plant (alkaloids in particular) actually increases in response to browsing pressure (Spooner and Roberts, 2005). A fascinating mutual relationship exists between an ascomycete (Ascomycetes are one of the three groups in the kingdom of Fungi), *Epichloë* in the family of ergots, Clavicipitaceae, its grass host and a dipteran fly (*Botanophila*). The fungus is commonly called 'choke disease' as it may prevent flowering and seed formation in the grass host. The fly deposits its eggs onto the fungus, which in this case is clearly visible as a raised crust on the grass stem. The male fly actively fertilizes the eggs by depositing faeces containing spermatia into the fungal crust and then the newly-hatched larvae have an assured source of food. This is the first and only documentation of this type of mutualism between a fungus and insect (Bultman and Leuchtmann, 2008).

Woodland

In woodland, and particularly in tropical forests, there is another habitat in which fungi have established themselves. This is on the surface of living leaves in the canopy of the trees and the colonizers are usually micro-fungi, collectively termed 'phylloplane fungi'. Besides these, there are saprotrophic macro-fungi that develop 'webs' of rhizomorphs just beneath the forest canopy that trap falling leaves. The fungi involved are *Marasmius* and *Crinipellis* and some xylariaceous ascomycetes (Spooner and Roberts, 2005) and their hyphae invade the trapped leaves, forming decaying tangles that often become so heavy that they fall to the forest floor where the degradation process continues.

Also in forests, the emission of blue-green light by luminescent fungi is a fascinating phenomenon. It is largely the mycelium of saprotrophic wood-rotters and litter fungi that glow in the dark although in some species the whole fruit body, or just the gills, stipe or only the fresh spores emit light. The biological advantage of having this trait is unknown although it has been suggested that nocturnal insects attracted to the light may have a role in spore dispersal (Bermudes et al, 1992). Of course there may be no ulterior motives – just a simple biochemical process during degradation where organic molecules are broken down in the presence of oxygen and 'luciferin', a phosphate-rich chemical, to release carbon dioxide and light. To date, over 60 species of fungi have been reported worldwide as being luminescent, with *Armillaria*, *Mycena* and *Omphalotus* being the most common genera having this mechanism (Desjardin et al, 2008) and *Filoboletus*, a rather unusual poroid agaric (see Box 6.1).

Orchids

Orchids are found in most biomes and have their own specific method of tapping into the carbon reserves of the ecosystem through endomycorrhizal fungi, They are totally dependent upon this association in which fungi penetrate the root cells (endo-) compared to the external sheath around the root in ecto-mycorrhizal associations. However, this association is entirely parasitic: the flow of nutrients is from fungus to orchid with little evidence that the fungus is actually benefitting from the deal. Green plants are autotrophic (i.e. manufacture their own food through photosynthesis) but some exceptions have been discovered: five green orchid species that thrive on mycorrhizal carbon (Bidartondo et al, 2004). These orchids are able to live in the deepest shade of the forest by tapping in to the fungal reserves without any herbaceous competition for light.

Orchid seeds are dust-like and contain limited reserves of starch so they are entirely dependent upon external supplies of carbohydrate and other nutrients for their growth. These supplies are provided by a fungus and the association begins soon after germination. The tiny 'protocorms' grow epidermal hairs that are soon penetrated by fungal hyphae which develop into branched coils within the orchid cells and remain within the plant's roots or stem. Some tropical epiphytic orchids are known to exist with wood-rotting fungi, including *Armillaria mellea* which is also a plant parasite. In this instance, the orchid is doubly parasitic, taking advantage of the fungus mycelium to derive its nutrients from host trees that the fungus has attacked (Spooner and Roberts, 2005). *Neottia* orchids parasitize *Sebacina* species (a gelatinous heterobasidiomycete);

BOX 6.1 FUNGI AND DIPTEROCARP FORESTS

Annemieke Verbeken

Forests of large parts of south and southeast Asia are dominated by Dipterocarpaceae.

These evergreen dipterocarp forests occur especially in the non-seasonal, humid zone and are characterized by tall trees (at least 30m high) with many thick lianas and abundant epiphytic plants. This biome covers at least three-quarters of the forest in Southeast Asia and forms a belt extending from Sumatra in the west to New Guinea in the east (Whitmore, 1984) where the forest extends from the coastline to the tops of all except the highest mountains. Extensions of these forest are also found in Thailand, Sri Lanka, India, South-China and Queensland.

Many species in Dipterocarpaceae are not only the most important source of timber in the area, but are also known to be ectomycorrhizal, such as *Dipterocarpus*, *Shorea*, *Anisoptera* and *Hopea*. Ectomycorrhizal Fagaceae such as *Lithocarpus*, *Castanopsis* and *Quercus* also occur in these forests at higher altitudes.

Though fungi are under-explored in many of these areas, some studies show that the mycodiversity is extremely high and ectomycorrhizal fungi seem to be dominant in dipterocarp forest. A study in Pasoh Forest Reserve (Malaysia) revealed 296 taxa likely to be ectomycorrhizal fungi with the most important families being Russulaceae, Amanitaceae, Cantharellacae and Boletaceae (Lee et al, 2003)

As in tropical Africa, members of the Cortinariaceae are rare, in contrast to what is observed in boreal forests (see Box 6.3 on Boreal Forest Fungi). As Corner (1935) already stated, most agaric fungi fruit more frequently in open places because this habitat is more exposed to alternate drying and wetting. This study also showed that the diversity of hypogeous fungi (truffle-like fungi with closed fruiting bodies and with a tendency to grow under the soil surface) is higher than presumed. This was also observed in Sri Lanka and Northern Thailand (Verbeken et al, in prep.) where hypogeous members of the Russulaceae are better represented than in tropical Africa. Dominance of *Russula*, *Lactarius*, *Amanita* and several boletes was also established from studies in Northern Thailand, India and Papua New Guinea. Many of these collections belong to currently undescribed taxa which are endemic to Southeast Asia or even to a more restricted area, such as the five endemic *Lactarius* species described for Pasoh forest in Malaysia, some of them with striking characters which have never been observed outside the region (Stubbe et al, 2007).

Many of the dominant ectomycorrhizal genera are also popular edible fungi and in several regions local people collect, eat and trade them. This is particularly well-studied in Yunnan, Southwest China (Wang, 2000) and in northern Thailand (Dell et al, 2005). Besides the ectomycorrhizal fungi, abundant saprotrophs occur on the leaf litter, fulfilling their role as wood-decayers (Figure 6.1). *Marasmius* is one of the most striking and well-represented genera and the polypores are the most important group. Some of the polypores are pantropical or paleotropical, but according to a study in Pasoh, Malaysia (Hattori and Lee, 2003) most of them seem to be typical tropical Asian species. Some agarics that decay wood are also very abundant in the forest, such as the bioluminescent *Filoboletus manipularis*. Some of these saprotrophic species are also used as human food, e.g. *Pleurotus* spp and *Lentinus* spp, while others are known for their medicinal uses (*Ganoderma* spp, *Wolfiopora cocos*).

Figure 6.1 *The bioluminescent* Filoboletus manipularis, *an agaric growing on decaying wood in Malaysian dipterocarp forest*

Photograph: R. Walleyn

Corallorhiza orchids invade *Thelephora* and *Tomentella* in Britain and invade some members of the Russulaceae in North America (Spooner and Roberts, 2005). The presence of fungi is evident in every niche of every biome and this fact alone stresses their importance in the maintenance of ecological balances within each habitat.

BEYOND PEOPLE: ANIMALS, FUNGI AND CONSERVATION

Animals and fungi can exist without human intervention but their conservation is in the hands of people who need knowledge of how they interact within their particular habitats. There is a three-way relationship going on in many forests, that of plant–fungus–animal, which is basic to the understanding of the ecology of both the forest and the animal (Reddell et al, 1997). The mycorrhizal status of a tree, for example, may be influenced by an animal's foraging behaviour and/or ingestion of a fungus because the dispersal of fungal spores is essential to the survival of the species through inoculation of new forest seedlings. There are several types of fungivory (eating of fungi): the consumer grazes on the mycelium; the fully developed fruiting bodies are consumed (Guevara et al, 2000); or incidental ingestion of spores and sporocarps while foraging in soil or humus (Reddell et al, 1997). Thus soil conservation within a habitat is an integral part of conserving the whole ecosystem. Soil fungal communities are characteristic of the vegetation cover in the various habitats (Christensen, 1981) and soil properties play an important role in each system. Perhaps then, a four-way relationship should be recognized and conserved accordingly: soil–plant–fungus–animal.

In conserving habitats, the fungivorous habit of soil-dwelling nematodes is worthy of further mention. These little animals penetrate the hyphae of the fungal mycelium and consume the contents. However, some fungi are able to retaliate by using several ingenious methods that have evolved separately to suit the fungus, and there is a record of a fossil nematode-trapping fungus preserved in amber dating back to 25 million years ago (Jansson and Poinar, 1986). There are over 150 species of predatory fungi that actively trap nematodes using various forms of sticky appendages, constricting and non-constricting nooses or webs of hyphae (Dix and Webster, 1995; Spooner and Roberts, 2005) and they all actively entice nematodes with chemical exudates (Field and Webster, 1977). The wood-rotting oyster mushroom (*Pleurotus*) is a familiar nematode-trapper and has evolved a system whereby an hour-glass-shaped projection from a hyphal strand exudes a sticky substance that traps the nematode. An immobilizing toxin is then released that rapidly paralyses the prey, after which hyphae grow into the nematode which then becomes just another source of nitrogen. Other nematodes ingest spores but then find themselves in the grip of a parasitic fungus: the spores lodge themselves in the digestive tract, produce hyphae and so infect their host from within.

Fungi are also predatory on other small creatures: amoebas, rotifers, arthropods and some fungi utilize bacteria as a food source (Raghukumar, 1992). These are mostly micro-fungi, but there is a remarkable story about a mushroom and an arthropod. The soil-dwelling springtails (collembolans) mentioned above, are not only fungivores but are also indirectly instrumental in the establishment of plant-fungal symbioses (Klironomos and Moutoglis, 1999) by carrying spores of mycorrhizal fungi and mycorrhizosphere bacteria on their body (these are bacteria that live among mycelial networks around a root). One fungal predator of the springtail *Folsoma candida* is the ectomycorrhizal mushroom *Laccaria bicolor*. The animal is captured and immobilized by a toxin secreted by the fungus which then infects the springtail with mycelia. The nitrogen from the prey is supplied to the mycorrhizal tree partner in exchange for photosynthetic carbon (Klironomos and Hart, 2001), taking the possibilities and mechanics of this ectomycorrhizal relationship one step further than ever imagined.

There are several small mammals and birds that are also agents of spore dispersal. In subalpine, coniferous forests in Europe, the red squirrel *Sciurus vulgaris* forages for hypogeous fungi in preference to epigeous species. This is an important seasonal food source for the squirrel and since it has a large home range, it may play an important role in spore dispersal through wide distribution of its scats (Bertolino et al, 2004). In the dry, sclerophyllous forests of southeast Tasmania, it was found that the foraging habits of the rat-kangaroo (*Bettongia gaimardi*) had a huge impact on the density of fungal fruiting bodies (Johnson, 1994). As with the squirrel in Europe, this animal and other bettong species on the Australian mainland may play a major role in maintaining species richness and abundance of ectomycorrhizal fungi through spore dispersal.

Domestic pigs and dogs are often trained to sniff out truffles, a delicacy in the European culinary market. In African miombo woodland (see Box 6.4) a small antelope (the common grey duiker, *Sylvicapra grimmia*) is known to actively uncover the 'truffle'

Figure 6.2 Mackintoshia persica

As its name implies, the peach odour may falsely attract frugivorous animals which then disperse the spores.

Photograph: C. Sharp

Mackintoshia persica (Pacioni and Sharp, 2000; Figure 6.2). In a natural situation, this too may contribute to spore dispersal by falsely attracting frugivorous (fruit-eating) animals with its odour of sweet peaches.

Fungal conservation has not grabbed the attention of the public or politicians as dramatically as has conservation of animals and plants. There is a general indifference to fungi until a traumatic poisoning case hits the media, which then taints the whole group. The lack of awareness of this fascinating hidden world may account for these attitudes and the overall cryptic nature of fungi does not make their investigation and research any easier. It cannot be said that any fungus has become 'extinct' in the manner of animal and plant species, as fungi can pop back into 'existence' after a century-long absence (Spooner and Roberts, 2005). In relation to a human lifespan this may well be a 'local extinction' but it is becoming increasingly clear that it is the change in habitat that shifts the status of individual fungal species. Together with the numerous interconnected responses to climatic conditions that trigger fungal development (Wilkins and Harris, 1946; Thoen, 1976; Watling, 1995; Sharp 2008), it is no wonder that habitat modification threatens fungal communities. Emphasis on the crucial role that fungi play in every niche of the biosphere will reinforce the need for their conservation along with and not distinct from animals and plants. Conservation of rare animals and plants may simultaneously conserve fungi. Loss of fungi will tip the balance of the whole ecosystem and it is quite an ironic thought that such disregard for the humble fungus could lead to an environmental collapse of the earth.

FUNGI AND NUTRIENT CYCLING

There are six major elements regulating nutrient cycling within ecosystems: hydrogen, carbon, nitrogen, oxygen, phosphorus and sulphur. These form the basis of all biological macro-molecules that are integral parts of the carbon, nitrogen and water cycles.

The breakdown of plant litter is one of the most central processes in the global carbon cycle and is an essential part of nature. Worldwide, vast quantities of debris are produced annually and continually recycled. For example, up to five tonnes of debris are produced per hectare per year in temperate woodland and up to 60 tonnes produced in tropical rain forest (Spooner and Roberts, 2005). Decomposition of this debris releases CO_2 to the atmosphere and provides nitrogen in various forms that can support new plant growth. On a global level, this process has been calculated to release 85 billion tonnes of carbon (as carbon dioxide) into the atmosphere (Spooner and Roberts, 2005) and fungi, bacteria and some invertebrates are the main agents responsible for this decay. It has been estimated that 90 per cent of all nutrient cycling in terrestrial environments is due to fungal activity, highlighting the crucial role that fungi have in the carbon cycle.

Nitrogen is intimately involved in controlling both plant growth and litter break-down and there is a need to understand what controls the rate of breakdown and nitrogen release into different environments for effective monitoring of climate change effects on the carbon balance of terrestrial ecosystems. The results of a ten-year research programme indicated that the amount of nitrogen released in all ecosystems (except dry grasslands) is controlled by the initial concentration of nitrogen in the litter and the mass remaining (Parton et al, 2007).

The carbon:nitrogen (C:N) ratio is a critical aspect of recycling and in a 'normal' decomposer system in the lower layers of woodland litter, ratios of between 25:1 and 50:1 may be attained. In comparison, woody substrates have a C:N ratio of 100:1 (Hedger and Basuki, 1982). During decomposition, nitrogen reserves are depleted by soil organisms and as competition for this resource increases, antagonism often develops between species.

Fungi that are involved in the decay of dead material are called saprotrophs and are most commonly found in forest and woodland where there is usually a substantial litter layer. Leaf litter is largely composed of cellulose and fungi have the appropriate enzymes to break this down into simpler compounds (e.g. glucose) which are then used as a food source. Some fungi will exhibit specific nitrogen requirements while others may be more flexible in their needs. Knowledge of this is important when considering the implications of fertilization on fungal communities (see 'Disturbance through habitat loss, fragmentation or modification', below).

There are other factors over and above nutritional and climatic ones that may influence fungal fruiting through the decomposition of litter:

- the presence of other fungi – for example, the mycorrhizal groups that compete for nitrogen and other nutrients, or other saprotrophs that compete antagonistically by release of suppressant substances into the litter (Hedger and Basuki, 1982);
- the presence of the surrounding microbial populations – these have their own demands on nutrient resources and may display either inhibitory or stimulating effects on the growth of saprotrophic fungi (Isaac, 1998).

It is becoming increasingly evident that mycorrhizal fungi have the potential to be the drivers in mobilization of nutrients in some ecosystems (Read and Perez-Moreno, 2003). The major role of these fungi is to improve the uptake of minerals by the 'host' plant in return for photosynthates. It has been shown that fungal sheaths of ectomycorrhizal roots absorb phosphorus five times as rapidly, and potassium twice as rapidly as non-mycorrhizal roots (many authors in Redhead, 1968). Mycorrhizae may also stimulate fine root development in the host tree and thereby lengthen the lifespan of the roots (Mason, 2001). The fungal mycelium itself has a potentially indefinite lifespan (Dahlberg, 1995) and in the temperate zones it has been calculated that under a single healthy tree, there are enough fungal threads to stretch around the equator five times – about 250,000kms! (McAllister, 1993). One can appreciate the volume of substances exchanged between tree and fungus and therefore how mycorrhizal plants are better able to cope with infertile soils or extreme soil pH levels.

HUMAN INFLUENCES ON FUNGI: DISTURBANCE AND RECOVERY

Human-induced changes in the environment often have dire effects on habitats and these effects are bound to impact on the hidden world of fungi. In a survey report of declining fungal species in Germany in 1996, it was found that 30 per cent of species were threatened by air pollution, 25 per cent by agriculture, 24 per cent by commercial forestry and 21 per cent by building and other developments (Spooner and Roberts, 2005). This gives an indication of how human activities in industrialized regions may impact on fungal communities. Consequences of habitat change include shifts in competitive strategies, population dynamics and species diversity, much of which is immeasurable. Without a doubt, fungi do adapt to their environment and their tolerance of change is fascinating.

Disturbance and landscape ecology

Fungi are affected by change at multiple scales, from changing climates through to habitat loss due to farming or grazing. Fungal communities are in a continual state of flux and after any disturbance they are sensitive to changes in nutritional levels. This often causes subsequent antagonism between competing species and, inevitably, this leads to a high rate of local extinction that is not compensated for by recruitment. With time, there develops a dominance of a few fungal species (Dix and Webster, 1995) and the whole structure of the community changes.

Disturbance through habitat loss, fragmentation or modification

There is a danger that habitat loss may result in fragmentation of the wider habitat resulting in 'islands' that are too small to support the original mycobiota (and flora and fauna) and which are still susceptible to the effects of human activities surrounding them.

On a global scale, climatic effects on soil development have a major impact on determining the type of mycorrhizal community formed (Read and Perez-Moreno, 2003), but at a local level, any change in quality of soil nutrient resource is of primary importance to mycorrhizal communities, more so than climate change (Read, 1991). Even within what appears to be climax vegetation, local changes in soil conditions may lead to development of distinctive plant communities with their own species composition and particular type of mycorrhizal system (Read, 1991; Newberry et al, 1988). Intensive farming and the consequent soil pollution through fertilization can be a major problem for the survival of natural fungal communities. In fertilized grasslands, Waxcaps (*Hygrocybe* spp) have been replaced by commonplace nitrophilic mushrooms (*Panaeolus, Coprinus, Psilocybe* and *Stropharia*) (Spooner and Roberts, 2005). Woodlands also suffer the consequences of chemical run-off from adjacent farmlands and changes in species composition have been noticed: *Clitocybe nebularis* and *Lepista inversa* are much more common in British woods than before but numbers of ectomycorrhizal species have decreased. Arbuscular mycorrhizal fungi (AM) are fungi from the third group in the kingdom of fungi called Zygomycetes that infect plant cells with their hyphal branches and swellings and thereby enhance the phosphorus supply to their host plant. For example, when native grassland is ploughed up for agriculture and wheat is planted in rotation with fallow land, the change in host for these AM fungi causes a shift in species dominance and the survival fitness of the species comes into play. The species unable to survive for two years without its preferred host will be replaced with one that can adapt (Allen, 1991).

Uncontrolled and disorganized practices of extensive deforestation, slash-and-burn and selective logging cause fragmentation of the habitat and will surely impact severely on mycorrhizal fungi. The disruption of the host-mycorrhizal connection will drive more adaptable species to replace those that cannot survive the change, either resulting in dramatic changes in the fungal assemblage or in islands of poorly inoculated soils. These islands would recover slowly, given the chance, but loss of organic matter is likely to slow the process of re-inoculation and result in a decrease in biodiversity of both tree and fungal species (McAllister, 1993). This was confirmed in Scotland where it was reported that fungi in disturbed locations were different from and less diverse than those in undisturbed sites (Mason, 2001). It is likely that this applies after habitat modification in Madagascar where much of the original forest has been replaced by exotic species (see Box 6.2). A similar scenario exists in the southeast lowveld of Zimbabwe where large areas of endomycorrhizal mopane (*Colophospermum mopane*) have been cleared for small-scale cropping. This area experiences extreme climatic conditions and is totally unsuited to agriculture of any sort but is part of that government's recent land-redistribution policy. In these situations it is almost certain that the crops will fail and the fields abandoned. Regeneration of mopane is very slow, and coupled with low rainfall and sparse ground cover these abandoned patches remain exposed to severe erosion and leaching of dissolved minerals. Whether mycorrhizae can survive such un-naturally long and extreme conditions remains doubtful.

BOX 6.2 MUSHROOMS IN MADAGASCAR

Paul Pirot

Madagascar is the fourth largest island in the world, having broken away from Gondwanaland and then from continental Africa. Its flora and fauna have evolved in isolation yet retain some similarities to Africa on the west and Asia on the east. Nearly all Madagascar's mammals and reptile species and almost 80 per cent of its plants are endemic, so it is likely that many of the mushrooms on the island are also endemic. Unfortunately this unique diversity is being severely threatened due to loss of the original habitat, which was primary forest. This is now mainly confined to the eastern part of the island where summer showers fall between November and March. The wettest place in Madagascar is on the Masoala peninsula (over 3500mm rain per annum) where the last remaining extensive coastal lowland rain forest is protected. This area was given World Heritage status in June 2007 and the biodiversity has been protected in a wide variety of habitats: rain forest, littoral forest, marsh, flooded forest, mangrove and coral reefs.

The Malagasy people have felled many of the original forest trees. Now, *Eucalyptus* has been planted to be used for the same needs and is cut at the height of the people's *borzina* (machete) so that they can re-grow (coppice). Outside the national parks there are few trees apart from exotics species planted in towns (*Jacaranda* for example) or those that provide edible fruits. In the open country north of Taomasina, mango, banana, papaya, guava, citrus fruits and especially litchi are grown for export to Europe at Christmas time.

A first impression of the mushrooms in Madagascar is that they look no different from those seen in Europe. The trees between Antananarivo and Antsirabe are mainly exotic species (*Pinus*, *Eucalyptus* or *Mimosa*) planted in order to reforest the island, and commonly support 'European' mushroom species like *Laccaria* cf. *laccata*, *Amanita muscaria* and *Suillusluteus* and *Coprinusplicatilis* in lawns.

In original primary forest in Ranomafana (50km northeast of Fianarantsoa) and Andasibe, the genera *Boletus*, *Russula* and *Hygrophorus* are particularly evident. The vegetation in this kind of forest is completely different from that in Europe: the trees are higher, often with pale bark, and except for the most well-known, many trees remain unnamed.

Ravenala is common everywhere and the three principal exotic trees seen in Andasibe are the *Ravenala*, *Pinus* and *Eucalyptus*. The *Ravenala* does not seem to host many mushrooms but under *Pinus* can be found *Lactarius* cf. *hepaticus*, and many kinds of *Boletus* are linked with *Eucalyptus*. The greatest numbers of fungal species are saprotrophic, growing on dead wood. Most common arepolypores and marasmioid fungi include the genera *Collybia*, *Mycena* and *Marasmius*, which are not easy to distinguish.

In the primary forest it is difficult to leave the footpaths as the vegetation is very dense to find the most interesting mushrooms. These are very different from what is known in Europe, for instance a *Russula* species with a ring on the stem or a thick veil at the margin, but which is also known from the miombo woodland in Africa (see Figure 6.3).

Another important, although peculiar, observation is a profusion of *Amanita*, *Russula* and bolete species growing along the roadsides, on steep slopes where the ground is bare. These are evidently associated with the overhanging trees.

Figure 6.3 Russula *cf.* heimii *in forest on Madagascar*

Photograph: Paul Pirot

The tropical Amazon forests are also subjected to large-scale logging to make space for small-scale agriculture and there is some concern about the overall effects this disturbance will have on the carbon status of the region, particularly in view of climate change. A severe drought in 2005 showed a positive response from an intact forest in actually greening-up rather that showing signs of die-back. This reaction is indicative of increased transpiration and carbon uptake and suggests that these deep-rooted forests are responding to the increased availability of sunlight rather than to water limitations (Saleska et al, 2007). In the later stages of succession in a tropical forest, it is known that plant species are dependent upon AM infection (Janos, 1980). It is also known that one of the ecological functions of endomycorrhizae is to enhance water supply to their hosts in drought–prone habitats and studies have shown that there are greater transpiration rates in infected plants compared to those not infected by AM (Read, 1991). This also ties in with the knowledge that mycorrhizal plants take up more carbon during drought cycles than do non-mycorrhizal plants (Allen, 1991). These observations give some hope that intact Amazon forests may be more resilient (at least to short-term climatic anomalies) than previously assumed, thus encouraging a need to better understand the conditions under which water limitations may actually trigger reductions in carbon uptake.

Modification of habitats may happen at a local level and cause changes in fungal communities. Although there is an unfounded fear that over-harvesting of edible mushrooms will result in reduced commercial pickings, there is a greater threat to the sustainability of mushroom harvesting from the behaviour of the collectors. In America, mushroom pickers rake through the leaf litter looking for the button stage of 'Matsutake' *Tricholoma magnivelare*, destroying the mycelium of the very species that they are collecting. Simultaneously, the mycelia of other ectomycorrhizal and saprotrophic species are being destroyed. Trampling of the habitat by collectors causes compaction of litter which, in turn, affects the dynamics of the soil and may impact on the fungal community. This can become a problem when thousands of mushroom pickers are involved (particularly in Italy), collecting from within peri-urban areas (Spooner and Roberts, 2005).

Atmospheric pollution and changes

The damaging effects of agro-industrial pollution have been known for over a century, particularly the response of lichens to sulphur dioxide. This reaction was so dramatic that a scale was established to assess levels of pollution using the presence or absence of certain epiphytic lichens on trees (Hawksworth, 1970).

Global changes in carbon dioxide levels in the atmosphere are the current concern of environmentalists. It is not known yet if changes to the C:N ratio of plant tissues will alter the balance in saprotrophic fungal communities (Peay et al, 2008) or have any influence on the performance of ectomycorrhizal associations. It is possible that shifts in the C:N ratio may alter the nutrient-foraging behaviour within and between trophic groups of fungi in different parts of the soil profile (Read, 1991). The impact of fungal activity in the soil has already been mentioned above (see 'Fungi and nutrient cycling') and is of huge dimensions. Soil respiration is a substantial part of the whole ecosystem's respiration and research has been done on boreal forest soils to determine where in the soil profile this process is most active (Pumpanen et al, 2008). It was found that the humus layer and top-soil contributed 69.9 per cent of the total carbon dioxide produced from the soil. Although not a part of that investigation and without a finer division of the top-soil, previous studies have demonstrated that fungal activity is likely to have produced a large portion of that carbon dioxide. The raw litter layer and fermentation layer within top-soil under deciduous woodland in both England and The Netherlands (see Box 6.5) supported the bulk of living mycelium (Frankland, 1975; Nagel-de Bois and Jansen, 1971). Ectomycorrhizal fungi have since been found to be particularly prevalent in the fermentation layer reflecting their preference in exploiting this quality of substrate (Read and Perez-Moreno, 2003). Meanwhile, the total biomass (living and dead mycelium) per gram of litter or soil from woods in The Netherlands was found to be greatest in the humus layer of the top-soil but interestingly, 95 per cent of this mycelium was found to be dead (Nagel-de Bois, 1971). It can be seen therefore that any changes in atmospheric carbon is more than likely to have a ripple effect all the way down to gaseous exchange in the soil.

Atmospheric pollutants are often dissolved in water and 'acid rain' is a very real threat to the environment, usually affecting regions well away from the industrial source. Sulphur dioxide and nitrogen dioxide are the main offenders in forming 'acid rain'. The major effects are the lowering of pH of the substrate on which it falls, physical damage to fungi and vegetation that are not tolerant to acid conditions and mineral leaching within soils which can then alter metabolic processes and ultimately influence degradation of litter. This 'acid rain' is therefore just as significant in soil carbon levels as are gaseous pollutants and has the potential to alter the balance within a fungal community. Physical effects of 'acid rain' can be seen in Sweden where the natural endophyte on conifer needles has been replaced by a more acid-tolerant species and the knock-on effect of that adaptation is a reduced resistance by the tree to insect damage on the needles (Spooner and Roberts, 2005).

The boreal forest ecosystem (see Box 6.3) is one of the main regulators of atmospheric carbon and stores more carbon than any biome on the planet (Jonsson and Wordle, 2009). These high-latitude systems are becoming increasingly more important as sources of carbon dioxide and methane for the atmosphere as regional warming is showing changes in the dynamics of colder ecosystems. Understanding carbon dynamics in high-latitude systems and the factors that may lead to changes in those dynamics is essential for appreciating the linkages and feedbacks between carbon reservoirs, ecosystems, land cover, hydrology and climate variability (US Global Change Research Program, 2009), not neglecting the integral role of fungi in these processes. However, the effects of anthropogenic nitrogen enrichment are reflected by decreases in the phosphorus:nitrogen ratio across the northern hemisphere which are likely to favour the dominance of AM-based communities (Read, 2003; Aerts, 2002).

To summarize this important section, fungi occupy the interface between plants (the sites of carbon fixation) and soil (in which carbon is stored) and thereby have enormous potential to influence the carbon source-sink interactions which ultimately impact on global climate systems (Read and Perez-Moreno, 2003). Human-induced nutritional disturbances are causing global changes in plant distribution and there is an essential need to determine how mycorrhizal fungi in particular (Figure 6.7) are involved in changes to these plant communities.

Fire

Whether man-induced or natural, fire regimes have a dramatic effect on woodland and their mushroom communities. Fire creates environmental mosaics that result in patches of habitat that differ in age and canopy structure and in altered soil nutrient supplies but nevertheless open up new ecological niches (Boerner, 1982). Most ecosystems have adapted to natural fire cycles and even the relatively fragile fungi have developed adaptive measures. Studies in a Californian pine forest showed that after a wildfire there was a major shift in the mushroom assemblage with the post-fire community dominated by species that had disturbance-resistant propagules already present in the soil (Baar et al, 1999).

In the miombo ecoregion (Figure 6.8) open *chipya* woodland has a predominance of endomycorrhizal and root-nodulating trees that seem better able to tolerate severe burning. However, fire-tolerant fungi occur with fire-tolerant *Uapaca* trees which, over time, invade heavily burnt areas of open *chipya* and develop a dense canopy. The increased shade excludes grass which in turn reduces the fuel load and therefore excludes fire. This vegetation succession allows protection for regeneration of

BOX 6.3 BOREAL FOREST FUNGI

Andy Taylor

The boreal forest (also known as Taiga) is the largest terrestrial biome on earth, forming a continuous zone between the more temperate vegetation in the south and the shrub vegetation of the arctic tundra in the north. It stretches across much of Alaska and Northern Canada, northern Scandinavia and right across northern Russia and Siberia (Figure 6.4). The climate has a major impact on the vegetation in this region, which is generally characterized by low plant diversity and low productivity. The over-storey is primarily coniferous trees (e.g. *Pinus*, *Picea* and *Larix* spp) and Birch (Betula), while woody ericaceous shrubs form the under-storey. Open heaths of lichen and moss are also a feature of boreal systems (Figure 6.5).

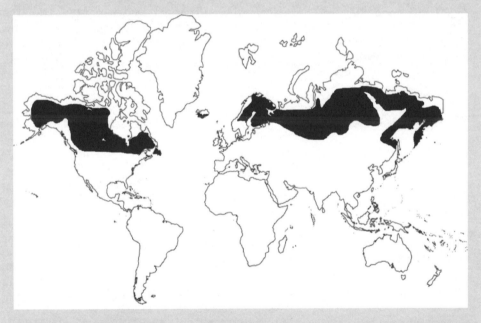

Figure 6.4 *World distribution of boreal forests*

Source: adapted from www.blueplanetbiomes.org/taiga.htm

Nutrient turnover rates are slow in these forests, with nitrogen (N) being the most limiting nutrient. In the absence of anthropogenic inputs from pollution, biologically active N comes from natural atmospheric deposition (1–3kg ha^{-1}/yr^{-1}) and N fixation (3–4kg ha^{-1}/yr^{-1}). Decomposition in boreal systems is therefore slow and organic matter accumulates at the soil surface and it is mainly within this substrate that fungi of the boreal forest grow and interact.

Figure 6.5   *Boreal forest in northern Sweden*

Photograph: A. F. S. Taylor

Above ground, the fungal communities in the boreal forest are in stark contrast to the poor species-richness in the plant communities. In particular, the numbers of ectomycorrhizal fungi are remarkable. In Scandinavia alone, there are an estimated 1700 species of ectomycorrhizal fungi with a large proportion of these in boreal forest. Within a single stand, it is possible to record >100 ectomycorrhizal species fruiting within a single hectare. So the fungi are not only species-rich over a large area but they also occur in high species-densities. The dominant genus is *Cortinarius* with an estimate 900 species in Scandinavia, many of which still remain to be described.

In general, the numbers of saprotrophic fungi that appear as fruiting bodies tend to be lower than ectomycorrhizal fungal species. Exceptions to this are in winter, when the saprotroph *Flammulina velutipes* can be abundant and is collected for eating, and in spring when large numbers of the edible false morel (*Gyromitra esculenta*) can be found. Although this morel is edible and collected and marketed commercially, it must first be repeatedly boiled in order to remove a toxin called 'gyromitrin'. When consumed in sufficient quantities this toxin can cause headaches and nausea, and eventually liver failure and death.

The harvesting of fungi for eating has a long tradition across the boreal region, with a variety of methods used to prepare and store them. These tend to vary with region. In Finland, for example, some species of *Lactarius* (which are impossible to eat raw as they contain chemicals which make them very acrid) are boiled for a short period in water then stored in salt. For later use they can then be soaked to remove the salt. This practice is absent from the neighbouring country of Sweden. Other *Lactarius* species without the acrid taste are cooked and eaten directly. The two genera *Boletus* (Figure 6.6, below) and *Cantharellus* contain the most sought after fungi in the boreal region and are increasingly collected to satisfy both domestic and commercial markets. Unfortunately, the increased harvesting of wild fungi has resulted in an increase in poisonings due to toxic fungi being mistakenly identified as edible.

Figure 6.6 Boletus pinophilus

Photograph: A. F. S. Taylor

ectomycorrhizal miombo and *Marquesia* woodland (Hogberg and Piearce, 1986). If it was possible to continually protect these woodlands from fire, they could develop into *mateshi* evergreen forest with both ecto- and endomycorrhizal tree species.

Fire does not only burn and sterilize a site but also changes the chemistry and structure of soil, most often increasing the surface alkalinity because of the remaining ash deposits. Fungi that respond to intense heat are called 'phoenicoid' fungi and often seem to prefer alkaline soils. Two examples are the cup fungus *Peziza violacea* and the morel *Morchella elata* though the latter also grows away from fire sites. Phoenicoid mushrooms were originally described as 'carbonicolous' because of their ability to colonize burnt vegetation and charcoal, but it appears that their ecology is more complex than this name suggests, as their spores need a heat-shock before germinating (Dix and Webster, 1995; Spooner and Roberts, 2005). There are a whole range of ecological groups within phoenicoid fungi and in contrast, most mycorrhizal species

Figure 6.7   *Ectomycorrhizal mushrooms typical of miombo woodland*

A. *Boletus spectabilissimus*; B. *Afroboletus luteolus*; C. *Amanita loosii*; D. *Russula heinemanniana*; E. *Lactarius velutissimus*; F. *Cantharellus rufopunctatus*.

Photographs: Cathy Sharp (A, C, D, E, F); B. Wursten (B).

Figure 6.8   Brachystegia spiciformis *woodland typical of the miombo ecoregion*

Photograph: Cathy Sharp

BOX 6.4 MUSHROOMS AND MIOMBO WOODLAND

Cathy Sharp

The term 'miombo' is derived from a Swahili word, used in Tanzania and Zambia (Wild and Barbosa, 1967) to describe a type of woodland dominated by tree genera within the Caesalpinioideae, namely *Brachystegia*, *Julbernardia* and *Isoberlinia*. White (1983) has divided Africa into simplified vegetation zones, and those that support Caesalpinioid trees (West and Central Africa) may share similarities with the mycobiota of miombo. However, true 'miombo' is characteristic of his 'Zambezian Regional Centre of Endemism' or the miombo ecoregion (WWF, 2001) (Figure 6.5.1). The above tree genera are known to be mycorrhizal as are *Marquesia*, *Afzelia* and *Pericopsis* in that same family, *Monotes* (Dipterocarpaceae) and *Uapaca* (Euphorbiaceae).

There are two broad types of miombo:

- Dry miombo is described as 'deciduous miombo savanna woodland' (Wild and Barbosa, 1967). It is the characteristic miombo in Zimbabwe, with large tracts in Zambia,

Mozambique and Tanzania. *B. spiciformis* (Figure 6.9), *J. globiflora* and *B. boehmii* are the dominant trees with *U. kirkiana* as an important associate.

● Wet Miombo is slightly more extensive than dry miombo and covers huge parts of Zambia, Angola, the southern Democratic Republic of Congo (DRC), eastern Malawi and Tanzania, and small patches of Mozambique. This ecotype is floristically richer than dry miombo (White, 1983), with the dominant trees being *B. floribunda* and *J. paniculata*.

Mushrooms typically found in miombo are from the genera *Russula*, *Lactarius*, *Cantharellus*, *Amanita* and several boletes. It is these ectomycorrhizal fungi that attract the most attention during the rains because they produce such a colourful array of mushrooms (see Figure 6.8). The advantage in being ectomycorrhizal is evident from the dominance of ectomycorrhizal trees in miombo woodland (Hogberg and Piearce, 1986; Frost, 1996). Two of these advantages are worthy of note as they contribute to improvement:

● The tree is tolerant to drought conditions. Fungal sheaths protect the fine roots from desiccation. Since miombo soils often experience moisture stress (between 3 and 9 months a year) this attribute is extremely advantageous. Moisture levels in the top 30cm of soil are often below wilting point (Frost, 1996; Sharp, 2008) and where there is erratic fluctuation in soil moisture the ectomycorrhizal zone ranges from 1–5cm beneath the litter level in *Uapaca* woodland (Thoen and Ba, 1989) and from 10–15cm under other miombo trees (Hogberg and Piearce, 1986). In higher rainfall areas of Zambia, chipya woodland seems to be dominated by endomycorrhizal trees where the need for drought tolerance is not as crucial.

● Uptake of minerals and since miombo soils are nutrient-poor and typically acid (mean pH ranging from 5.3 to 5.6) and low in nitrogen and available phosphorus, this function is most advantageous to the tree.

Fire regimes have a dramatic effect on woodland, determined by two types of burn in African woodlands:

● 'Early burn' occurs early in the cool/dry season when the climatic conditions limit rapid spread of fire, i.e. wind speeds and day temperatures are low and nights are cool, often with dew that can extinguish a fire overnight. The fuel load is usually fairly low, with just enough un-burnable, green grass to cause a patchwork of burnt and un-burnt areas. The intensity of an early burn is 100–300kJ/s/m.

● 'Hot burn' occurs later at the end of the cool/dry and into the hot/dry season. Wind speeds have picked up by then and the hot and dry conditions allow fires to burn continually, often for several months, consuming all the grass and dead wood and raging at intensities of 500–5000kJ/s/m (Robertson, 1993).

Leaf litter is at risk of being burnt by wildfires and repeated burnings every dry season have a detrimental effect on the biodiversity of saprotrophic fungi (De Kesel and Guelly, 2007). On a single excursion in Benin, 97 per cent of collected macro-fungi were symbionts (De Kesel, pers.comm.) and since litter had been destroyed by fire, saprotrophs were sparse.

Figure 6.9 Pycnoporus sanguineus, *a polypore capable of growing on burnt substrates*

Photograph: C. Sharp

However, some wood-rotting species are able to grow on burnt substrates (e.g. *Pycnoporus sanguineus* (Figure 6.9) and *Trametes cingulata*). Environmental conditions play an important role in controlling the rate of litter decomposition in miombo woodland, particularly seasonal moisture regimes (Frost 1996). In Wet Miombo, and depending on tree species, more than 90 per cent of leaf litter has decayed within a year compared to about 60 per cent in Dry Miombo. Termites and saprophytic fungi are the major contributors to this decay.

Some termites actively cultivate fungi (*Termitomyces*) which are a source of food that sustains the termite colony. The fungus is a specialized saprotroph in that it utilizes the organic matter in the comb (constructed by the termites) as its source of nutrient. There is a seasonal eruption of fruiting bodies upon the termitarium that in turn provides food for humans and animals. *T. microcarpus* is rather small to harvest because rain-splash renders them gritty but the larger species are a special delicacy not usually sold along the roadside. Other mushrooms which provide a popular, seasonal source of income are *Amanita loosii* (*A. zambiana*) (Figure 6.10), the chanterelles (Figure 6.7F) and *Lactarius kabansus* (Figure 6.7E).

The miombo ecotype is one of diverse vegetation that supports an extensive range of mushrooms, particularly ectomycorrhizal species that share the same European genera but with a huge variety of different species. The full extent of the species diversity is nowhere near realization since vast tracts of woodland and forest still remain unexplored and it is hoped that the current deforestation in Africa will not eradicate species before they have even been discovered.

Figure 6.10   *A good harvest of* Amanita loosii

Photograph: C. Sharp

cannot tolerate fires at all. Manzanita plants (*Arctostaphylos*) along the Pacific Coast of North America are common in the chapparal and arable to regrow after fire, soon re-establishing themselves with certain AM fungi that are able to survive such a severe disturbance, out-competing those that cannot (Allen, 1991).

Recovery and landscape ecology

Disturbed ecosystems rarely re-establish themselves from 'scratch' but are dependent upon residual micro-organisms in patches of soil (especially mycorrhizal fungi) to hold the system together and 'pull it up by its bootstraps', so described as the 'bootstrap hypothesis' (Perry et al, 1989). Restoration of disturbed lands has prompted a need to understand the involvement of mycorrhizae at a landscape level. Early studies on land reclamation showed that re-establishment of new trees on mine-waste were generally unsuccessful. Through the realization that these trees were dependent upon mycorrhizae in order to thrive, inoculation of plants in disturbed areas was encouraged. Now, slag heaps, coal tips, mine-dumps and landfill sites are routinely planted with trees that have deliberately been inoculated with mycorrhizal fungi. It is those fungi that have a wide range of hosts which are used; in Britain these are the earthball *Scleroderma citrinum* and the agaric *Paxillus involutus* (Spooner and Roberts, 2005). In America, *Pisolithus arhizus* is used to inoculate pines planted on sites of industrial waste.

Furthermore, awareness that wind and animals are important vectors of spore dispersal has advanced recovery programmes by using these tools in appropriate land management (Allen, 1991). During the establishment of AM plants on Mount St. Helens in the Pacific Northwest of the US, it was found that animals dispersed spores from one patch of vegetation to another as the plants re-established themselves across the site (Allen, 1988). This emphasizes how ecology of mushrooms goes way beyond people, using animals and other agents in a fine-tuned balance with the environment.

During the natural process of decomposition many bacteria and fungi are able to break down toxic chemicals into simple compounds which may have beneficial effects. This 'bioremediation' process is used in the clean-up of oil spillages where some fungi are known to thrive on hydrocarbons, degrading them into simpler and 'safer' substances (Spooner and Roberts, 2005). Although many of the fungi involved in bioremediation are microfungi, there are examples of macro-fungi serving the same useful purpose. The oyster mushroom (*Pleurotus ostreatus*) is known to break down hydrocarbons in crude oil while the corticioid fungus *Phanerochaete chrysosporium* breaks down creosote and other oils, and is even involved in the clean-up of explosive waste on the ground. Bioremediation of toxic metal-rich effluents and contaminated sites can also be achieved through the activity of fungi that are able to absorb and accumulate metals. 'Biosorption' is the process whereby fungi absorb metals (arsenic, cadmium, cobalt, copper, mercury, selenium, uranium and zinc) which can then be recovered and disposed of safely or recycled (Spooner and Roberts, 2005). Many of the fungi capable of this function are ascomycetes and therefore beyond the scope of this chapter. However, mushrooms are susceptible to uptake of radioactive compounds and are therefore good bio-indicators of radioactive contamination. After the Chernobyl disaster in 1986 the contamination of edible mushrooms in Ukraine exceeded limits of safety but the levels lowered as the wind-masses moved westward across the continent.

Fungi are continually expanding their range, and disturbances such as those discussed above provide a huge opportunity for fungi to establish themselves in newly-formed habitats. With this in mind, it cannot be denied that there is great potential for use of fungi in managing the processes of recovering and maintaining the landscape ecology after such human-induced disturbances.

FUNCTIONAL ECOLOGY OF FUNGI

Functional ecology in plants uses morphological traits of a species (specific leaf area, pod numbers, seed size, etc.) as a tool in measuring and interpreting changes in community structure (Peay et al, 2008). The extension of this ecological research to the understanding of fungal community is more difficult as there are more biochemical functional traits than morphological ones. Cultured fungi under laboratory conditions seldom equate to what is happening in the field, particularly since the majority of fungi are non-culturable (Peay et al, 2008).

Some morphological traits which may determine the functional ecology of fungi include: hyphal morphology of ectomycorrhizae (Agerer, 2001); hyphal abundances (Koide et al, 2007); surface area of functional hymenium in polypores (Guevara et al, 2000) and numbers of entry points of mycorrhizal infection per centimetre of host root (Smith et al, 1986). At a molecular level, functional genes may be used as an ecological tool but these may not necessarily express themselves in the field and only a few have been identified (Read and Perez-Moreno, 2003). However, laccase genes are thought to be important in the decomposition of high-lignin plant litter and changes in gene abundance appear to be linked with the presence of particular wood-decay fungi (Blackwood et al, 2007). The ability to assign a value to functional traits in fungi would enable interpretation of changes in community structure at both landscape and species-assemblage levels and an appreciation of the link between community structure and function of the ecosystem (Figure 6.12).

FUTURE RESEARCH NEEDS

Research in fungal ecology has advanced dramatically since the use of molecular tools but the importance of basic field knowledge of mushrooms cannot be stressed enough. Apart from the exciting discovery of the molecular fingerprint of a mushroom, this genetic identification is almost valueless without knowledge of the morphology and ecology of the specimen. It is a frightening thought that a molecular biologist may become so wrapped up in the fascinating test-tube world that there is no appreciation of the equally fascinating life-history of the organism that is under such avid scrutiny. Natural history data of fungi automatically lead to ecological and phylogenetic questions and therefore provide opportunity for research and experimentation. From this develops a need for user-friendly tools with which to capture that data and 'bioinformatics' is one such avenue of research that is rapidly advancing.

BOX 6.5 TEMPERATE BROAD-LEAFED DECIDUOUS FORESTS

Annemieke Verbeken and Cathy Sharp

Deciduous forest covers the eastern half of North America, the middle of Europe, eastern parts of Asia (southwest Russia, Japan and eastern China), together with some forests in South America, southeastern Australia and New Zealand. The southern hemisphere biomes differ in their vegetation on account of the more humid, subtropical climate.

In North America almost all the forests are secondary, but they still have a large diversity of flora and fauna and this is especially true for the Appalachian Plateau in the east. In Europe, most of the forest has been cleared for agriculture, with remnants surviving in protected nature reserves and some royal hunting estates. The broad-leafed deciduous forests of China are known primarily from fossil records because intensive agriculture in this region has caused clearance of natural vegetation over the last 4000 years. However, what remains in central China is rich and most distinctive as are the forests in the Caucasus and the Himalaya. Japan has a largely artificial forest, but in the mountains of Korea the forest is more or less intact. Of all the biomes, deciduous forest is the most altered of any habitat on earth due to rich, fertile soils which are suited to agricultural practices.

Temperate forests experience a wide range of variability in temperature and rainfall and have four distinct seasons: spring, summer, autumn and winter. In regions where rainfall is broadly distributed throughout the year, deciduous trees mix with species of evergreens. Among the most common deciduous genera are *Quercus* (oak), *Acer* (maple), *Fagus* (beech), *Betula* (Birch), *Castanea* (chestnut), *Carya* (hickory), *Ulmus* (elm), *Tilia* (basswood or linden), *Juglans* (walnut) and *Liquidambar* (sweet gum). Different species within these genera occur on each continent and *Northofagus* is a genus typical of the New Zealand forests. The broad-leafed biome is renowned for its spectacular autumn (fall) display of red, orange and yellow foliage prior to leaf-drop. This is an adaptation by the tree to reduce transpiration loss and prevent foliage freezing during the long winter months.

Structurally, these forests are characterized by four layers and in contrast to tropical rain forests, most biodiversity is concentrated close to the forest floor:

- The first zone is the tree canopy composed of mature full-sized dominant species mentioned above and these range from 20m to over 30m in height.
- The second layer is the shrub zone comprising, for example, rhododendrons, azaleas and mountain laurel.
- The herbaceous layer is an under-storey of grass and other herbaceous plants, many of which are perennial forbs that bloom primarily in early spring before the full canopy develops and shades them out.
- The final zone is the ground layer, which contains lichen, club mosses, true mosses and fungi. Fungi and lichens also inhabit tree trunks in all the other layers.

Broad-leafed trees tend to be nutrient-demanding and their leaves bind the major nutrient bases. Thus the litter under this forest is not as acidic as that under coniferous trees and

Figure 6.11 *A.* Mycena crocata, *a decomposer of* Fagus *in richer deciduous woods;* *B.* Lactarius camphoratus, *a common ectomycorrhizal species in both deciduous and coniferous temperate woodland on rather poor soils.*

Photographs: R. Walleyn

consequently differs in its fungal communities. (As a comparison, examples of acid-loving mushrooms are *Paxillus involutus*, *Amanita citrina* and *Hygrophoropsis aurantiaca*). Autumn leaf fall produces rich humus which begins to decay rapidly in spring just as the growing season begins. On sandy substrates, pines replace broadleaf species and on waterlogged sites in more northerly latitudes, bogs develop, each habitat having their own distinctive mycobiota. Ectomycorrhizal fungi are a major component of this biota, favouring the Fagaceae (oak and beech) and Betulaceae (birch) woodlands. Examples are shown in Figure 6.12.

Harvesting of edible fungi is particularly important in Eastern Europe and has been for aeons. Boletes are a favourite, with *Boletus edulis* the most popular species. Chanterelles are another favourite and truffles are a prized delicacy that fetch high prices on the commercial market. The Japanese shiitake mushroom (*Lentinula edodes*) is an important edible mushroom that is now grown commercially in Europe and America and, being a saprotrophic species, is relatively easy to cultivate. The commercial cultivation of the temperate oyster mushroom (*Pleurotus*) has extended to Africa in an attempt to provide an extra food source and household income.

Phylogeny (the evolutionary history and relationships of a group of organisms) is not usually considered in ecological studies but is used to assign organisms to functional or trophic groups (e.g. mycorrhizal, saprotrophic, parasitic, etc.), particularly where little taxonomic data is available (Peay et al, 2008). Studies in community ecology and root-inhabiting fungi have shown that phylogeny is a good start in recognizing major ecological traits and this needs to be extended to fungal communities. Peay et al have wrapped this up very concisely: 'Thus, a little natural history and good phylogenetics have the potential to go a long way in helping to characterize the ecological role of fungi identified in environmental studies, even if the fungi have not been formally described'.

As often happens in any field of research, the more one finds out, the more questions arise. The way forward in fungal ecology is paved with exciting research possibilities, some of which are highlighted below:

- Renewed focus on fundamental knowledge of the natural history of mushrooms by continued compilation of field data, particularly over many years, so as to capture evidence of ecological changes in fungal community structure.
- Maintenance of basic fungal biology in order to better understand molecular based identification (Peay et al, 2008).
- Identification of the link between competitive strategies in fungi and their life history (Peay et al, 2008).
- The application of molecular techniques to overcome sampling barriers and thereby derive more accurate estimates of fungal species richness (Peay et al, 2008).
- The linking of established patterns of niche partitioning with functional gene approaches in order to gain a better understanding of the structure of fungal communities and functioning of the ecosystem (Peay et al, 2008).

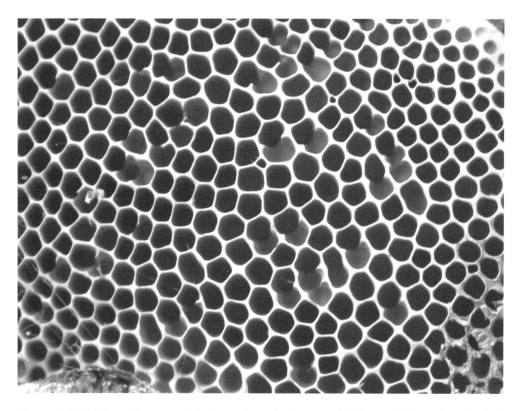

Figure 6.12   *The surface area of the hymenium of polypores might be a suitable trait with which to determine functional ecology of fungi; this is* Hexagonia.

Photograph: C. Sharp

- Determination of the causes of fine-scale variability in fungal assemblages (Peay et al, 2008) – influence of soil moisture and organic matter particularly in miombo woodland (Sharp, 2008).
- Quantification of landscape-scale patterns of fungal dispersal and linkage of this knowledge with ecological patterns such as succession (Peay et al, 2008) and biogeography (Allen, 1991).
- Investigation of the gaps in the understanding of mycorrhizal fungi in order to better understand ecological processes: the extent of fungal diversity; the mechanics of the exchange between plant and fungus (A. Fitter in Whitfield, 2007); the influence of phenology of woodland and forest on mycorrhizal status below-ground (Sharp, 2008); the survival strategies of ectomycorrhizae during extended periods of drought (Sharp, 2008); identification of the roles played by complex 'hidden' fungi (*Tomentella, Tomentellopsis* and *Tylospora*) in nutrient economics of forest systems (Read and Perez-Moreno, 2003); and the importance of fungivorous animals in the structure and maintenance of fungal communities in miombo woodland (Sharp, 2008) and at a landscape level (Allen, 1991).
- Understanding the effects of fire on fungal communities in order to implement appropriate sustainable management techniques and thereby conserve the habitat.

- Understanding of mycorrhizal dynamics in response to climate change. The ability of the mycorrhizal fungus to adapt to change and the responses of the host plant to climatic changes are likely to be major determinants in the maintenance of productive ecosystems and are well worth investigating (Allen, 1991; Read and Perez-Moreno, 2003).

In conclusion, when encountering mushrooms on a woodland walk or during a forestry management exercise, one should be aware of their secret life below ground. There is literally 'more than meets the eye' and fungal ecology is a treasure trove of opportunity. With the rapid advancement in molecular technology alongside fieldwork and laboratory experimentation, there will be a chance to take a peek into this hidden world of fungi and appreciate, even more, their crucial role in the ecology of our environment.

REFERENCES

Aerts, R. (2002) 'The role of various types of mycorrhizal fungi in nutrient cycling and plant competition', in M. G. A. van der Heijden and I. Sanders (eds) *Mycorrhizal ecology*, Springer-Verlag, Berlin, pp117–133

Agerer, R. (2001) 'Exploration types of ectomycorrhizae', *Mycorrhiza* 11, pp107–114

Allen, M. F. (1988) 'Re-establishment VA of mycorrhizae following severe disturbance: comparative patch dynamics of a shrub desert and a sub-alpine volcano', *Proceedings of the Royal Society of Edinburgh* 94B, pp63–71

Allen, M. F. (1991) *The ecology of mycorrhizae*, Cambridge University Press, Cambridge

Arnold, A. E., Maynard, Z., Gilbert, G. S., Coley, P. D. and Kursar, T. A. (2000) 'Are tropical endophytes hyperdiverse?' *Ecology Letters* 3, pp267–274

Arnolds, E. (1981) 'Ecology and coenology of macro-fungi in grassland and moist heathland in Drenthe, the Netherlands. Part 1. Introduction and synecology', *Bibl. Mycol.* 83, 407

Baar, J., Horton, T. R., Kretzer, A. and Bruns, T. D. (1999) Mycorrhizal recolonization of *Pinus muricata* from resistant propagules after a stand-replacing wildfire. *New Phytologist* 143, pp409–418

Bermudes, D., Peterson, R. H. and Nealson, K. N. (1992) 'Low-level bioluminescence detected in *Mycena haematopus* basidiocarps', *Mycologia* 84, pp799–802

Bertolino, S., Vizzini, A., Wauters, L. A. and Tosi, G. (2004) 'Consumption of hypogeous and epigeous fungi by the red squirrel (*Sciurus vulgaris*) in subalpine conifer forests', *Forest Ecology & Management*, 202, pp227–233

Bidartondo, M. I., Burghardt, B., Gebauer, G., Bruns, T. D. and Read, D. J. (2004) 'Changing partners in the dark: isotopic and molecular evidence of ectomycorrhizal liaisons between forest orchids and trees', *Proc. R. Soc. Lond.* B271, pp1799–1806

Blackwood C. B., Waldrop M. P., Zak, D. R. and Sinsabaugh, R. L. (2007) 'Molecular analysis of fungal communities and laccase genes in decomposing litter reveals differences among forest types but no impact of nitrogen deposition', *Environmental Microbiology* 9, pp1306–1316

Boa, E. (2004) *Wild edible fungi*, FAO, Rome

Boerner, R. E. J. (1982) 'Fire and nutrient cycling in temperate ecosystems', *BioScience*, 32, pp187–192

Bultman, T. L. and Leuchtmann, A. (2008) 'Biology of the *Epichloe-Botanophila* interaction: An interesting association between fungi and insects', *Fungal Biology Reviews* 22, pp131–138

Christensen, M. (1981) 'Species diversity and dominance in fungal communities', in D. T. Wicklow and G. C. Carroll (eds) *The Fungal Community*, Marcel Dekker, New York, pp201–232

Corner, E. J. H. (1935) 'The seasonal fruitings of Agarics in Malaya', *Gardens' Bulletin, Straits Settlements* 9, pp79–88

Dahlberg, A. (1995) 'Somatic incompatibility in ectomycorrhizas', in A. Varma and B. Hock (eds) *Mycorrhiza*, Springer-Verlag, Berlin, pp116–137

De Kesel, A. and Guelly, A. (2007) 'Seminaire de mycologie. Togo (Afrique de l'Ouest), 2–26 Juillet 2007', *Final Report Global Taxonomy Initiative Project*, National Botanic Garden, Belgium

Dell, B., Sanmee, R., Lumyong, P. and Lumyong, S. (2005) 'Ectomycorrhizal fungi in dry and wet dipterocarp forests in northern Thailand—diversity and use as food', *Proceedings of the 8th Round Table Conference on Dipterocarps*, Ho Chi Minh City, 15–17 November 2005

Desjardin, D. E., Oliveira, A. G. and Stevani, C. V. (2008) 'Fungi bioluminescence revisited', *Photochem. Photobiol. Sci.* 7, pp170–182

Dix, N. J. and Webster, J. (1995) *Fungal Ecology*, Chapman and Hall, London

Field, J. I. and Webster, J. (1977) 'Traps of predaceous fungi attract nematodes', *Trans. Br. mycol. Soc.* 68, pp467–469

Frankland, J. C. (1975) 'Fungal decomposition of leaf litter in a deciduous wood', in G. K. Kilbertus, O. Reisinger, A. Mourey and J. A. Cancella de Fonseca (eds) *Biodegradation et Humification*, Pierron, Sarreguemines, pp33–40

Frost, P. (1996) 'The ecology of miombo woodlands', in B. Campbell (ed) *The miombo in transition: Woodlands and welfare in Africa*, CIFOR, Bogor, Malaysia

Gelfand, M. and Harris, C. (1982) 'Poisoning by *Amanita pantherina*: A description of two cases', *C. Afr. J. Med.* 28, pp159–163

Gelfand, M., Mavi, S., Drummond, R. B. and Ndemera, B. (1985) *The traditional medical practitioner in Zimbabwe. His principles of practice and pharmacopoeia*, Mambo Press, Gweru

Gould, S. J. (1992) 'A humongous fungus among us', *Natural History* 7, 10–16

Guevara, R., Rayner, A. D. M. and Reynolds, S. E. (2000) 'Effects of fungivory by two specialist ciid beetles (*Octotemnus glabriculus* and *Cis boleti*) on the reproductive fitness of their host fungus *Coriolopsis versicolor*', *New Phytologist* 145, pp137–144

Haaramo, M. (2008) *Mikko's Phylogeny Archive – Collembola*, www.helsinki.fi/~mhaaramo/, accessed 31 July 2010

Harris, C. (1981) 'More on mushroom poisoning', *C. Afr. J. Med.* 27, pp208–209

Hattori, T. and Lee, S. S. (2003) 'Community structure of wood–decaying basidiomycetes in Pasoh', in T. Okuda et al (eds) *Pasoh. Ecology of a lowland rainforest in Southeast Asia*, Springer, Tokyo

Hawksworth, D. L. and Rose, F. (1970) 'Qualitative scale for estimating sulphur dioxide air pollution in England and Wales using epiphytic lichens', *Nature* 227, pp145–148

Hawksworth, D. L. (1991) 'The fungal dimension of biodiversity: Magnitude, significance and conservation', *Mycol. Res.* 95, pp641–655

Hawksworth, D. L. (2001) 'The magnitude of fungal diversity: The 1.5 million species estimate revisited', *Mycol. Res.* 105, pp1422–1432

Hedger, J. N. and Basuki, T. (1982) 'The role of basidiomycetes in composts: A model system for decomposition studies', in J. C. Frankland, J. J. Hedger and M. Swift (eds) *Decomposer basidiomycetes: Their biology and ecology*, Cambridge University Press, Cambridge, pp263–305

Hogberg, P. and Piearce, G. D. (1986) 'Mycorrhizas in Zambian trees in relation to host taxonomy, vegetation type and successional patterns', *Journal of Ecology* 74, pp775–785

Horton, T. R. and Bruns, T. D. (2001) 'The molecular revolution in ectomycorrhizal ecology: Peeking into the black box', *Molecular Ecology* 10, pp1855–1871

Isaac, S. (1998) 'To what extent does fungal activity contribute to the processes of decomposition in soils and in composts?' *Mycologist* 12, pp185–186

Janos, D. P. (1980) 'Mycorrhizae influence tropical succession', *Biotropica* 12, pp56–64

Jansson, H.-B. and Poinar, G. O. (1986) Some possible fossil nematophagous fungi. *Trans. Br. mycol. Soc.* 87, pp471–474

Johnson, C. N. (1994) 'Mycophagy and spore dispersal by a rat-kangaroo: Consumption of ectomycorrhizal taxa in relation to their abundance', *Functional Ecology* 8, pp464–468

Jonsson, M. and Wordle, D. A. (2010) 'Structural equation modelling reveals plant-community drivers of carbon storage in boreal forest ecosystems', *Biology Letters* 23, vol 6, no 1, pp116–9

Klironomos, J. N. and Hart, M. M. (2001) 'Animal nitrogen swap for plant carbon', *Nature* 410, pp651–652

Klironomos, J. N. and Moutoglis, P. (1999) 'Colonization of nonmycorrhizal plants by mycorrhizal neighbours as influenced by the collembolan *Folsomia candida*', *Biology and Fertility of Soils* 29, pp277–281

Koide, R. T., Shumway, D. L., Xu, B. and Sharda, J. N. (2007) 'On temporal partitioning of a community of ectomycorrhizal fungi', *New Phytologist* 174, pp420–429

Lee, S. S., Watling, R. and Turnbull, E. (2003) 'Diversity of putative ectomycorrhizal fungi in Pasoh Forest Reserve', in T. Okuda et al (eds) *Pasoh. Ecology of a lowland rainforest in Southeast Asia*, Springer, Tokyo

Mason, P. (2001) 'Looking below the surface', *Trees: Journal and Yearbook of the International Tree Foundation* 61, pp16–17

McAllister, D. E. (1993) 'Vast soil fungal networks sustain forests. Is the hidden tree-fungus partnership in crisis?' *Global Diversity*, vol 3, no 1, pp32–34

Mueller, G. M., Schmit, J. P., Leacock, P. R., Buyck, B., Cifuentes, J., Desjardin, D. E., Halling, R. E., Hjortstam, K., Iturriaga, T., Larsson, K.-H., Lodge, D. J., May, T. W., Minter, D., Rajchenberg, M., Redhead, S. A., Ryvarden, L., Trappe, J. M., Watling, R. and Wu, Q. (2007) 'Global diversity and distribution of macrofungi', *Biodivers. Conserv.* 16, pp37–48

Nagel de Bois, H. M. and Jansen, E. (1971) 'The growth of fungal mycelium in forest soil layers', *Revue d'Ecologie et de Biologie du Sol* 8, pp509–520

Newberry, D. M., Alexander, I. J., Thomas, D. W. and Gartlan, J. S. (1988) 'Ectomycorrhizal rain-forest legumes and soil phosphorus in Korup National Park, Cameroon', *New Phytologist* 109, pp433–450

Pacioni, G. and Sharp, C. (2000) '*Mackintoshia*, a new sequestrate basidiomycete genus from Zimbabwe', *Mycotaxon* 75, pp225–228

Parton, W., Silver, W. L., Burke, I. C., Grassens, L., Harman, M. E., Currie, W. S., King, J. Y., Adair, E. C., Brandt, L. A., Hart, S. C. and Fasth, B. (2007) 'Global scale similarities in nitrogen release patterns during long-term decomposition', *Science* 315, pp361–364

Peay, K. G., Kennedy, P. G. and Bruns, T. D. (2008) 'Fungal community ecology: A hybrid beast with a molecular master', *BioScience* 58, pp799–810

Pegler, D. N. (1997) *The larger fungi of Borneo*, Natural History Publications, Kota Kinabalu

Perry, D. A., Amaranthus, M. P., Borchers, S. L. and Brainerd, R. E. (1989) 'Bootstrapping in ecosystems', *BioScience* 39, pp230–237

Piearce, G. D. and Sharp, C. (2000) 'Vernacular names of Zimbabwean fungi: A preliminary checklist', *Kirkia* 17, pp219–228

Pirot, P. (2006) *Olatra, champignons d'Andasibe*, Mitsinjo Association, Madagascar, www.madagascar-library.com/r/1374.html

Pole Evans, I. B. (1918) 'Note on the genus *Terfezia*: A truffle from the Kalahari', *Trans. Royal Soc. S. Afr.* 7, pp117–118

Pumpanen, J., Ilvesniemi, H., Kulmala, L., Siivola, E., Laakso, H., Kolari, P., Helenelund, C., Laakso, M., Uusimaa, M. and Hari, P. (2008) 'Respiration in boreal forest soil as determined from carbon dioxide concentration profile', *Soil Sci. Soc. Am. J.* 72, pp1187–1196

Raghukumar, S. (1992) 'Bacterivory – a novel dual role for thraustochytrids in the sea', *Marine Biology* 113, pp165–169

Read, D. J. (1991) 'Mycorrhizas in ecosystems', *Experientia* 47, pp376–391

Read, D. J. and Perez-Moreno, J. (2003) 'Mycorrhizas and nutrient cycling in ecosystems – a journey towards relevance?' *New Phytologist* 157, pp475–492

Reddell, P., Spain, A. and Hopkins, M. (1997) 'Dispersal of spores of mycorrhizal fungi in scats of native animals in tropical forests of Northeastern Australia', *Biotropica* 29, pp184–192

Redhead, J. F. (1968) 'Mycorrhizal associations in some Nigerian forest trees', *Trans. Br. mycol. Soc.* 51, pp377–387

Robertson, F. (1993) 'Early burning in the Brachystegia woodland of the Parks and Wildlife Estate', *Zimbabwe Science News* vol 27, nos 7–9, pp68–71

Sabatini, M. A. and Innocenti, G. (2001) 'Effects of collembola on plant-pathogenic fungus interactions in simple experimental systems', *Biology and Fertility of Soils* 33, pp62–66

Saleska, S. R., Didan, K., Huete, A. R. and da Rocha, H. R. (2007) 'Amazon forests green-up during 2005 drought', *Science* 318, p612

Sharp, C. (2008) 'Macrofungi in a miombo woodland in Central Zimbabwe', MPhil thesis, University of Aberdeen

Simon, L., Bousque, J., Levesque, R. C. and Lalonde, M. (1993) 'Origin and diversification of endomycorrhizal fungi and coincidence with vascular land plants', *Nature* 363, pp67–69

Smith, M. L., Bruhn, J. N. and Anderson, J. B. (1992) 'The fungus *Armillaria bulbosa* is among the largest and oldest living organisms', *Nature* 356, pp428–431

Smith, S. E., Tester, M. and Walker, N. A. (1986) 'The development of mycorrhizal root systems in *Trifolium substerraneum* L. Growth of roots and the uniformity of spatial distribution of mycorrhizal infection units in young plants', *New Phytologist* 103, pp117–131

Spooner, B. M. and Roberts, R. (2005) *Fungi*, Collins, London

Stubbe, D., Verbeken, A. and Watling, R. (2007) 'Blue staining species of Lactarius subgenus Plinthogalus in Malaysia', *Belg. J. Bot.*, vol 140, no 2, pp197–212

Thoen, D. (1976) 'Facteurs physiques et fructification des champignons supérieurs dans quelques pessières d'Ardenne méridionale (Belgique)', *Bulletin de la Société Linnéenne de Lyon* 45, pp269–284

Thoen, D. and Ba, A. M. (1989) 'Ectomycorrhizas and putative ectomycorrhizal fungi of *Afzelia africana* Sm. and *Uapaca guineensis* Mull. Arg. in Southern Senegal', *New Phytologist* 113, pp549–559

Trappe, J., Claridge, A. W., Arora, D. and Smit, W. A. (2008) 'Desert truffles of the African Kalahari: Ecology, ethnomycology and taxonomy', *Economic Botany* 62, pp521–529

US Global Change Research Program (2009) 'The global carbon cycle', *Annual Report: Our changing planet*

Van Wyk, B.-E., Van Oudtshoorn, B. and Gericke, N. (2000) *Medicinal plants of South Africa*, Briza, Pretoria

Wang, X. H. (2000) 'A taxonomic study on some commercial species in the genus *Lactarius* (Agaricales) from Yunnan province, China', *Acta Bot. Yunnanica*, vol 22, no 3, pp419–427 (in Chinese)

Watling, R. (1995) 'Assessment of fungal diversity: Macromycetes, the problems', *Can. J. Bot.* 73, S15–S24

White, F. (1983) *The vegetation of Africa*, UNESCO, Paris

Whitfield, J. (2007) 'Underground networking', *Nature* 449, pp136–138

Whitmore, T. C. (1984) *Tropical rainforests of the Far East* (2nd edition), Oxford University Press, Oxford

Wild, H. and Barbosa, L. A. G. (1967) 'Vegetation map of the Flora Zambesiaca area', *Flora Zambesiaca* (Supplement), M. O. Collins, Salisbury, Rhodesia [sic]

Wilkins, W. H. and Harris, G. C. M. (1946) 'The ecology of the larger fungi V. An investigation into the influence of rainfall and temperature on the seasonal production of fungi in a beechwood and a pinewood', *Annals of Applied Biology* 33, pp179–188

Wilkins, W. H. and Patrick, S. H. M. (1939) 'The ecology of the larger fungi III. Constancy and frequency of grassland species with special reference to soil types', *Annals of Applied Biology* 26, pp25–46

Wilkins, W. H. and Patrick, S. H. M. (1940) 'The ecology of the larger fungi IV. The seasonal frequency of grassland fungi with special reference to the influence of environmental factors. *Annals of Applied Biology* 27, pp17–34

World Wide Fund for Nature (WWF) (2001) 'Conserving the Miombo Ecoregion, Reconnaissance Summary', H. O. Kojwang (ed), WWF, Southern Africa Regional Programme Office, South Africa

CHAPTER 7

Ensuring Sustainable Harvests of Wild Mushrooms

David Pilz

> *As if some joy*
> *As yet unexpressed*
> *Sends up mushrooms*

(Robert Mainone, *Parnassus flowers: Haiku poems*)

INTRODUCTION

People around the world have always found uses for the fruit bodies (sporocarps) of fungi. Edible mushrooms and truffles are used as food, flavouring and medicine; even woody conks (bracket fungus) are used medicinally (Halpern and Miller, 2002; Hobbs, 1986; Stamets and Yao, 2002) or for fibre, e.g. fire-starting tinder (Stamets 2002). Boa (2004; 2006) coined the term 'wild useful fungi' to capture the diversity of uses for wild fungi. Frequently, deep cultural traditions have developed around their harvest and these vary as widely as the fungi themselves. Boa (2004, 2006) has documented more than 2000 useful fungal species worldwide. They are harvested in habitats ranging from tropical deserts to boreal tundra. This book focuses on harvested fungi found in forests, especially edible mushrooms. Certain tree species produce some of the most abundantly collected edible mushrooms: morels, boletes, chanterelles, matsutake, russulas and a host of others (Hall et al, 2003). The diversity of wild edible mushrooms, the forest habitats where they grow and the cultures that harvest them makes it impossible to prescribe standard methods of ensuring sustainable harvests that would apply to all situations. There are, however, underlying principles for how best to address sustainability issues and a suite of approaches to monitoring that can be tailored to local circumstances.

ASPECTS OF SUSTAINABILITY

When sustainable mushroom harvesting is discussed, the typical meaning is non-declining levels of production (quantity/area/time-period), but there are other meanings too. For instance, some land managers are more interested in sustaining viable populations of the harvested fungus or ensuring fungal diversity in a particular habitat or land management unit. Sustaining mushroom production also has economic and social components. For example, Pilz (2004) concluded that commercial harvesting of the medicinal conk chaga (*Inonotus obliquus* (Pers.) Pilát) in no way endangered this extremely widespread and abundant pathogen of birch trees in the boreal forests of Russia, but that the species could be locally over-harvested. Without efforts at enhancing production, the harvest might become economically unsustainable, as collectors need to travel further from towns and cities to find specimens.

Mushroom harvesting is also strongly interwoven with sustaining cultural and social traditions. Arora (1999) provides colourful examples of traditions from around the world mixing in the mushroom harvesting camps of western North America. By contrast, Trappe et al (2008a; 2008b) compare ancient cultural traditions of desert truffle harvesting among indigenous peoples of the Australian Outback and the African Kalahari. Yamin-Pasternak (2008) describes the very different cultural traditions regarding mushrooms between otherwise similar cultures on either side of the Bering Straight. Winkler (2008) investigates traditions of harvesting the medicinal fungus, yartsa gunbu (*Cordyceps sinensis* (Berk.) Sacc.) in the grasslands of Tibet. The literature describing cultural aspects of mushroom harvesting is voluminous, but these recent examples illustrate the incredible richness of such customs around the world and the importance of mushroom harvesting in communicating intergenerational cultural practices and identity.

BIOLOGY AND ECOLOGY OF HARVESTED FUNGI

Understanding the biology and ecology of harvested fungi is integral to sustaining their populations and fruit body production. Fungi constitute a large and very important branch on the tree of life (Maddison and Schulz, 2007). Although mushrooms, conks and truffles are macroscopic, the fungi that produce them are considered micro-organisms in their biology and ecology (Carlile et al, 2001). For instance, they can establish new clonal colonies from single cells and their fundamental reproductive structures (spores) are typically single-celled. They are heterotrophs (i.e. organisms that have different forms at different stages of their life cycle) and absorb nutrients from their environment, typically the substrate they occupy.

Importantly, their aptitude for dispersal (clonal or sexual) tends to be prodigious, as spores are produced in copious quantities and may be spread by wind, animals, insects, water or other mechanisms. When fungal propagules encounter habitat to which they are well adapted, they are competitive colonizers. As with all organisms, available habitat is essential to healthy populations. Forest fungi occupy several habitat types.

For instance, the commonly cultivated shiitake (*Lentinula edodes* (Berk.) Pegler) and oyster (*Pleurotus ostreatus* (Jacq.: Fr.) P. Kumm.) mushrooms are examples of fungi that decay wood and produce edible fruit bodies. Although these fungi grow wild in forests, the vast majority of commerce in these species derives from cultivation because it is relatively simple to provide the substrate and growing conditions for inexpensive and reliable production (Przybylowicz and Donoghue, 2008; Stamets, 2000).

Some forest fungi that produce edible mushrooms are soil saprobes that decay organic detritus on or in the soil profile, e.g. some woodland *Agaricus* species, the blewitt (*Lepista nuda* (Bull.: Fr.) Cook) and shaggy manes (*Coprinus comatus* (O. F. Müll.) Gray). These forest saprobes may be common in the wild, but not abundant in any one location. They require specific substrates and habitat conditions to be competitive with other decay fungi; when they have depleted their food supply, they must colonize new habitats. Edible mushrooms produced by saprobic forest fungi are harvested worldwide, but their collection is typically opportunistic. Fruiting may last less than a decade unless a continuous supply of new food resources becomes available.

By contrast, ectomycorrhizal forest fungi, such as those mentioned in the introductory paragraph, produce large quantities of edible mushrooms, often annually for decades. The reason is their food source. Mycorrhizal fungi form symbiotic associations (Smith and Read, 1997) with plant roots, forming a dual plant–fungus nutrient exchange structure called mycorrhizae or mycorrhizas (literally 'fungus'–'roots'). The fungus absorbs water and minerals from the soil and transfers these to the plant, greatly enlarging its effective root system. The plant in return provides the fungus with carbohydrates it has produced through photosynthesis (Allen, 1992). There are many types of mycorrhizal relations. Ectomycorrhizae (Marks and Kozlowski, 1973) refer to a type of mycorrhiza typically formed by some genera of Basidiomycetes with certain genera of tree species (Cairney and Chambers, 1999). The fungus forms a sheath around the tree's root tips, hence the modifier 'ecto-' or 'on the outside'. Importantly, this group of fungi produces the most abundant and widely collected edible forest mushrooms precisely because their food source is so abundant and reliable. Forest trees produce large quantities of photosynthates each year and share a significant proportion with their ectomycorrhizal fungal symbionts. This abundant and fairly reliable source of energy allows these fungi to fruit prolifically during years when weather conditions cooperate, as long as their host trees remain healthy. Good mushroom collecting areas can persist for decades as forests slowly mature.

Additionally, unlike edible species of wood decay fungi, ectomycorrhizal mushrooms are typically difficult and expensive to cultivate in plantations. Other than a few high value, easily inoculated species (such as certain culinary truffles), growing ectomycorrhizal fungi in plantations of inoculated trees cannot compete economically with abundant crops of wild mushrooms and their international trade.

MANAGING FOREST HABITAT

The population viability and fruit body production of edible forest mushrooms are so intimately connected with their food source, the forest trees, that sustaining the edible mushroom resource requires appropriate forest management (Wiensczyk et al, 2002).

The many popular ectomycorrhizal mushroom species require certain tree host species, although most can associate with several tree species, often in several genera. For instance, the name of the prized Japanese matsutake (*Tricholoma matsutake* (S. Ito et Imai) Sing) means 'pine mushroom', because it fruits prolifically with pine trees. However, a very similar species in North America, the white or American matsutake (*Tricholoma magnivelare* (Peck) Redhead) has a very broad host range, including trees in five widespread genera (Hosford et al, 1997). In order for a desired edible mushroom to occur in a forest, its preferred host tree species must grow there. Productivity of the mushroom is dependent, at least in part, on the abundance, growth and health of appropriate host tree species.

Forests are dynamic assemblages of organisms that change through time. As stands (plant populations) age, food supplies and habitat conditions shift for fungi. Young stands, less than a decade old, rarely produce significant quantities of edible ectomycorrhizal mushrooms, presumably because the trees are too small to produce sufficient quantities of surplus carbohydrates. In cold or dry climates, where host trees grow slowly, this initial period without fruiting may last several decades. As stands become established, the trees begin growing vigorously and the canopy begins to close; at this stage prolific fruiting of some edible species, such as chanterelles (*Cantharellus* spp), often commences and persists for decades as the stand matures (Love et al, 1998). Pilz et al (2006a) speculate that thinning these forests to reduce competition might extend this period of abundant fruiting by prolonging the period of vigorous tree growth among the residual trees. As such stands reach maturity and trees begin to senesce, the productivity of chanterelles can drop off as the diversity of competing ectomycorrhizal species increases (Smith et al, 2002). Other prized edible fungi, such as the American matsutake fruiting in British Columbia, apparently fruit only in late seral (secondary succession) stands (Kranabetter et al, 2005).

Similarly, some edible mushrooms, such as the winter chanterelle of western North America (*Craterellus tubaeformis* (Fries) Quélet), seem to grow best in dense moist forests with ample quantities of well-rotted coarse woody debris (Trappe, 2004) whereas others, such as the Japanese matsutake, fruit best in open pine forests with little understorey vegetation and thin litter layers (Hosford et al, 1997).

Because edible mushroom species, forest types, geography, soil conditions, climate and human uses of the forest vary so widely around the world, one must understand the specific habitat conditions that allow each species of edible mushroom to thrive in each locale. Such information allows forest managers to tailor forest conditions across large areas, so that some accessible forest stands will always be producing valuable mushroom crops. This information also provides the foundation for GIS (Geographic Information System) modelling of suitable mushroom habitats across broad landscapes (Yang et al 2006). With further understanding of the drivers of ectomycorrhizal mushroom productivity, the average size of mushroom crops across the landscape over multiple years can also be modelled (Bonet et al, 2008; Pilz et al, 2002).

ENHANCING PRODUCTION

Understanding how edible species of fungi respond to forest habitat provides the opportunity to increase their population densities and enhance their productivity. For instance, wood saprobes need wood to decompose, so ensuring that new dead trees or logs are regularly recruited as structural elements of the forest in turn provides potential habitats for the fungi and other organisms. A more proactive approach would involve inoculating live trees or not yet rotted logs with the edible fungus of choice. Although not as cost-effective as cultivating these edible mushrooms in grow houses, field inoculation could enhance the recreational and household commodity value of forests (Stamets, 2005) while providing other ecosystem benefits such as wildlife habitat (Marcot, 2002).

Scientists have long sought to artificially inoculate tree seedlings with ectomycorrhizal fungi to produce crops of selected mushrooms upon planting out. Edible ectomycorrhizal fungi vary widely in how readily they can be used to colonize seedlings under nursery conditions. For instance, the Périgord black truffle (*Tuber melanosporum* Vitt.) is relatively easy to inoculate on tree seedlings using spores, which are also easy to collect en mass (Hall et al, 2007). Other species, such as chanterelles (*Cantharellus cibarius* Fr.), require exacting sterile chamber conditions and mycelial inoculum in order to become established on seedlings (Danell and Camacho, 1997; Pilz et al, 2003:25–28). Yet other prized species, such as the Japanese matsutake, appear to prefer growing with older trees. Ectomycorrhizae can be formed on the roots of young seedlings in nurseries, but rarely persist upon planting out, which has led to the development of methods to inoculate older trees in situ (Guerin-Laguette et al, 2005). Developments in this field continue to progress, so planting inoculated seedlings will likely become more common (Wang and Hall, 2004). So far, only truffles are valuable enough to justify the expense of intensively managing tree plantations solely for production of culinary fungal fruit bodies. That does not preclude foresters or private landowners from planting inoculated seedlings to enhance harvests of edible mushrooms from less intensively managed forests. Given the right host trees and ideal habitat, such efforts might very well improve yields of the selected fungus, but without controlled comparisons, it will be hard to determine if the selected fungus might not have colonized the forest anyway.

Lastly, many conscientious mushroom harvesters attempt to enhance reproduction and productivity of harvested mushrooms by spreading the spores of the mushrooms they collect. For example, loose weave plastic baskets or buckets with holes drilled in the bottom are sometimes used as collection containers. The intent is to facilitate dissemination of spores while the harvesters walk around collecting. Unfortunately, most commercially harvested mushrooms are most valuable when collected young, because they have longer shelf life during transport to markets than older specimens. Typically spores mature and are released as the sporocarp itself matures, hence this good-intentioned practice might not always be effective, although it certainly does no harm. Other collectors will spread old fruit bodies with no monetary value into areas where the mushroom does not yet fruit. Anecdotal accounts of successfully spreading mushroom patches are common, but no controlled trials have demonstrated the efficacy of this practice; once again, it is likely harmless. On a larger scale, when mature morel mushrooms are dried in heated rooms, they frequently release huge quantities of spores that can be collected. Some speculate whether spreading collected morel spores from aircraft would be useful for improving future yields. The efficacy of this approach could be tested using molecular methods of genetic analysis (Pilz et al, 2007:120–121).

THE IMPACT OF MUSHROOM HARVESTING

Can forest mushrooms be over-harvested? What are the impacts of heavy commercial harvesting on the productivity and population viability of harvested forest fungi?

These are among the first questions that come to mind among forest managers tasked with ensuring sustainability and members of the public who value their forests and forest resources. Understanding the nature of ectomycorrhizal relations between edible mushrooms and healthy trees, and the fact that the mushroom, not the body of the fungus, is the reproductive structure, helps to alleviate some of these concerns. Indeed, Norvell (1995) showed that a decade of careful harvesting had no impact on chanterelle fruiting. Egli et al (2006) also showed no impact on subsequent fruiting from two decades of carefully harvesting all species in the study plots. Importantly, the later study noted that trampling did impair fruiting in a given season, most likely from direct damage to young mushroom 'buttons' (primordial) that had not yet expanded. This has implications for monitoring methods, as will be discussed in the next section. Both of these studies also compared careful mushroom plucking with cutting the mushroom off at the base and found no differences between these harvest methods.

Unfortunately, not all mushrooms are harvested carefully. For instance, matsutake are most valuable when they are quite young and the expanding cap has not yet broken the veil between the edge of the cap and the stem. These prized and valuable young specimens are often sought before they emerge from under the forest floor litter layer. Experienced harvesters who visit the same spot annually can find these mushrooms by the bumps they create in the litter layer. Typically they will excavate the mushroom carefully and hide the evidence of their harvest so others do not learn where their mushroom patches are located. In North America, new or transitory harvesters who have little intention of returning in subsequent years will sometimes rake the litter from large areas of the forest floor in search of young matsutake. This can depress subsequent fruiting for several years, depending on how deeply the soil is raked and how much the mycelium is disturbed (Luoma et al, 2006).

Humans have harvested edible ectomycorrhizal mushrooms since ancient times and yet they are still abundant in most forests with appropriate host trees. Picking impact studies show that no harm is caused by careful harvesting over several decades. As micro-organisms with prodigious reproductive mechanisms, populations and productivity seem to be driven more by the quality of habitat than by harvesting pressures. When declines in harvests have been noted, frequently they are related to forest health (Arnolds, 1991) or increased competition. In spite of all these considerations, widespread and intensive commercial harvesting of edible forest mushrooms for global trade is a new phenomenon in recent decades. No long-term, landscape-scale, replicated monitoring efforts have yet focused on the sustainability of intensive commercial mushroom harvesting (Pilz and Molina, 1998; 2002). Is trampling a concern in heavily harvested areas? Does harvesting most mushrooms, year after year, before they have a chance to release their spores, depress reproductive success or genetic diversity? Do harvesters spread spores of harvested mushrooms to new areas with their shoes? Do they spread competitive fungi into otherwise productive areas? These, and many other, questions can be addressed with research and monitoring.

Meanwhile, some simple conservation measures can be adopted if concerns are serious. Many harvested mushrooms fruit in areas too steep or remote for easy harvesting. These areas can act as reservoirs of spore dispersal. In some instances, like National Parks or wilderness areas in the US, commercial harvesting of any product is prohibited. Alternative conservation measures might entail rotating areas where harvesting is permitted or setting harvest seasons that allow some mushrooms to mature and spread their spores. Such restrictions should be designed in collaboration with the harvesters themselves to avoid unnecessary, ill-designed or onerous regulations. Moore et al (2001) address a range of fungal conservation issues.

MONITORING MUSHROOM DIVERSITY

Resource managers commonly wish to monitor edible mushroom productivity within the context of overall mushroom or fungal diversity in an ecosystem. Approaches can range from sampling the occurrence of all detectable fungal species in a given area to focusing on certain types of fruit bodies, e.g. fungi that produce macroscopic hypogeous (below-ground fruiting) or epigeous (above-ground fruiting) sporocarps. Purposes, approaches and resources for biodiversity monitoring can vary greatly, and methods for sampling are equally diverse. Mueller et al (2004) provide a comprehensive guide to methods for sampling fungal diversity. These guidelines can be adapted to include edible mushrooms as a subset. Ingleby et al (2004) is a more user-friendly illustrated guide for collecting, identifying and using an array of edible ectomycorrhizal mushrooms associated with forest trees.

MONITORING EDIBLE MUSHROOM POPULATIONS

Until the last decade, monitoring the population structure of ectomycorrhizal fungi depended on indirectly monitoring their sporocarps, a method fraught with inaccuracies. This situation has changed dramatically with the advent of relatively inexpensive molecular techniques of genetic analysis (Horton and Bruns, 2001; Martin, 2007). Importantly, species-specific probes can be developed to ascertain the abundance of the mycelium of a given species in the soil of a forest stand (Gordon, 2003).

Soil samples collected throughout a forest stand and then bulked and mixed, could provide inexpensive measures of the abundance of the mycelium of a given target species in that stand. Such measures would be useful for tracking seasonal fluctuations in mycelial density, as well as annual trends. Sampling soil mycelial densities would be exceptionally useful for determining how silvicultural activities like thinning or prescribed fire might affect the abundance and mycelial extent of harvested mushroom species. For instance, a fungus might persist in the soil even though fruiting is suppressed for some years. Used in conjunction with monitoring fruit body production, this method could provide a very detailed understanding of how harvested ectomycorrhizal fungi respond to changes in their environments and mushroom harvesting activities across larger spatial scales. To the author's knowledge, no such studies have yet been conducted.

MONITORING EDIBLE MUSHROOM PRODUCTIVITY

There are many publications that discuss general inventory or monitory strategies for various types of wild organisms. For this discussion, inventory is defined as a one-time quantification of a biological population or commercial resource. Monitoring consists of repeated sampling to detect trends over time. Monitoring of trends requires consistent sampling protocols across sampling periods, otherwise the results are difficult to compare statistically. Elzinga et al (2001) provide a comprehensive overview of how to monitor plant and animal populations. Wong et al (2001) discuss inventory and monitoring of non-timber forest products within the socio-economic context of involving local participants. Kerns et al (2002) also examine a variety of approaches and methods for monitoring non-timber forest products.

The following discussion focuses on important considerations for practical, efficient and statistically valid monitoring of the productivity of edible ectomycorrhizal fungi. Mushrooms harvested as commercial products have an unusual set of characteristics that affect the goals, design and sampling protocols of monitoring projects.

Biological or commercial productivity

Is the monitoring intended to measure biological or commercial productivity, or both? Biological productivity is defined as the quantity (fresh weight, dry weight or numbers) of fruit bodies produced in a given spatial area per unit of time (we suggest during an entire annual fruiting season, as described below). Commercial productivity is defined as the amount which is actually harvested for sale within a certain area over a given time.

For instance, commercial productivity could be measured with weigh stations at checkpoints for a given road system through which all harvesters must travel. Or collaborative arrangements could be made with harvesters to record their harvests each season in return for benefits or favours such as exclusive access to the harvest area or exemptions from fees or taxes. In whatever manner that commercial harvest quantities are sampled or measured (100 per cent sampling), the evaluation of trends must account for changes in prices (depending on harvest season) which directly influence incentives to harvest more or less intensively. Monitoring commercial productivity by quality grades is possible, but it can be difficult since buyers have varied quality criteria depending on the intended end product or market.

Large annual fluctuations in productivity

In many habitats there can be very large annual fluctuations in fruiting, not infrequently correlated with weather patterns shortly before and during the fruiting season. In the case of ectomycorrhizal mushrooms, productivity in any given annual fruiting season likely corresponds to the following (simplified) factors:

● the quantity of surplus carbohydrates which the host tree has to share with its fungal symbionts during the growing season;

- the amount of rainfall available to wet the upper soil profile and facilitate mycelial growth and primodia formation;
- weather conditions that allow fruit bodies to grow and mature without drying or freezing.

The potential productivity in a given season (as in the first two factors) might be great, but dry weather during the fruiting season can abort a crop. Indeed, any two of the above factors might be favourable and the third could diminish productivity: they act in combination. The extent of variation in these factors varies by location, forest biome and climate (typical weather patterns). In some locations, rainfall and fruiting seasons are relatively reliable and consistent; in others not. The design of monitoring programmes should take into account the anticipated variation in productivity between fruiting seasons so that adequate sampling is conducted, while excessive effort is avoided. Consultation with statisticians during the design phase of a monitoring project will greatly improve the probability that plot size and number of plots will be adequate to keep variation low enough to detect differences or trends with a reasonable level of confidence while avoiding the unnecessary expenditure of resources to conduct too much sampling.

Detection error

Although some mushrooms (like orange coloured chanterelles) are easy to spot against the forest floor, others (like morels) are well camouflaged and can be difficult to find. Sampling errors which derive from overlooking specimens are called detection errors. If all the sampling occurs in the same habitat, with the same crew, at the same time of day (since illumination and shadows affect the visibility of mushrooms), then detection error might not affect the results. However, if any of these factors differ, results might be affected. In general, it is important to pick a sampling method that minimizes the risk of inaccurate results by standardizing methods and effort as much as possible. It is also helpful to choose sampling designs and methods that improve detection rates. Narrow strip plots, approximately 2m wide, allow two sampling team members to walk along either side searching for specimens from opposite perspectives, improving the likelihood of detecting elusive species.

Trampling

Narrow strip plots, as mentioned above, also allow team members to sample the plot without walking on it, thus diminishing the probability that trampling the plot has crushed potential fruiting bodies which might have grown later in the season.

Clustered fruiting

Edible mushrooms tend to fruit in clustered patterns, within stands and across the landscape. Fruiting clusters, commonly called mushroom patches, indirectly reflect the spatial extent of the mycelial thallus (body) of the fungus in the soil. If the target

Table 7.1   *Sample plot size, number and total sample area adequate for sampling edible mushrooms in forest stands with relatively dense mushroom fruiting patterns*

Mushroom	Plot dimensions (metres)	Plot size (square metres)	Number of plots	Total sample area per stand (square metres)	Citation
Chanterelles	8 x 100	800	5	4000	(Pilz et al, 1998)
American matsutake	2 x 50	100	6	600	(Pilz et al, 1999)
Morels	2 x 100	200	10	2000	(Pilz et al, 2004)
Chanterelles	5 x varied lengths	700 to 2000	5	3500 to 10,000	(Pilz et al, 2006)

mushroom fruits sparsely across the sample area, plots must be quite large to avoid many plots yielding zero values. Thompson and Seber (1996) describe an alternative, but statistically robust, adaptive sampling approach for clustered populations. This approach involves protocols for intensive sub-sampling in the local area when a specimen of a clustered population is encountered. This approach is probably more efficient when sampling widely scattered clusters than very large plots. The sub-sampling protocols are complex and sampling crews must be well-trained to implement the method consistently under varied field conditions; advanced statistical expertise is also required for the analysis and its interpretation.

Long narrow strip plots, systematically transecting a forest stand, have proved practical for obtaining sufficient statistical power in the case of mushroom species that fruit in clustered patterns, but at relatively high densities. Table 7.1 shows the combinations of plot shape, size, number of plots per site or stand, and total sample area which were adequate for the author in four landscape scale studies.

Other researchers have used large circular or square plots for mushroom diversity studies that included edible mushrooms. Trampling impacts were considered acceptable because sampling crews learned where mushroom patches were located and avoided walking there (see Martínez de Aragón et al, 2007).

Random sampling of habitats

When the goal of a monitoring project is to estimate the average productivity of a forest habitat type, or to compare different habitats or silvicultural treatments on a landscape scale, the proper biometrical approach is to determine the location of the plots randomly (or systematically from a random starting point) before knowing whether or where the target mushrooms fruit within the selected forest stand. In the case of mushrooms that occur sporadically in a given habitat, this statistical requirement can pose practical difficulties because some plots or sampled stands may have few or no populations of the targeted mushroom. This results in frustration or wasted time, effort and expense sampling empty plots. For unbiased landscape scale habitat productivity estimates there is no simple solution, because areas with low or no productivity are part of the habitat. Adaptive sampling protocols could be the best approach for this situation. For comparisons of the effects of silvicultural treatments on mushroom productivity, the experiment can be located in areas of known productivity, but plots laid out without knowledge of where specific mushroom patches are located.

Dynamic fruit bodies and mushroom flushes

Mushrooms tend to fruit during a specific season and in a specific location. The season can be as short as a couple of weeks or as long as several months, but corresponds generally with the time of year when both moisture and temperatures are favourable for fruit body development. A typical mushroom will grow, mature and decay in a period ranging from one to six weeks, depending on species and weather patterns. Individual mushrooms may start to grow at different times during a fruiting season. Commonly there will be several flushes of fruiting during seasons that last a month or more. Flushes are the simultaneous growth of many fruit bodies and usually occur in response to rainfall events or temperature patterns.

In order to estimate annual mushroom productivity, it is necessary to sample all the fruiting that occurs during the season. If the season is long enough for mushrooms to develop at different times during the season (either individually or in flushes), then the site must be visited repeatedly during the season to sample all the mushrooms that develop. This need posits several considerations:

- If the monitoring location is distant, it becomes important to be familiar with the mushroom's typical fruiting season and to watch weather patterns, in order to plan when to begin sampling. Arrangements may be made with individuals living near the monitoring site or those who visit regularly to harvest mushrooms; they can inform researchers when mushrooms begin to grow.
- The repeat sampling interval should be shorter than the average lifespan of the targeted mushrooms so that no specimens or flushes are missed.
- If biomass (wet or dry weight) is being sampled, then a minimum size criterion is required so that mushrooms are not measured before they reach their potential size. This criterion can reflect the size at which they are typically harvested or their maximum size, depending on the monitoring goals.
- If the mushrooms are counted or measured on the site (without harvesting), the sampled specimens must be marked to avoid repeat sampling during the next sampling interval. A toothpick placed on the same side (cardinal direction) of each sampled mushroom works fairly well, although animals can displace them; sampled mushrooms can also be marked with ink. This is not necessary if the sampled mushrooms are harvested.

What to measure

If mushrooms are plucked when they are sampled, their fresh and dry weights can be measured directly. If dry weight is measured, it is important to dry the mushrooms very soon after they are harvested (usually the same night) or they may start to decay. Commercially available home food driers work well because they provide a constant flow of warm dry air. For driers with temperature controls, 35 to 45 degrees centigrade is a good range of temperature settings.

Mushroom weight can also be estimated from measuring fruit body dimensions. The easiest dimension to measure in the field is cap diameter because measuring the length of the stem often requires crawling on the ground and often a substantial part of the stem is in the soil and requires excavation to measure. If the mushroom caps are more or less round (e.g. boletes), then one measurement of cap diameter is usually adequate. If the caps are irregular in shape (for instance, chanterelles), an average of the maximum and minimum cap diameters works best. For mushrooms like morels that have heads rather than caps, the height and average width of the head can be used to calculate its volume. In whatever manner the fruit body is measured, 20 or more mushrooms, representing a range of sizes, are harvested outside of the sample plots, measured and then weighed. A regression equation is then developed to estimate mushroom weight from size measurements taken on non-harvested mushrooms within the plot. Such estimates of weight are inherently less precise than actually weighing the mushrooms, but tend to be sufficiently robust when used consistently across all sampling plots or areas (Pilz et al, 1998; 1999; 2004; Luoma et al, 2006).

The easiest aspect of productivity to measure is simply the number of mushrooms. Counting and marking the counted mushrooms is quick, and therefore researchers can sample more plots and larger areas during a day in the field. The four datasets listed in Table 7.1 involved sampling both weights and numbers of fruit bodies. In no instance (unpublished data) did the results of the statistical analyses differ among these types of measures of productivity. Sometimes the mushroom weight productivity of an area is a goal of the project, for instance to provide commercial value estimates. In these instances, fruit bodies could still be merely counted and then the counts multiplied by the average mushroom weight at the size they are typically harvested. If this approach is followed, be sure to include a typical range of mushroom moisture contents in calculating the average weight because fresh weight can vary significantly in the field depending on rainfall and humidity.

COLLABORATIVE MONITORING

Humans are now integral participants in almost all forest ecosystems and the management of forest resources such as mushrooms must take human society and its needs into account (Pilz et al, 1996; Molina et al, 1997). In some instances, the forest resource property rights of indigenous communities are important considerations in monitoring and management activities; there is extensive literature on this topic, e.g. Tedder et al (2002) and Bray et al (2003). However, some mushroom harvesters migrate in the search for harvesting opportunities and these individuals are also important stakeholders in managing sustainable mushroom harvests (McLain and Jones, 1997). There are many other stakeholders involved in management of the edible forest mushroom resource, including mushroom buyers and purveyors, other forest users, land managers and local communities. Since so many stakeholders, such deep cultural traditions and such important economic benefits are involved, the most effective form of management is the collaboration of all interested parties.

However, different stakeholder groups commonly have different or conflicting goals and distrust among these groups is all too common. Collaborative monitoring yields two important benefits. Firstly, it provides basic information about the resource that can be trusted by all involved parties. Secondly, the very involvement with a collaborative monitoring project helps build trust among stakeholder groups. Both benefits can lead to more effective resource management and more equitable arrangements for using the resource.

The international literature on collaborative or participatory monitoring and forest management is extensive; the following works are recommended to provide the reader with a starting point.

- Carter (1996) is a textbook that analyses commonalities among participatory forest resource assessment projects in seven countries.
- Lynch et al (2004) make the case for involving US non-timber forest product harvesters in inventory and monitoring activities.
- Pilz et al (2006b) provide a handbook for scientists and managers on the factors to consider when developing participatory monitoring projects; it includes checklists and an annotated bibliography.

Some of the most innovative programmes for sustainable management of edible mushroom resources integrate all aspects of the resource and its utilization: biological monitoring, forest management, harvest regulation, marketing, economic development, local cuisine and tourism. Plan Conservación y Uso Sostenible de las Setas y Trufas de Andalucía (CUSSTA) in the autonomous community of Andalucía, Spain is a prime example: organizers of the regional plan also hosted the World Fungi conference in Cordoba in 2007; conference participants developed a proposal for Mycoparks modelled after the UNESCO Geopark programme (Arroyo et al, 2007). Their goals include an integrated package of cooperative conservation, education, cultural heritage preservation, sustainable economic development and tourism.

CONCLUSION

For many citizens of the planet, harvesting wild products from the forest is one of the most enjoyable and fulfilling activities imaginable. It recalls memories of humanity's hunter/gatherer heritage, and offers rich rewards: the fun of the hunt; the joy of discovery; affinity with nature; the satisfying art of keen observation; and a sumptuous meal at the end of the day. The sustainable harvesting of any wild organism ultimately requires respect. The respectful harvesting of mushrooms is enshrined in ten simple principles:

- Obtain permission to collect from the landowner.
- Be certain of your identification.
- Collect only what you will use.
- Leave small mushrooms to grow larger and old mushrooms to spread their spores.
- Pluck mushrooms carefully or cut them off; don't disturb the mycelium.

- Collect mushrooms in well-ventilated containers so they don't decay.
- Remove dirt as you collect the mushrooms so they do not spoil in the container.
- Clean and dry or refrigerate mushrooms promptly upon return to avoid spoilage and waste.
- Be courteous to wildlife and other forest visitors, and leave only footprints, not damage or rubbish.
- Value and appreciate the fungus and the mushrooms it produces, and educate others to do so.

REFERENCES

Allen, M. F. (1992) *Mycorrhizal Functioning: an integrative plant-fungal process*, Chapman and Hall, New York

Arnolds, E. (1991) 'Decline of ectomycorrhizal fungi in Europe', *Agricultural Ecosystems & Environment*, vol 35, pp209–244

Arora, D. (1999) 'The way of the wild mushroom', *California Wild*, vol 52, no 4, pp8–19, www.researcharchive.calacademy.org/calwild/1999fall/stories/mushroom.html, accessed 8 February 2009

Arroyo, B. M., Perini, C., Cazares, E., de Diego Calonge, F., Claridge, A., de Miguel, A. M. and Dávalos, L.G. (2007) 'Fungi of the earth: Declaration of Cordoba', La Consejería de Medio Ambiente, La Junta de Andalucía, www.ima-mycology.org/doc/Declaration%20CordobaIng.pdf, accessed 1 March 2009

Boa, E. (2004) *Wild edible fungi: A global overview of their use and importance to people*, Non-Wood Forest Products 17, FAO, Rome

Boa, E. (2006) *Wild useful fungi*, CABI, Egham, UK, www.wildusefulfungi.org/index.asp, accessed 8 February 2009

Bonet, J. A., Pukkala, T., Fischer, C. R., Palahí, M., de Aragón, J. M. and Colinas, C. (2008) 'Empirical models for predicting the production of wild mushrooms in Scots pine (*Pinus slyvestris* L.) forests in the Central Pyrenees', *Annuals of Forest Science*, vol 65, no 2, art 206, www.afs-journal.org/, accessed 21 Feb 2009

Bray, D. B., Merino-Pérez, L., Negreros-Castillo, P., Segura-Warnholtz, G., Torres-Rojo, J. M. and Vester, H. F. M. (2003) 'Mexico's community-managed forests as a global model for sustainable landscapes', *Conservation Biology*, vol 17, no 3, pp672–677

Cairney, J. W. G. and Chambers, S. M. (eds) (1999) *Ectomycorrhizal fungi: key genera in profile*, Springer-Verlag, New York

Carlile, M. J., Watkinson, S. C. and Gooday, G. W. (2001) *The fungi* (2nd edition), Elsevier Academic Press, London

Carter, J. (ed) (1996) *Recent approaches to participatory forest resource assessment*, Rural Development Forestry Study Guide 2, Overseas Development Institute, London

Danell, E. and Camacho, F. J. (1997) 'Successful cultivation of the golden chanterelle', *Nature*, vol 385, p303

Egli, S., Peter, M., Buser, C., Stahel, W., and Ayer, F. (2006) 'Mushroom picking does not impair future harvests – results of a long-term study in Switzerland', *Biological Conservation*, vol 129, pp271–276

Elzinga, C. L., Salzer, D. W., Willoughby, J. W. and Gibbs, J. P. (2001) *Monitoring plant and animal populations*, Blackwell Science, Malden, MA

Gordon, M. J. (2003) 'A species-specific molecular probe for *Tricholoma magnivelare*, the American matsutake', MS thesis, Department of Biology, Portland State Unversity, OR

Guerin-Laguette, A., Matsushita, N., Lapeyrie, F., Shindo, K. and Suzuk, K. (2005) 'Successful inoculation of mature pine with *Tricholoma matsutake*', *Mycorrhiza*, vol 15, pp301–305

Hall, I. R., Stephenson, S. L. Buchanan, P. K., Wang, Y. and Cole, A. L. J. (2003) *Edible and poisonous mushrooms of the world*, Timber Press, Portland, OR

Hall, I. R., Brown, G. T., and Zmambonelli, A. (2007) *Taming the truffle: The history, lore, and science of the ultimate mushroom*, Timber Press, Portland, OR

Halpern, G. M. and Miller, A. H. (2002) *Medicinal Mushrooms: Ancient remedies for modern ailments*, M. Evans, New York

Hobbs, C. (1986) *Medicinal Mushrooms: An exploration of tradition, healing, and culture*, Botanica Press, Summertown, TN

Horton, T. R. and Bruns, T. D. (2001) 'The molecular revolution in ectomycorrhizal ecology: Peeking into the black-box', *Molecular Ecology*, vol 10, no 8, pp1855–1871

Hosford, D., Pilz, D., Molina, R., and Amaranthus, M. (1997) 'Ecology and management of the commercially harvested American matsutake', General Technical Report PNW-GTR-412, USDA Forest Service, Pacific Northwest Research Station, Portland, OR, www.treesearch.fs.fed.us/pubs/7599, accessed 1 March 2009

Ingleby, K., Thanh, V. X. and Mason, P. A. (2004) *Manual for the collection, identification and use of edible mycorrhizal mushrooms associated with forest trees*, Centre for Ecology and Hydrology, Midlothian, UK, www.edinburgh.ceh.ac.uk/tropical/mushroommanual.htm, accessed 28 February 2009

Kerns, B. K., Liegel, L., Pilz, D. and Alexander, S. J. (2002) 'Biological inventory and monitoring', in Jones, E., Mclain, R. and Weigand, J. (eds) *Nontimber forest products in the United States*, University Press of Kansas, Lawrence, pp237–269

Kranabetter, J. M., Friesen, J., Gamiet, S., and Kroeger, P. (2005) 'Ectomycorrhizal mushroom distribution by stand age in western hemlock – lodgepole pine forests of northwestern British Columbia', *Canadian Journal of Forest Research*, vol 35, pp1527–1539

Love, T., Jones, E., and Liegel, L. (1998) 'Valuing the temperate rainforest: Wild mushrooming on the Olympic Peninsula Biosphere Reserve', *Ambio*, Special Report, no 9, pp16–25

Luoma, D. L., Eberhart, J. L., Abbott, R., Moore, A., Amaranthus, M. P., and Pilz, D. (2006) 'Effects of mushroom harvest technique on subsequent American matsutake production', *Forest Ecology and Management*, vol 236, pp65–75

Lynch, K. A., Jones, E. T. and McLain, R. J. (2004) *Nontimber forest product inventorying and monitoring in the United States: Rationale and recommendations for a participatory approach*, National Commission on Science for Sustainable Forestry, Washington, DC, www.ifcae.org/projects/ncssf1/, accessed 28 February 2009

Maddison, D. R. and Schulz, K.-S. (eds) (2007) *The Tree of Life Web Project*, www.tolweb.org/tree, accessed 31 July 2010

Mainone, R. F. (1982) *Parnassus flowers: haiku poems* (3rd edition), Wonderland Press, New York

Marcot, B. C. (2002) 'An ecological functional basis for managing dead wood decay elements for wildlife', in W. F. Laudenslayer, Jr., P. J. Shea, B. E. Valentine, C. P. Weatherspoon and T. E. Lisle (eds) *Proceedings of the symposium on the ecology and management of dead wood in western forests*, General Technical Report PSW-GTR-181, USDA Forest Service, Pacific Southwest Station, Berkeley CA, www.treesearch.fs.fed.us/pubs/6718, accessed 22 February 2009, pp895–910

Marks, G. C. and Kozlowski, T. T. (1973) *Ectomycorrhizae*, Academic Press, New York

Martin, K. J. (2007) 'Introduction to molecular analysis of ectomycorrhizal communities', *Soil Science Society of America Journal*, vol 71, pp601–610, www.soil.scijournals.org/cgi/reprint/71/2/601, accessed 22 February 2009,

Martínez de Aragón, J., Bonet, J. A., Fischer, C. R. and Colinas, C. (2007) 'Productivity of ectomycorrhizal and selected edible saprotrophic fungi in pine forests of the pre-Pyrenees mountains, Spain: Predictive equations for forest management of mycological resources', *Forest Ecology and Management*, vol 252, pp239–256

McLain, R. J. and Jones, E. T. (1997) *Challenging 'community' definitions in sustainable natural resource management: The case of wild mushroom harvesting in the USA*. Gatekeeper Series No. 68, IIED Sustainable Agriculture Programme, www.iied.org/pubs/display.php?o=6130IIED&n=1 &l=1&t=Challenging%20'Community', accessed 28 February 2009

Molina, R., Vance, N., Weigand, J. F., Pilz, D. and Amaranthus, M. P. (1997) 'Special forest products: Integrating social, economic, and biological considerations into ecosystem management', in K. A. Kohm and J. F. Franklin (eds) *Creating a forestry for the 21st century: The science of ecosystem management*, Island Press, Washington DC, pp315–336, www.treesearch.fs.fed.us/pubs/6031, accessed 22 February 2009

Moore, D., Nauta, M. M., Evans, S. E. and Rotheroe, M. (2001) *Fungal conservation: Issues and solutions*, Cambridge University Press, Cambridge

Mueller, G. M., Bills, G. F. and Foster, M. S. (2004) *Biodiversity of fungi: Inventory and monitoring methods*, Elsevier, New York

Norvell, L. L. (1995) 'Loving the chanterelle to death? The ten-year Oregon chanterelle project', *McIlvainea*, vol 12, pp6–25

Pilz, D. (2004) *Chaga and Other Fungal Resources: Assessment of sustainable commercial harvesting in Khabarovsk and Primorsky Krais, Russia*, Report prepared for Winrock International, Morrilton, Arkansas and the FOREST Project, Khabarovsk,

Russia. PilzWald—Forestry Applications of Mycology, Susanville CA, www.fsl.orst.edu/mycology/PilzPage_files/Pilz2004ChagaReport.pdf, accessed 24 August 2010

Pilz, D. and Molina, R. (1998) 'A proposal for regional monitoring of edible forest mushrooms', *Mushroom, The Journal of Wild Mushrooming*, Summer Issue 60, vol 16, no 3, pp19–23

Pilz, D. and Molina, R. (2002) 'Commercial harvests of edible mushrooms from the forests of the Pacific Northwest United States: Issues, management, and monitoring for sustainability', *Forest Ecology and Management*, vol 155, nos 1–3, pp3–16

Pilz, D., Molina, R., Amaranthus, M. Castellano, M. and Weber, N. S. (1996) 'Forest fungi and ecosystem management', in D. Pilz and R. Molina (eds) *Managing forest ecosystems to conserve fungus diversity and sustain wild mushroom harvests*, General Technical Report PNW-GTR-371, USDA Forest Service, Pacific Northwest Research Station, Portland OR, pp86–103, www.treesearch.fs.fed.us/pubs/5634, accessed 28 February 2009

Pilz, D., Molina, R. and Liegel, L. H. (1998) 'Biological productivity of chanterelle mushrooms in and near the Olympic Peninsula Biosphere Reserve', in L. H. Liegel (compiler) *The biological, socioeconomic, and managerial aspects of chanterelle mushroom harvesting: The Olympic Peninsula, Washington State, USA*, Ambio, Special Report No 9, Royal Swedish Academy of Sciences, Stockholm, pp8–13

Pilz, D., Smith, J., Amaranthus, M. P., Alexander, S., Molina, R. and Luoma, D. (1999) 'Mushrooms and timber: Managing commercial harvesting in the Oregon Cascades', *Journal of Forestry*, vol 97, no 3, pp4–11

Pilz, D., Molina, R., Danell, E., Waring, R. H., Rose, C., Alexander, S., Luoma, D., Cromack, K. and Lefevre, C. (2002) 'SilviShrooms: Predicting edible ectomycorrhizal mushroom productivity', in A. C. Johnson, R. W. Haynes, R. A. Monserud (eds) *Congruent management of multiple resources: Proceedings from the Wood Compatibility Initiative workshop*, General Technical Report PNW-GTR-563, USDA, Forest Service, Pacific Northwest Research Station, Portland OR, pp199–207, www.treesearch.fs.fed.us/pubs/4936, accessed 22 February 2009

Pilz, D., Norvell, L., Danell, E. and Molina, R. (2003) *Ecology and management of commercially harvested chanterelle mushrooms*, General Technical Report PNW-GTR-576, USDA Forest Service, Pacific Northwest Research Station, Portland OR, www.treesearch.fs.fed.us/pubs/5298, accessed 22 Feb 2009

Pilz, D., Weber, N. S., Carter, C., Parks, C. G. and Molina, R. (2004) 'Productivity and diversity of morel mushrooms in healthy, burned, and insect-damaged forests of northeastern Oregon', *Forest Ecology and Management*, vol 198, pp367–386, www.treesearch.fs.fed.us/pubs/7345, accessed 28 Feb 2009

Pilz, D., Molina, R., and Mayo, J. (2006a) 'Effects of thinning young forests on chanterelle mushroom production', *Journal of Forestry*, vol 104, no 1, pp9–14, www.treesearch.fs.fed.us/pubs/24570, accessed 28 Feb 2009

Pilz, D., Ballard, H. L. and Jones, E. T. (2006b) *Broadening participation in biological monitoring: a handbook for scientists and managers*, General Technical Report PNW-GTR-680, USDA Forest Service, Pacific Northwest Research Station, Portland OR, www.treesearch.fs.fed.us/pubs/24897, accessed 28 February 2009

Przybylowicz, P. and Donoghue, J. (2008) *Shiitake Growers Handbook: The art and science of mushroom cultivation*, Kendall/Hunt Publishing Company, Dubuque IA

Smith J. E., Molina, R., Huso, M. M. P., Luoma, D., McKay, D., Castellano, M. A., Lebel, T. and Valachovic, Y. (2002) 'Species richness, abundance, and composition of hypogeous and epigeous ectomycorrhizal fungal sporocarps in young, rotation-age, and old-growth stands of Douglas-fir (*Pseudotsuga menziesii*) in the Cascade Range of Oregon, U.S.A.', *Canadian Journal of Botany*, vol 80, pp186–204

Smith, S. E. and Read, D. J. (1997) *Mycorrhizal symbiosis* (2nd edition), Academic Press, London

Stamets, P. (2000) *Growing gourmet and medicinal mushrooms* (3rd edition), Ten Speed Press, Berkeley CA

Stamets, P. (2002) 'Novel antimicrobials from mushrooms', *Herbalgram*, vol 54, pp28–33, www.fungi.com/pdf/pdfs/articles/HerbalGram.pdf, accessed 8 February 2009

Stamets, P. (2005) *Mycelium running: How mushrooms can help save the world*, Ten Speed Press, Berkeley CA

Stamets, P. and Yao, D. W. (2002) *Mycomedicinals: An informational treatise on mushrooms*, MycoMedia Productions, Olympia WA

Tedder, S., Mitchell, D. and Hillyer, A. (2002) *Property rights in the sustainable management of non-timber forest products*, Forest Renewal BC, British Columbia Ministry of Forests, Victoria, www.for.gov.bc.ca/hre/ntfp/#Older_Publications, accessed 28 February 2009

Thompson, S. K. and Serber, G. A. F. (1996) *Adaptive sampling*, Wiley, New York

Trappe, M. (2004) 'Habitat and host associations of *Craterellus tubaeformis* in northwestern Oregon', *Mycologia*, vol 96, no 3, pp498–509

Trappe, J. M., Claridge, A. W., Claridge, D. L. and Liddle, L. (2008a) 'Desert truffles of the Australian outback: Ecology, ethnomycology, and taxonomy', *Economic Botany*, vol 62, no 3, pp497–506

Trappe, J. M., Claridge, A. W., Arora, D. and Smit, W. A. (2008b) 'Desert truffles of the African Kalahari: Ecology, ethnomycology, and taxonomy', *Economic Botany*, vol 62, no 3, pp521–529

Wang, Y. and Hall, I. (2004) 'Edible ectomycorrhizal mushrooms: Challenges and achievements', *Canadian Journal of Botany*, vol 82, pp1063–1073

Wienszyk, A. M., Gamiet, S., Durall, D. M., Jones, M. D. and Simard, S. W. (2002) 'Ectomycorrhizae and forestry in British Columbia: A summary of current research and conservation strategies', *B.C. Journal of Ecosystems and Management*, vol 2, no 1, www.forrex.org/JEM/Article.asp?Article=41, accessed 28 Feb 2009

Winkler, D. (2008) 'Yartsa gunbu (*Cordyceps sinensis*) and the fungal commodification of Tibet's rural economy', *Economic Botany*, vol 62, no 3, pp291–305

Wong, J. L. G., Thornber, K. and Baker, N. (2001) *Resource assessment of non-wood forest products*, Non-Wood Forest Products Series, Issue 13, FAO, Rome, www.fao.org/docrep/004/y1457e/y1457e00.HTM, accessed 8 February 2009

Yamin-Pasternak, S. (2008) 'From disgust to desire: Changing attitudes toward Beringian mushrooms', *Economic Botany*, vol 62, no 3, pp214–222

Yang, X., Skidmoreb, A. K., Melicka, D. R., Zhoua Z., and Xu, J. (2006) 'Mapping non-wood forest product (matsutake mushrooms) using logistic regression and a GIS expert systems', *Ecological Modelling*, vol 198, nos 1–2, pp208–218

CHAPTER 8

Mushrooms, Health and Nutrition

Zhu L. Yang

INTRODUCTION

A large number of wild or cultivated fungi are appreciated by people in many cultures for food. Wild collected mushrooms are particularly appreciated for their pleasant aroma, flavour and texture. Although a few wild species, like *Tricholoma matsutake* and *Thelephora ganbajun*, have an unusual taste, different cultures have developed delicious recipes using mushrooms found in their locality (Ying and Zang, 1994; Sanmee et al, 2003; Wang et al, 2004).

The nutritional value of mushrooms has already been mentioned (see Chapter 1). In general, mushroom fruiting bodies, on a dry weight basis, contain about 39.9 per cent carbohydrate, 17.5 per cent protein and 2.9 per cent fats, the rest being the minerals (Latiff et al, 1996). Chang and Bushwell (1996) showed that cultivated mushrooms normally contain 19 to 35 per cent protein. Sanmee et al (2003) reported that *Phlebopus portentosus*, a wide edible mushroom in palaeotropical regions, had a protein content as high as 24.2 per cent. Moreover, mushroom proteins contain all the essential amino acids, and are especially rich in lysine and leucine which are lacking in most staple cereal foods. The low total fat content and the high proportion of polyunsaturated fatty acids (72 to 85 per cent) relative to total fatty acids is considered a significant contributor to the health value of mushrooms (Buswell and Chang, 1993; Chang and Buswell, 1996). Fresh mushrooms contain relatively large amounts of carbohydrate and fibre, ranging from 51 to 88 per cent and 4 to 20 per cent respectively for the major cultivated species. Mushrooms also appear to be a good source of vitamins, including B vitamins, vitamin D, vitamin K, and sometimes vitamins A and C (Arora, 1986; Racz et al, 1996; Manzi et al, 1999; Mattila et al, 2001; Demirbaş, 2001; Agrahar-Murugkar and Subbulakshmi, 2005; Gençcelep et al, 2009).

Being low in calories and high in proteins, fibre, vitamins and minerals, edible mushrooms are healthy foods. Thus the consumption of cultivated and wild edible mushrooms, a popular delicacy in many countries, has been increasing rapidly. Consequently, the world mushroom industry has a bright future (Chang, 2006b; Chang and Buswell, 2008).

The medicinal properties of mushrooms have long been recognized by people in many countries such as China, Japan and Mexico (Liu, 1984; Ying et al, 1987; Chang, 2006a; Guzman, 2008; Dai and Yang, 2008; Holliday and Cleaver, 2008). Mushrooms

Figure 8.1   Lactarius tenuicystidiatus *mushrooms for sale at a market in southwest China*

Photograph: Prof. Xinghua Wang

Figure 8.2   *The medicinal fungus* Shiraia bambusicola *has a long history of use in traditional medicine in China*

Photograph: Prof. Xinghua Wang

in traditional Chinese medicine have been used for more than 3000 years for the prevention and treatment of diseases (Chang, 2006a; Figure 8.2). The entomophagus medicinal fungus *Cordyceps sinensis* is a good example of a new interest based on this long tradition (Zhu et al, 1998; Box 8.1). The efficacy of mushrooms in medicine is due to their chemical composition (Liu, 2004).

The potential of mushrooms as a source of biological active compounds of medicinal value including anti-cancer, anti-viral, immunopotentiating, hypocholesterolaemic and hepatoprotective agents has caused a recent surge of interest. As a result, mushroom nutriceuticals, extracted from either the fungal mycelium or fruiting body, are becoming an important component of the expanding mushroom biotechnology industry (Chang and Buswell, 1996). However, scientific validation of culinary–medicinal mushroom products are badly needed (Chang, 2006a).

It should be noted that many cultivated and wild mushrooms have the capacity to bio-accumulate metal ions including toxic heavy metals, metalloids or noble metals (Byrne et al, 1979; Byrne and Tušek-Žnidarič, 1990; Aruguete et al, 1998; Cihangir and Saglam, 1999; Kalač and Svoboda, 2000; Demirbaş, 2001; Borovička and Řanda, 2007). Some species of *Agaricus, Macrolepiota, Lepista* and *Calocybe* accumulate high levels of cadmium and mercury even in unpolluted and mildly polluted areas. The concentrations of cadmium, lead and mercury increase considerably in heavily polluted sites, such as in the vicinity of metal smelters (Kalač and Svoboda, 2000). In addition, a few macro-fungi such as *Amanita strobiliformis* and *A. solitaria* have recently been found to hyper-accumulate silver (Ag). The Ag content in the soils is 0.07–1.01 mg kg^{-1}, while the Ag contents of both *Amanita* species were mostly in the range of 200–700 mg kg^{-1} d.w. Silver concentrations in macro-fungal fruit bodies were commonly 800–2500 times higher than in underlying soils (Borovička et al, 2007). Moreover, saprobic macro-fungi usually have a higher Ag content (median 3.61 mg kg^{-1} Ag d.w.) than ectomycorrhizal fungi (median 0.65 mg kg^{-1} Ag d.w.) (Borovička et al, 2007). Kalač and Svoboda (2000) suggested that metal levels in fruiting bodies of wild growing mushrooms are considerably affected by the age of mycelium and by the interval between the fructifications. The highest metal levels have been detected after the first harvest. Consumption of these metal-accumulating species should be restricted. However, because the ability of many edible mushroom species to bio-accumulate metal ions is still unknown, eating excessive amounts of wild collected mushrooms should be avoided.

BOX 8.1 ENTOMOPHAGOUS MEDICINAL FUNGI

Anthony B. Cunningham

Most fungi are traded commercially as food, rather than medicine. In his review of wild edible and medicinal fungi use in 110 countries, Eric Boa (2004) found that only 6 per cent (133 species) were used solely for medicinal purposes, with an additional 10 per cent being used medicinally or with edible/food uses. In China, the most commonly traded medicinal fungi are *Cordyceps* (*C. sinensis, C. militaris, C. sobolifera*) (Clavicipitaceae), *Ganoderma* (*G. lucidum, G. sinense*) (Polyporaceae) and *Shiraia bambusicola* (Hypocreaceae) (Figure 8.2).

The best known of all medicinal fungi come from the genus *Cordyceps*, which contains over 300 species of entomophagous fungi. *Cordyceps* are known to a range of indigenous and local people across the world for a variety of uses. In Aotearoa/New Zealand they were traditionally used as one of the ingredients in making pigments for tamoko (Maori tattoos). In Papua New Guinea, *Cordyceps* is used as an antibiotic to treat skin infections and tropical ulcers. In China, two *Cordyceps* species are traded commercially (Figure 8.3).

Cordyceps sinensis in particular has been well known and highly valued in Tibetan and Chinese medicine for centuries (Winkler, 2008). One of the earliest western accounts of *Cordyceps* trade was by Du Halde (1736) at a time when *C. sinensis* were worth four times their weight in silver (Pegler, Yao and Li, 1994). In medieval Europe naturalists considered *Cordyceps* to be an example of transmutation from an animal to a plant (Willis, 1941). It was only in the 19th century, however, that western naturalists started to gain an understanding of the link between *Cordyceps* and insects.

Today, *C. sinensis* has been well documented precisely because of its medicinal value, with over 150 scientific papers published in the past 15 years covering its biology (Steinkraus, 1994; Zang, 1990), genetic variation in the wild populations (Chen et al, 1999), efficacy (Chiou, 2000), the quality of commercially sold *C. sinensis* (Wu et al, 1996), the artificial culture of the mycelia (Kiho, 1999) and reviews by Zhu, Halpern and Jones (1998a; 1998b). Recent molecular techniques give a clear understanding of the phylogeny of *Cordyceps* (Sung et al, 2007). Most *Cordyceps* are endoparasitic on insects (beetles, cicadas, moths (mainly Hepialidae), spittlebugs and scale insects). Remarkably, Nikoh and Fukatsu (2000) have shown that inter-kingdom host jumping has occurred, with a shift from insect host to Hart's truffles in 6.7 per cent (i.e. 20) of the 300 described *Cordyceps* species.

C. sinensis is commonly considered to be declining due to overexploitation (Negi et al, 2006) combined with habitat loss (Liang et al, 2008). Winkler (2008) suggests that *C. sinensis* is only moderately vulnerable to overharvest – a conclusion I agree with, apart from one concern: climate change. Not only is resource management made more complex by the life cycle of this entomophagous fungus and its high price (US$12,000 per kg), but also by the effects of a warmer world on the high altitude habitat (3000–5000m asl) of *C. sinensis*. Climate change is widely recognized across the Himalayas, exemplified by the Minyong glacier retreating over 200m in just four years (Miura, 2007). Dr Yang Da-Rong has observed that prime *C. sinensis* habitat has shifted 500m higher than 20 years previously, equating this to a 70 to 97 per cent decline in *C. sinensis* biomass (Stone, 2008). Neither Stone (2008) nor other researchers working on *Cordyceps* harvesting have mentioned climate change, however. Interestingly, Hong et al (1997), working on *Metarhizium flavoviride*, an entomophangous fungus in the same family (Clavicipitaceae) as *Cordyceps*, showed that spore viability and spore survival rates declined rapidly under moister, warmer conditions. Add to this dependence on the population dynamics of Hepialid moths and their food-plants, and a complex set of circumstances, which must be managed on multiple levels, becomes apparent.

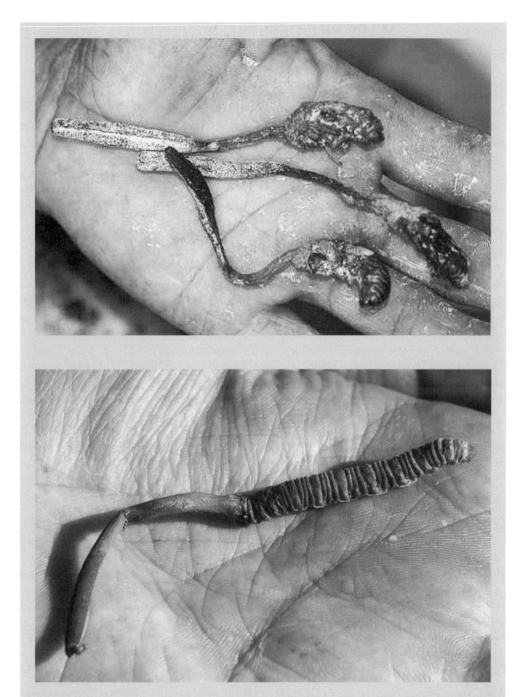

Figure 8.3 *A.* Cordyceps sobolifera, *which occurs on cicada nymphs; B.* Cordyceps sinensis, *which is found on Hepialid moth caterpillars*

Photographs: Anthony B. Cunningham

MAIN PROCESSING METHODS
OF EDIBLE MUSHROOMS

Mushrooms are highly perishable, mainly due to the high water content (approximately 90 per cent), the high level of enzyme activity and the presence of micro-flora (Jaworska and Bernaś, 2009). After harvesting, many wild or cultivated mushrooms are used within a short period. They are cleaned and washed with water, and then cooked, fried or toasted in traditional ways.

To keep mushrooms fresh after collection for long-term use is often difficult. People have tried to use different methods. Due to their metabolism and the external environment, the freshness of mushrooms is affected by temperatures, and processing and packing methods. Many patents for the processing of edible mushrooms have been developed. Generally, fresh mushrooms are processed by drying, freeze-drying, freezing or canning for preservation.

Each processing method has its own advantages and disadvantages. Although drying is the most common method for preserving mushrooms, freezing has become increasingly popular. The main advantage of freezing is that it allows the best retention of nutritional values as well as sensory qualities, such as colour, aroma, taste and texture. Moreover, advances in freezing technology indicate a growing trend towards the production of convenience foods which are 'ready to cook' or 'ready to eat' (Jaworska and Bernaś, 2009). Canned mushrooms lose some of their antioxidant qualities as a consequence of industrial processing (Murcia et al, 2002). Kalač and Křížek (1997) observed "no unambiguous effect" of storage temperature on the amine levels (histamine and tyramine) of wild growing and cultivated mushrooms stored at 6°C or 20°C as intact fruiting bodies, wet slices and stewed slices for at least two days. Chi et al (1996) found that sealing in polyethylene bags with holes and storage at low temperature can prolong the life of *Pleurotus ostreatus* and *Flammulina velutipes*, and prevent deterioration of quality during storage. Coated mushrooms were found to have a better appearance, a better colour and an advantage in weight in comparison with uncoated mushrooms (Hershko and Nussinovitch, 1998).

For some mushrooms, special processes are necessary to avoid being poisoned. For example, *Bulgaria inquinans* (Pers.) Fr., which is saprobic mainly on decaying oak sticks and logs, and widely distributed in temperate areas of the northern hemisphere. This fungus is often regarded as inedible in the west (Jordan, 1995; Arora, 1986) but is a delicacy in Northeastern China (Li and Bau, 2003) although it is poisonous (Mao, 1987). Due to phytochromes in the fruit body, this mushroom can cause serious food-sensitized solar dermatitis (Li and Bau, 2003; Bao, 2006). Harvested in summer, the mushroom must be treated with washing lye, plant ash or salt water for 12 to 24 hours, and then washed with fresh water before cooking (Bao, 2006).

How to identify toxic mushrooms

Mushroom poisoning is caused by toxins present in the fruiting bodies. The toxins in some mushrooms will not be destroyed even by cooking. There are 14 major syndromes of mushroom poisoning (Diaz, 2005); several are quite common e.g. phalloides

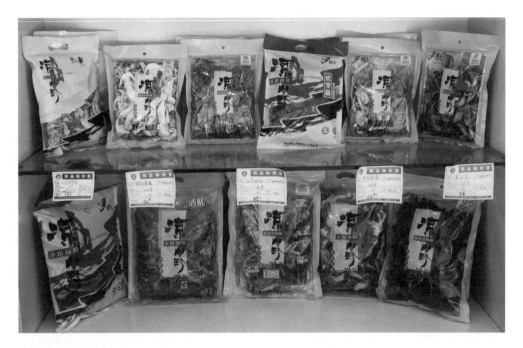

Figure 8.4 *Dried mushrooms packed for commercial sale from a high quality retail store in Sichuan, China*

Photograph: A. B. Cunningham

syndrome, orellanus syndrome, gyromitra syndrome, muscarin syndrome, pantherina syndrome, psilocybin syndrome, gastrointestinal syndrome, paxillus syndrome and coprine syndrome (Deshmukh et al, 2006; Mao, 2006; Saviuc and Danel, 2006). In East Asia, *Russula subnigricans* can cause serious rhabdomyolysis (the breakdown of skeletal muscle tissue) (Takahashi et al, 1993; Diaz, 2005).

Mushrooms are varied in morphology, colour, smell and habitat (Hall et al, 2003) and, because of the several hundred different species encountered in the field, it is difficult even for professional mycologists to separate toxic mushrooms from edible ones based on their macro-morphological characters alone (see Chapter 2). Many poisonous or lethal mushrooms grow in the same habitat as edible ones; it is unreliable and even risky to separate edible ones from poisonous ones according to places where they prefer to grow. When collecting mushrooms which are unfamiliar, it is strongly recommended to find a professional taxonomist of fungi to help with identification. When such help is unavailable, a good field-guide to mushrooms is an option. These guides require knowledge of basic terminology and the keys to the species. In some cases, a microscope may also be helpful for a correct identification of mushrooms (see Chapter 2). Local people may also have insights into the characteristics of closely related fungi, and may know which of similar mushroom species are edible and which are toxic (Box 8.2).

It is easier to identify toxic mushrooms when there is a good knowledge about edible mushrooms and their similar poisonous doubles. For example, the edible *Kuehneromyces mutabilis* can be confused with poisonous *Galerina autumnalis* and the edible *Pleurotus*

BOX 8.2 LOCAL KNOWLEDGE OF MUSHROOMS CAN BE VITAL TO ONE'S HEALTH!

Cathy Sharp

One of the downsides of urban migration on all continents is loss of traditional knowledge. Together with loss of knowledge comes the common assumption that what is familiar 'at home' also applies in the new places to which people have moved. This can be particularly dangerous in the case of confusing edible mushrooms as mentioned in Chapters 2, 6 and 8. Local people's knowledge can be useful in order to become familiar with local edible or toxic mushrooms. Of course, each individual has the choice to accept the advice of local people or not. In Zimbabwe there was a case where an elderly Shona woman advised an equally old white man not to eat the *Amanita* with which his arms were laden. He had been out collecting mushrooms in the miombo woodland and told her that he ate this kind of mushroom every season and chose not to heed her warnings. Five days later he was dead. In Zimbabwe, a preliminary checklist of vernacular names has been compiled (Piearce and Sharp, 2000) and new names are continually being added. With due caution, such a

Figure 8.5   Lactarius kabansus *is commonly known as 'nzeve ambuya' or 'old mother's ear' and often sold along the roadsides in miombo woodland regions*

Photograph: D. H. C. Plowes

list may offer a short-cut to identifying common species. Often, one name will apply to a particular group of mushrooms but the information within that name will sometimes give an indication of its edibility. For example, a mushroom with the name '*Kuneguva*' that translates as 'where there is a grave', is obviously toxic and should therefore avoided. The name '*Howa mapengu*' means 'the mushroom that makes you go mad' and applies to both *Amanita muscaria* and *A. pantherina*. Interestingly, the Vikings are reported to have nibbled *A. muscaria* before going into battle and poisoning cases of *A. pantherina* have indicated periods of raving lunacy as the toxin goes through the body (Gelfand and Harris, 1982). Although there are no known toxic *Lactarius* species in Zimbabwe, '*chivandukira*' is the name given to the two varieties of *L. baliophaeus* which have blood-like latex that rapidly blackens; they certainly look unappealing and are not eaten by the local people (Verbeken et al, 2000). Other mushroom names are purely descriptive and confirmation of their edibility is advised before indulging in 'liver of the dog', 'tongue of the cow', 'cock's comb', 'baboon's snuff' or 'old mother's ear' (Figure 8.5)!

ostreatus resembles *Lampteromyces japonicus*. The edible *Amanita hemibapha* subsp. *javanica* is widely distributed in southeast Asia and east Asia and sold on the markets, but it should be avoided because it can easily be confused with the lethal *A. subjunquillea*. Poisonous cases have been reported almost every year in the last ten years in Yunnan, southwestern China due to eating lethal *A. subjunquillea*. Both species have yellow to yellowish fruiting bodies with an annulus and a membranous volva around the base of the stipe. They can be distinguished by radial striations along the pileal margin, a cylindrical stipe base, common clamps and non-amyloid spores formed by *A. hemibapha* subsp. *javanica*, while *A. subjunquillea* possesses no striations (or faint striations when old) along the pileal margin, a bulbous stipe base, no clamps and amyloid spores.

How to eat wild mushrooms safely

To avoid eating poisonous mushrooms, one principle should be maintained: never eat a mushroom that you don't know, or rather, only eat mushrooms that have been proved edible. There are some 'rules' for recognizing poisonous mushrooms in folklore, e.g. 'mushrooms with bright colours or a pileus with warts are poisonous'; 'mushrooms which aren't bitten by worms or maggots are poisonous'; 'mushrooms, when bruised with colour changes, are poisonous'; 'if during cooking mushrooms, the silverware, garlic or rice in the cooker have turned, they are poisonous'. Unfortunately, each rule is only true for a very limited numbers of species of mushrooms. It is true that pigments within fruit bodies of the poisonous *Cordierites frondosa* can turn the rice colour, but the lethal dull-coloured *A. fuliginea* never discolours the silverware, garlic or rice! There are no simple rules to separate toxic mushrooms from edible ones.

When you have moved to a new place, do not eat the mushrooms that look like edible ones from your earlier surroundings, as they may be poisonous. In mid-March 2000 a disaster occurred in Guangzhou, southern China: nine people cooked and ate a mushroom and only one of them survived. They came from Hunan Province, and had worked and lived in Guangzhou for only a few months. They had found a white mushroom with many fruit bodies in a forest in Guangzhou, and supposed the mushroom was the same edible one occurring in Hunan. Uncooked remnants of the lethal mushroom and additional material subsequently gathered from the original collecting site were studied taxonomically. It turned out to be *A. exitialis* (Yang et al, 2001), a species containing many kinds of toxic peptides and a very high amount of toxins (Chen et al, 2003).

Perhaps the best approach is to remember the old adage: 'There are old mushroom eaters and bold mushroom eaters – but no old, bold mushroom eaters.'

REFERENCES

Agrahar-Murugkar, D. and Subbulakshmi, G. (2005) 'Nutritional value of edible wild mushrooms collected from the Khasi hills of Meghalaya', *Food Chemistry* 89, pp599–603

Arora, D. (1986) *Mushrooms Demystified* (2nd edition), Ten Speed Press, Berkeley CA

Aruguete, D. M., Aldstadt, J. H. and Mueller, G. M. (1998) 'Accumulation of several heavy metals and lanthanides in mushrooms (Agaricales) from the Chicago region', *Science of The Total Environment*, vol 224, pp43–56

Bao, H. Y. (2006) *Studies on Chemical Compositions and Pharmacological Action of Some Toadstools*, Inner Mongolian Science Press, Huhehaote

Boa, E. (2004) *Wild edible fungi: A global overview of their use and importance to people.* Non-wood Forest Products 17, FAO, Rome

Borovička, J. and Řanda, Z. (2007) 'Distribution of iron, cobalt, zinc and selenium in macrofungi', *Mycological Progress*, vol 1, no 6, pp249–259

Borovička, J., Řanda, Z., Jelínek, E., Kotrba, P. and Dunn, C. E. (2007) 'Hyperaccumulation of silver by *Amanita strobiliformis* and related species of the section *Lepidella*', *Mycological Research*, vol 111, pp1339–1344

Buswell, J. A. and Chang, S. T. (1993) 'Edible Mushrooms: Attributes and Applications', in S. T. Chang, J. A. Buswell and P. G. Miles (eds) *Genetics and Breeding of Edible Mushrooms*, Gordon and Breach Scientific Publishers, Philadelphia

Byrne, A. R. and Tušek-Žnidarič, M. (1990) 'Studies on the uptake and binding of trace metals in fungi. Part I: Accumulation and characterization of mercury and silver in the cultivated mushroom', *Agaricus bisporus. Applied Organometallic Chemistry* 4, pp43–48

Byrne, A. R., Dermelj, M. and Vakselj, T. (1979) 'Silver accumulation by fungi', *Chemosphere* 8, pp815–821

Chan T. Y., Chan, J. C., Tomlinson, B. and Critchley J. A. (1994) 'Poisoning by Chinese herbal medicines in Hong Kong: A hospital-based study', *Veterinary and Human Toxicology*, vol 36, no 6, pp546–547

Chang, S. T. (2006a) 'The need for scientific validation of culinary-medicinal mushroom products', *International Journal of Medicinal Mushrooms* 8, pp187–195

Chang, S. T. (2006b) 'The world mushroom industry: Trends and technological development', *International Journal of Medicinal Mushrooms* 8, pp297–314

Chang, S. T. and Buswell, J. A. (1996) 'Mushrooms nutriceuticals', *World Journal of Microbiology and Biotechnology* 12, pp473–476

Chang, S. T. and Buswell, J. A. (2008) 'Development of the World Mushroom Industry: Applied Mushroom Biology and International Mushroom Organizations', *International Journal of Medicinal mushrooms* 10, pp195–208

Chen Y., Zhang Y. P., Yang Y., Yang D. (1999) 'Genetic diversity and taxonomic implication of *Cordyceps sinensis* as revealed by RAPD markers', *Biochem. Genet.*, vol 37, nos 5–6, pp201–213

Chen, S. J., Yin, D. H., Li, L., Zha, X., Shuen, J. H. and Zhama, C. (2000) 'Resources and distribution of *Cordyceps sinensis* in Naqu Tibet' [Chinese, with English abstract], *Zhong Yao Cai*, vol 23, no 11, pp673–675

Chen, S. J., Yin, D. H., Zhong, G. Y. and Huang, T. F. (2002) 'Study on the biology of adult parasite of *Cordyceps sinensis, Hepialus biruensis*' [Chinese, with English abstract], in *Zhongguo Zhong Yao Za Zhi*, vol 27, no 12, pp893–895

Chen, Z. H., Hu, J. S., Zhang, Z. G., Zhang, P. and Li, D. P. (2003) 'Determination and analysis of the main amatoxins and phallotoxins in 28 species of *Amanita* from China', *Mycosystema* 22, pp565–573

Chi, J.-H., Ha, T.-M., Kim, Y.-H. and Ju, Y.-C. (1996) 'Effects of storage temperature and packing method for keeping freshness of fresh mushrooms', *RDA Journal of Agricultural Science Farm Management Agricultural Engineering Sericulture Mycology and Farm Products Utilization* 38, pp915–921

Chiou, W. F., Chang, P. C., Chou, C. J. and Chen, C. F. (2000) 'Protein constituent contributes to the hypotensive and vasorelaxant activities of Cordyceps sinensis', *Life Sciences*, vol 66, no 14, pp1369–1376

Cihangir, N. and Saglam, N. (1999) 'Removal of cadmium by *Pleurotus sajor-caju* basidiomycetes', *Acta Biotechnologica*, vol 19, pp171–177

Dai, Y. C., and Yang, Z. L. (2008) 'A revised checklist of medicinal fungi in China', *Mycosystema*, vol 27, pp 801–824

Demirbaş, A. (2001) 'Heavy metal bioaccumulation by mushrooms from artificially fortified soils', *Food Chemistry*, vol 74, pp293–301

Deshmukh, S. K., Natarajan, K. and Verekar, S. A. (2006) 'Poisonous and hallucinogenic mushrooms of India', *International Journal of Medicinal Mushrooms*, vol 8, pp251–262

Diaz, J. H. (2005) 'Syndromic diagnosis and management of confirmed mushroom poisonings', *Critical Care Medicine*, vol 33, pp427–436

Du Halde, P. (1736) *The general history of China*, vol 4, John Watts, London, pp 41–42 [cited by Pegler et al, 1994]

Gelfand, M. and Harris, C. (1982) 'Poisoning by *Amanita pantherina*: A description of two cases', *Central African Journal of Medicine*, vol 28, pp159–163

Gençcelep, H., Uzun, Y., Tuncturk, Y. and Demirel, K. (2009) 'Determination of mineral contents of wild-grown edible mushrooms', *Food Chemistry*, vol 113, pp1033–1036

Goldstein, M. C. (1996) *Nomads of Golok, Qinghai: A Report*, available for download at www.case.edu/affil/tibet/CollectedArticles.htm

Guzman, G. (2008) 'Diversity and use of traditional Mexican medicinal fungi, a review', *International Journal of Medicinal mushrooms*, vol 10, pp209–217

Hall, I. R., Stephenson, S. T., Buchanan, P. K., Yun, W. and Cole, A .L. J. (2003) *Edible and Poisonous Mushrooms of the World*, The New Zealand Institute for Crop and Food Research Limited, Christchurch, New Zealand

Hershko, V. and Nussinovitch, A. (1998) 'Relationships between hydrocolloid coating and mushroom structure', *Journal of Agricultural and Food Chemistry* 46, pp2988–2997

Holliday, J. C. and Cleaver, M. (2008) 'Medicinal value of the caterpillar fungi species of the genus *Cordyceps* (Fr.) Link (Ascomycetes), a review', *International Journal of Medicinal Mushrooms*, vol 10, pp219–234

Hong, T. D., Ellis, R. H. and Moore, D. (1997) 'Development of a Model to Predict the Effect of Temperature and Moisture on Fungal Spore Longevity', *Annals of Botany* 79, pp121–128

Jaworska, G. and Bernaś, E. (2009) 'The effect of preliminary processing and period of storage on the quality of frozen *Boletus edulis* (Bull: Fr.) mushrooms', *Food Chemistry*, vol 113, pp936–943

Jordan, M. (1995) *The Encyclopedia of Fungi of Britain and Europe*, David and Charles, Newton Abbot, UK

Kalač, P. and Křížek, M. (1997) 'Formation of biogenic amines in four edible mushroom species stored under different conditions', *Food Chemistry* 58, pp 233–236

Kalač, P. and Svoboda, L. (2000) 'A review of trace element concentrations in edible mushrooms', *Food Chemistry* 69, pp273–281

Latiff, L. A., Daran, A. B. M. and Mohamed, A. B. (1996) 'Relative distribution of minerals in the pileus and stalk of some selected edible mushrooms', *Food Chemistry* 56, pp115–121

Li, Q. S., Zeng, W., Yin, D. H. and Huang, T. F. (1999) 'A Preliminary Study on Alternation of Generations of *Cordyceps sinensis*' [Chinese, with English abstract], in *Zhongguo Zhong Yao Za Zhi [China Jour. Chin. Mat. Med.]*, vol 23, no 4, pp210–212

Li, Y. and Bau, T. (2003) *Mushrooms of Changbai Mountains, China*, Science Press, Beijing

Liu, B. (1984) *Medicinal Fungi in China* (3rd edition), Shanxi People's Publishing House, Taiyuan

Liu, J. K. (2004) *Mycochemistry*, China Science and Technology Press, Beijing

Manzi, P., Gambelli, L., Marconi, S., Vivanti, V. and Pizzoferrato, L. (1999) 'Nutrients in edible mushrooms: An inter-species comparative study', *Food Chemistry* 65, pp477–482

Mao, X. L. (1987) *Guide to Poisonous Mushrooms*, Popular Science Press, Beijing

Mao, X. L. (2006) 'Poisonous mushrooms and their toxins in China', *Mycosystema* 25, pp345–363

Mattila, P., Könkö, K., Eurola, M., Pihlava, J. M., Astola, J., Vahteristo, L., Hietaniemi, V., Kumpulainen, J., Valtonen, M. and Piironen, V. (2001) 'Contents of vitamins, mineral elements, and some phenolic compounds in cultivated mushrooms', *Journal of Agricultural and Food Chemistry* 49, pp2343–2348

Murcia, M. A., Martinez-Tome, M., Jimenez, A. M., Vera, A. M., Honrubia, M. and Parras, P. (2002) 'Antioxidant activity of edible fungi (truffles and mushrooms): Losses during industrial processing', *Journal of Food Production* 65, pp1614–1622

Nikoh, N. and Fukatsu, T. (2000) 'Interkingdom host jumping underground: Phylogenetic analysis of endoparasitic fungi of the genus *Cordyceps*', *Molecular Biology and Evolution* 17, pp629–638

Pegler, D. N., Yao, Y.-J. and Li, Y. (1994) 'The Chinese "caterpillar fungus"', *Mycologist*, vol 8, no 1, pp1–4

Piearce, G. D. and Sharp, C. (2000) 'Vernacular names of Zimbabwean fungi: A preliminary checklist', *Kirkia* 17, pp219–228

Rácz, L., Papp, L., Prokai, B. and Kovács, Z. (1996) 'Trace element determination in cultivated mushrooms: An investigation of manganese, nickel, and cadmium intake in cultivated mushrooms using ICP atomic emission', *Microchemical Journal* 54, pp444–451

Sanmee, R., Dell, B., Lumyong, P., Izumori, K. and Lumyong, S. (2003) 'Nutritive value of popular wild edible mushrooms from northern Thailand', *Food Chemistry* 82, pp527–532

Saviuc, P. and Danel, V. (2006) 'New syndromes in mushroom poisoning', *Toxicological Reviews* 25, pp199–209

Steinkraus, D. (1994) 'Chinese caterpillar fungus and world record runners', *American Entomologist*, vol 40, no 4, pp235–239

Stone, R. (2008) 'Last Stand for the Body Snatcher of the Himalayas?' *Science* 322, p1182

Strong, D. R., Maron, J. L., Connors, P. G., Whipple, A., Harrison, S., and Jeffries, R. L. (1995) 'High mortality, fluctuation in numbers, and heavy subterranean insect herbivory in bush lupine, *Lupinus arboreus*', *Oecologia* 104, pp85–92

Sung, G. H., Sung, J. M., Hywel-Jones, N. L., Luangsa-ard, J. J., Shrestha, B., and Spatafora, J. W. (2007) 'Phylogenetic classification of *Cordyceps* and the clavicipitaceous fungi', *Studies in Mycology* 57, pp5–59

Takahashi, A., Agatsuma, T., Ohta, T., Nunozawa, T., Endo, T. and Nozoe, S. (1993) 'Russuphelin-B, Russuphelin-C, Russuphelin-D, Russuphelin-E and Russuphelin-F, New cytotoxic substances from the mushroom *Russula subnigricans* Hongo', *Chemical and Pharmaceutical Bulletin* 41, pp1726–1729

Verbeken, A., Walleyn, R., Sharp, C. and Buyck, B. (2000) 'Studies in tropical African *Lactarius* species 9. Records from Zimbabwe', *System. Geogr. Pl.* 70, pp181–215

Wang, X. H., Liu, P. G. and Yu, F. Q. (2004) *Color Atlas of Wild Commercial Mushroom in Yunnan,* Yunnan Science and Technology Press, Kunming

Willis, J. H. (1941) *Victorian fungi,* Field Naturalists' Club of Victoria, Melbourne, Australia

Winkler, D. (2008) 'Yartsa Gunbu (*Cordyceps sinensis*) and the Fungal Commodification of Tibet's Rural Economy', *Economic Botany* 62, pp291–305

Wu, T. N., Yang K. C., Wang C. M., Lai J. S., Ko K. N., Chang P. Y. and Liou S. H. (1996) 'Lead poisoning caused by contaminated *Cordyceps,* a Chinese herbal medicine: Two case reports', *Science of the Total Environment,* vol 182, no 1–3, pp193–195

Yang, Z. L. and Li, T. H. (2001) 'Notes on three white amanitae of section *Phalloideae* (Amanitaceae) from China', *Mycotaxon* 78, pp439–448

Ying, J. Z. and Zang, M. (1994) *Economic Macrofungi from Southwestern China,* Science Press, Beijing

Ying, J. Z., Mao, X. L., Ma, Q. M., Zong, Y. C. and Wen, H. A.(1987) *Icones of Medicinal Fungi from China,* Science Press, Beijing

Zang, M. and Kinjo, N. (1998) 'Notes on the Alpine Cordyceps of China and Nearby Nations', *Mycotaxon* 66, pp215–229

Zhu J. S., Halpern, G. M. and Jones, K. (1998) 'The scientific rediscovery of an ancient Chinese herbal medicine. Part I: *Cordyceps sinensis*', *Journal of Alternative and Complementary Medicine* 4, pp289–303

Fungi and the Future: Policy and Practice for Sustainable Production and Conservation

Anthony B. Cunningham

INTRODUCTION

In 1992, the Convention on Biological Diversity (CBD) raised international awareness about the need for biodiversity conservation, sustainable resource use and issues of access and benefit sharing. With an estimated 1.5 million species, fungi are a very significant part of that diversity (Hawksworth, 2003), yet even macro-fungi have generally stayed 'below the radar screen' of policymakers, despite their ecological importance and multiple values.

Experts around the world have recognized that many of the ambitious goals of the CBD have not been achieved and that the world's biological diversity continues to be lost at a rapid rate. This recognition of declining biodiversity is widespread in international policy meetings, from the Johannesburg World Summit on Sustainable Development (2002) to the ASEAN (Association of Southeast Asian Nations) Biodiversity Conference (2009) and the Subsidiary Body on Scientific, Technical and Technological Advice to the Convention on Biological Diversity (SBSTTA) in Nairobi (2010).

This chapter begins with an outline of the complexities that challenge policy implementation in practice. It will then review steps that have been suggested and which need to be taken within the three major components of the CBD, and conclude with recommendations for the future.

THE COMPLEXITIES OF PUTTING POLICIES INTO PRACTICE

Policy goals are more easily written than implemented. One might say that achieving CBD goals in terms of forests and macro-fungi demonstrates that, as Thomas and Bunnell (2001) succinctly put it, forest management is not rocket science – it is far more complex'. Policies and practices are necessary that promote fungus conservation and use through integration of resource management, ecological restoration, local livelihood improvement and governance at multiple scales. This makes policy development and implementation a complex task, as discussed below.

Complexity in diversity: The challenge of the endangered mycologist

Although awareness of the diversity and importance of fungi has increased, basic mycological knowledge is limited, particularly in the tropics where fungal diversity is probably highest. Although about 100,000 species of fungi have been described, Hawksworth (2003) has estimated that there are likely to be about 1.5 million species of fungi worldwide. Yet there are very few mycologists to deal with this complexity and even fewer dealing with conservation or resource management issues. Hyde (2003) points out that number of fungal systematists has declined rapidly across most of the world. In a survey of 22 Asian countries, Hyde (2003) found that China and Japan were the most active, but in 16 of the countries surveyed there were no publications during survey period and therefore no productive taxonomic mycologists. In Europe, the number of professional mycologists dealing with macro-fungi is also very low. In a survey of 26 European countries by Senn-Irlet et al (2007), they found that only six countries (Finland, Poland, Russia, Spain, Sweden and Turkey) have more than ten professional mycologists working with macro-fungi.

Fungi and bio-complexity

Fungi are not only diverse and poorly known, but are part of complex trophic relationships. Conservation and resource management of fungi is therefore challenging and, as Cathy Sharp (Chapter 6) and David Pilz (Chapter 7) point out, fungi are affected by different factors operating at multiple spatial and time scales. A good example is in the northwest US, where close links exist between northern spotted owls (*Strix occidentalis*), their main prey (the northern flying squirrel), truffles (the squirrels favourite food) and the trees in these forests whose ability to take in water and nutrients are enhanced by mycorrhizal fungi. These fungi are, in turn, part of the mycorrhizosphere with its diversity of bacteria, insects, microbes and nematodes (Carey, 2003; Maser et al, 2008). In a recent article Jim Trappe estimates that 2000 species of ectomycorrhizal fungi are associated with Douglas firs, one of the dominant tree species in these forests (Trappe and Claridge, 2010). In Australia, mycophagy is also widespread, particularly among kangaroo-rats (Potoroidae). In Australia, the links between fungi (truffles, false-truffles and sporocarpic Endogonaceae) and the ecology of the plants with which these fungi have mycorrhizal relationships is as complex as that in North America (Claridge and May, 2006). The populations of many kangaroo-rats have fallen sharply due to changing fire ecology, feral animals and habitat loss. The loss of kangaroo-rats, even aside from their role as dispersers of fungal spores, has widespread ecological implications, in part due to their role as browsers and as 'landscape engineers' (Noble et al, 2007). It is clear from research in Australia and North America that many factors have to be taken into account in a hierarchical approach (as defined by Noss, 1990) to conservation, management and monitoring of fungi. Molina et al (2003) have practised this approach in temperate coniferous forests, providing a model for other places.

Complexities of land and resource tenure

Clear land tenure and rights to accessing fungi are crucial to successful conservation and resource management. Clear rights of access also help to ensure that mushroom harvesters benefit and have an incentive to conserve habitat or follow harvest guidelines. Across the world, however, there are variations in the bundle of land and resource rights, with different forms of ownership and the time-scales over which those rights are held, as Eric Boa discusses in Chapter 1. In Japan, for example, a bidding system for rights to harvest matsutake shifts resource tenure (but not land tenure) from the landowner to successful bidders who then have exclusive rights to gather, sell or give away matsutake as gifts; these rights vary from year to year through the bidding process (Saito and Mitsumata, 2008). Despite having been in place for centuries, the outcomes of bidding systems varied in different parts of Japan and were more effective at maintaining matsutake habitat in communal lands with a strong tradition of *iriai*, a form of community-based resource land management.

By contrast, in several Scandinavian countries, long-established systems of 'everyman's rights' (*allemansrätten*) has enabled anyone to walk through private land and collect berries and mushrooms. This system has worked for centuries, but is being challenged by globalization. In Stockholm, the majority of people selling high value mushrooms and berries are Turkish (Figure 9.1). Depending on the season, the *Boletus* and *Cantharellus* they sell are from Sweden or may be imported from Estonia.

High local labour costs and the efficiency of foreign workers have also played an important role in a global world. In Sweden and Norway, for example, thousands of 'guest-workers' are flown in from China, Thailand or Vietnam to pick berries during the berry fruiting season. In Finland this has raised public concerns about immigration, labour practices and tax policies (Richards and Saastamoinen, 2010). It may also place the 'everyman's right' under strain in one of the few areas of the world where forestry policy has taken non-timber forest product harvests into account.

Cultivation and complexity

On the surface, production from cultivation to meet commercial demand for mushrooms seems simple. Tenure issues are usually clear. Harvest pressure is taken off wild stocks in multiple-use forests and intensive production of species like *Auricularia* (wood-ear mushrooms), shiitake (*Lentinula edodes*) and oyster mushroom (*Pleurotus ostreatus*) is economically viable and efficient. Greater efficiency through cultivation can bring significant economic benefits to many rural farmers, such as *Letinula edodes* producers in Shaanxi (Figure 9.4).

In other cases, cultivation comes at a price because it does not necessarily mean and end to the need for management plans for forested landscapes. In China, for example, *Auricularia auricula* production now takes place on a massive scale, using *qing gang* (*Quercus*) stems harvested from natural forests (Figure 9.2). To be sustained this requires forest management plans for oak forests (which contain several endemic *Quercus* species) or a shift to other substrates for intensive mushroom production.

In other cases, such as morel cultivation in China, overharvest of large poplar trees (*Populus rotundifolia* var. *bonatii*) is also a concern, and cultivation of relatively fast growing trees has been suggested (Box 9.1).

Figure 9.1   *Mushroom trade and traders are affected by globalization: A. At this market in Stockholm, Sweden, most of the traders were Turkish; early in the season, most* Cantharellus *and* Boletus *sold were from Estonia; B. A* matsutake *picker in Zhongdian, southwest China, preparing her product for a bidding process in the local market that will end up in most of her product being air-freighted to Japan.*

Photographs: A: Anthony B. Cunningham; B: Kunming Institute of Botany

Limited policy recognition of strong links to livelihoods

We know from reviews and research that a high diversity of fungi are used for food (Chapter 1). Detailed studies of the contribution that fungi make to local people's livelihoods or to household income are relatively scarce, yet we know from recent research that commercial trade in fungi can be extremely important to the local household economies in high mountain areas of the Himalaya. In a detailed survey of fungus use in 17 districts of Nepal, Christensen et al (2008) recorded 228 species used for food. In their study Christensen et al (2008) found that mushrooms were important for food whether households were poor or relatively wealthy. Households collected an average of 18.1kg of mushrooms per household, but 7 per cent collected more than 50kg per year and 3 per cent over 100kg of mushrooms per year. In terms of commercial use, poorer households were more involved; in a single mushroom harvest season individuals could earn up to the equivalent of six months' salary in terms of agricultural wage rates. In high altitude areas of Tibet, Winkler (2008) records that

Figure 9.2 *Intensive production of* Auricularia auricula *(wood-ear mushrooms) in Sichuan, China, uses hundreds of tonnes of* Quercus *logs*

Photograph: Anthony B. Cunningham

income from sale of *Cordyceps sinensis* frequently represents between 70 per cent and 90 per cent of household income. In Yunnan, China, the commercial trade in matsutake (*Tricholoma matsutake*) has transformed whole villages (Figure 9.3), earning households in Zhongdian area (Diqing Autonomous Tibetan Prefecture) a higher income than that from any other local product, including timber and livestock (Arora, 2008).

More work on micro-economics is needed. Detailed research protocols such as the approach used by the Poverty and Environment Network (PEN) are therefore very useful, even if they show a relatively low use of fungi in some locations (Box 9.2).

CONSERVATION OF FUNGAL DIVERSITY

There is no point in reinventing the wheel. It is far better to support the practical steps that have already been suggested. Hawksworth (2003) has proposed MycoAction Plans that operate on global, national and regional levels, with strong links between each level; actions would be grouped according to the key themes such as collaboration, education and conservation. These interlinked levels make sense because the CBD is implemented through national governments which are signatories to the Convention. However, regional and international collaboration would be needed on a larger scale

BOX 9.1 POPLAR TREES AND MOREL CULTIVATION IN NORTHWEST YUNNAN, CHINA

Yongchang Zhao

Morels (*Morchella* spp) are highly prized mushrooms harvested mainly from the wild. In many parts of the world, mushroom pickers know the close association between morels and the fire ecology of forests. In North America, pickers target areas that have been recently burnt, since rich patches of morels grow there. In Finland, the Finnish name for morels (*huhtasieni*) refers to *huhta*, a woodland area cleared for farming through slashing and burning. In the Central Himalaya of India, local people deliberately burn montane forest in October and November to stimulate wild morel production (Prasad et al, 2002). This use of fire in the Himalaya has raised concerns in terms of biodiversity conservation, with a call for morel cultivation in order to improve local people's economic opportunities and for conservation reasons (Prasad et al, 2002).

Recent technological developments have made the cultivation of the morel possible in various parts of the world. Several of these are patented (e.g. Miller, 2005). One of the complexities of cultivation is the genetic variation in *Morchella esculenta* and other species (Dalgleish and Jacobson, 2005; Masaphy et al, 2010). In their review of the potential for morel cultivation, Stott and Mohammed (2004) suggest two needs of successful morel cultivation: firstly, to focus on the environmental and nutritional requirements for the reliable production of abundant sclerotia; and secondly, for research on the conditions needed for ascocarp initiation and maturation. In northwest Yunnan, China, the yellow morel (*Morchella esculenta*), is cultivated using the 'semi-artificial/semi-natural' cultivation method (known as *banrengong zaipei*).

The process comprises four parts: spawn preparation, selection of proper cultivation site, prepare of substrate and fruiting management.

- The grain spawn is prepared in May and planting spawn is prepared in July. Places with sandy soil, good irritation opportunities and winter snowfall are preferred. Poplar (*Populus rotundifolia* var. *bonatii*) stumps are used as growing material, with 2m^3 per 666m^2 (1mu in Chinese units). The stumps are prepared for 3 to 10 days and hewn into 40–100cm. Soil beds are prepared at the size of 120×60cm with 40cm intervals. The stumps are squared off and placed in the soil beds. The spawn is spread on the stump and covered with soil.
- Shade, weed, water and disease are the most important factors in fruiting management. When the surface temperature starts to increase after winter, the area is watered once or twice a week to maintain soil water content at 50 per cent. Morel start to flush when the temperature reaches 15°C.
- The duration of fruiting is 50 to 60 days, with harvests for two to three years after each inoculation. Production is 6–10 kg of dry morels per 666m^2 during three years. The total income is thus about 4000–5000 Yuan (US$588–735) per year. However, such production is kept at small scale.

The main limiting factor is the supply of poplar stumps. Large-scale morel production will consume huge amount of poplar tree trees and may eventually threaten this resource. Therefore, planting poplar trees is an essential part of this process.

Figure 9.3 *Rammed earth houses in northwest Yunnan, China, built through income from trade in wild harvested* Tricholoma matsutake *and* Cordyceps sinensis

Photograph: T. Cunningham

to avoid a scattered approach. It is also critical to establish priorities where funding is increasingly scarce and problems urgent. This has been done by Hawksworth (2003):

● Agreement on a list of priority fungal groups to be surveyed during rapid site assessments.
● Development of a list of criteria that can be used to assess and evaluate the sites of greatest scientific importance for fungal conservation.
● Compilation of a list of specialists willing to undertake identifications of fungi, indicating which identifications will be done free of charge and which require payment, and making the list available at least online via the International Mycological Association (IMA) home page (www.ima-mycology.org).
● Development of complementary accession policies through discussions between the major fungal culture collections.

Steps have been taken to develop national and regional strategies for macro-fungi, following a similar approach for 'Important Fungus Areas' (IFAs) to the CBD's Global Strategy for Plant Conservation (GSPC). Following the GSPC 'model' seems like a good idea, firstly since a close relationship exists between plants and fungi and, secondly, as it will aid momentum if a sister strategy has already been ratified by the CBD. The first step in this process was taken by Evans et al (2002) in the UK and since then at a regional scale within Europe (Senn-Irlet et al, 2007). There is no doubt that regional

BOX 9.2 FUNGI, LIVELIHOODS AND MICRO-ECONOMICS: THE PEN METHODOLOGY

Nick Hogarth

In many countries the value of NTFPs (Non-timber Forest Products) – including fungi – contributes as much, if not more, to national product as industrial round-wood (Chapter 5). Produced and consumed largely outside the cash economy, NTFPs have attracted only limited attention and even less in the way of measurement and research. But the detailed nature of the PEN methodology, allows the annual cash and subsistence value of NTFPs such as fungi to be quantified at the household and/or village level, and also compared to sites across the world.

What is PEN?

The Poverty and Environment Network (PEN) is an ambitious international research programme administered by the Forests and Livelihoods Program of the Center for International Forestry Research (CIFOR). Launched in 2004, at the core of PEN is the collection of uniform, detailed socio-economic data at household and village level, conducted at 38 study sites in 26 countries. The aim of the research is to inform and improve forest policy formulation and implementation, and to influence mainstream policies towards rural poverty alleviation on a regional and global scale.

The PEN methodology represents a new and innovative way of doing research. It involves a large number of partners in global data collection using comparable definitions, questionnaires and methods. The data collection, which was completed in 2009, carefully records all forest and environmental values. All income data are collected using four quarterly surveys designed to capture seasonal variations, shorten recall periods and increase accuracy. Standardized information on cash and subsistence incomes from all major sources is obtained by collecting data during one full year for: amounts of products and services collected, sold or purchased; costs incurred in processing and marketing; and prices. The questionnaires are devised to capture data related to the role of forest and forest products for households living in different forest environments, institutional arrangements and market contexts.

Application of the PEN Method for fungi research

Because the PEN surveys capture information on cash and subsistence incomes from all major sources, the analysis offers the scope to focus on the significance of either one or many forest or agricultural products, livestock, wages, remittances or other income sources. For example, PEN data can be used to calculate who 'depends' on fungi according to income categories, i.e. are the poor more dependent? Also, the significance of fungi in household livelihoods can be determined by calculating the relative income share of fungi compared to other forest-derived income (Figure 9.4), or as a contribution to total household income.

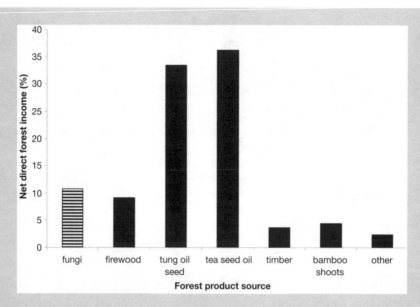

Figure 9.4 *The role of fungi in household direct-forest income*

Nala Administrative Village, Nabi Township, Tianlin County, Guangxi Zhuang Autonomous Region (China). PEN survey conducted in 2007 (n=40). Income includes cash and non-cash equivalent values from natural and plantation forests (Chinese definition of 'forestry' is used).

Source: Nick Hogarth

Although the main function of the PEN methodology is to capture economic information, it is not limited to economics. Information is also gathered about the people who collect the forest products (gender, age, education, etc.), the type of land from which they are collected, land tenure, subsistence versus commercial use, market information and processing/value adding information. For example, in addition to the income information in Figure 9.4 above, the PEN method revealed the following:

- 41 per cent of fungi were collected by adult female household members; 47 per cent was collected by both adult males and adult females participating equally; and 12 per cent was collected by the adult male household members.
- 94 per cent was collected from natural forest, with 6 per cent from plantation forest (no cultivation recorded).
- 88 per cent of households collected fungi for sale only (not for home consumption), selling to private wholesale buyers within the village.

For research specifically on fungi, the PEN data can complement other more focused methodologies such as taxonomic studies, in-depth market-chain analyses or more qualitative methods of capturing the medicinal or cultural values of fungi. For an example of PEN methodology used to complement other methods, see Christensen et al (2008).

Figure 9.5 *Co-operation between small-scale farmers meets large-scale market demand in Dacigou village, Shaanxi province*

a) Low cost tunnels (a shade-cloth over locally cut withies and poles from agroforestry systems) used for intensive production of shiitake mushrooms in Shaanxi, China.

b) Intensive production on sawdust or crop surplus within log-shaped plastic pouches inoculated with pure shiitake mushroom spores. This method was introduced to farmers in Java in the mid-1990s.

c) Shiitake mushrooms ready for harvest.

d,e) In addition to sales of fresh mushrooms, appropriate technology driers in each household enable surplus to be dried to prolong shelf-life, increase the ease of transport and reach a wider market.

Photographs: Anthony B. Cunningham

and national associations of mycologists can play an important part in this process in other parts of the world too. Just as Senn-Irlet et al's (2007) guidelines for conservation of macro-fungi in Europe are linked to the European Council for the Conservation of Fungi (ECCF) (see www.wsl.ch/eccf/publications-en.ehtml), so other regional, national or even continent-wide associations and networks can play an important role. In addition to the ECCF, important professional associations are:

- Africa: the African Mycological Association (www.africanmycology.org);
- The Asia-Pacific region: the Asian Mycology Committee (www.fungaldiversity.org);
- Australia: the Australasian Mycological Society (www.australasianmycology.com);
- Latin America: the Asociación Latinoamericana de Micología (www.almic.org); and
- North America, the Mycological Society of America (MSA) (www.msafungi.org).

In terms of developing conservation action plans, mycologists have an important role to play in networking regionally and communicating with national governments. Mycologists' knowledge will be crucial in developing understanding of, and monitoring changes in, fungal biodiversity. Very few fungi are on the current International Union for Conservation of Nature (IUCN) Red List. With limited monitoring across large spatial scales, changes in populations may not be detected, but the extent of change illustrated by two lichen species on the IUCN Red List gives an example of how a range of other fungi may be influenced. The boreal felt lichen (*Erioderma pedicellatum*), a species with narrow habitat requirements in old growth coniferous forests near the sea, has completely disappeared from its former distribution in Norway and Sweden. In Canada, this lichen species has also disappeared from New Brunswick and in Nova Scotia its populations declined by more than 95 per cent. The largest remaining population in Newfoundland, found in an area of just 23.35km^2, is also in decline (Scheidegger, 2003). From a global perspective, this lichen has declined by more than 80 per cent, primarily due to air pollution and habitat loss due to logging, resulting its listing as a Critically Endangered Species by IUCN. Stochastic events also need to be taken into account in long-term conservation, management and recovery plans for fungi, adding to the complexities (and time-scales) of conserving lichens and possibly restricted range fungi. In addition to habitat loss and the effects of changing fire ecology on the Florida perforate reindeer lichen (*Cladonia perforata*), hurricanes have impacted populations of this endangered species. In 1996, for example, a hurricane wiped out two of the three subpopulations, with a third subpopulation declining by over 70 per cent (Yahr, 2003).

In Europe, the main threats to macro-fungi identified by Senn-Irlet et al (2007) are habitat fragmentation and a decline in areas with old-growth forests and dead wood availability. In addition, there is a decline of old semi-natural and unfertilized grasslands due to fertilization, reforestation or lack of grazing and the high levels of nitrogen added by people to areas with nutrient poor soils. The challenge of trying to attain the CBD's goals through balancing biodiversity conservation objectives with those of sustainable use, development and livelihoods requires both ground-level attention to landscape change and conservation at multiple-scales with multiple stakeholders.

It is widely recognized that single-species conservation and protected areas are insufficient for protecting biodiversity. Lindenmayer and Franklin (2002), recognizing that 'since species loss is predominantly driven by habitat loss, the overarching goal of matrix management must be to prevent habitat loss', suggested five general principles for forest biodiversity conservation, namely the maintenance of:

- connectivity;
- landscape heterogeneity;
- stand structural complexity;
- the integrity of aquatic systems by sustaining hydrologic and geomorphological processes; and
- risk-spreading i.e. adoption of various strategies linked to the principles listed above between different stands and landscapes ('don't do the same thing everywhere').

SUSTAINABLE USE

As Egli et al's (2005) long-term study in Switzerland showed, harvesting mushrooms is sustainable. Some exceptions occur, such as the white ferula mushroom (*Pleurotus nebrodensis*); this is on the IUCN red list and has been highly prized for over a century. It is worth €50 to €70 (approximately US$60–86) per kilogram (Venturella, 2006). Even in such an extreme case, where only 250 fruiting bodies (mushrooms) are produced annually and harvesting impacts are of concern, the exception proves the rule: maintaining or restoring habitat remains a key issue. *Pleurotus nebrodensis* occurs in highly fragmented populations in an area of Sicily less than 100km^2. It is very habitat-specific and is restricted to limestone areas in association with a plant species in the Apiaceae (*Cachrys ferulacea*).

A common conservation goal is for protected areas to cover 10 per cent of national land area. The question is: 'what about the other 90 per cent'? As Nix (1997) points out, 'it is certain that the […] park and reserve system will be totally inadequate for conservation of the products of four billion years of evolution […] a new ecocentric paradigm, that integrates biodiversity conservation with the totality of human activities, is long overdue'.

Applying Lindenmayer and Franklin's (2002) principles requires an integrated, ecosystem approach in landscapes often occupied by people. Participatory research on *Telophora ganbajun* in Yunnan, China is an example of this (Box 9.3).

Research in the temperate coniferous forests of the northwestern US on how to manage for heterogeneity and complexity also holds lessons for many others parts of the world. So do approaches to resource economics (Chapter 4) and sustainable use (Chapter 7) that have been developed in the northwestern US. In the Pacific Northwest, researchers have developed a good knowledge of the community structure of ectomycorrhizal fungi in different age-classes of forests after disturbance (Carey, 2003) and the trade-offs required in forest management (Lehmkuhl et al, 2007). Similar knowledge would be extremely useful for forest policy and management practices in other parts of the world for the conservation and sustainable use of fungi. In Asia and Africa, much less research has been done on this topic and conceptual ideas on links between macro-fungi forest successional stages need to be tested (Figure 9.7).

BOX 9.3 INTERDISCIPLINARY RESEARCH ON THE COMMERCIAL MUSHROOM (*THELEPHORA GANBAJUN*)

He Jun

Managing wild fungi harvests needs to be interdisciplinary, with biophysical processes considered in the context of a wide range of social, economic, political and ecological questions. The World Agroforestry Centre, ICRAF-China is currently leading an action research project that applies an interdisciplinary approach to integrated management of wild fungi. The current focus is on *Thelephora ganbajun*, an endemic and economically valuable species in Yunnan, southwest China (He et al, in press). The pilot study was carried out in Baoshan prefecture of Yunnan where *T. ganbajun* populations are concentrated. In combination with participatory methods, the research team adopted an interdisciplinary approach to assess the biophysical and socioeconomic factors that influence the production and sustainable use of *T. ganbajun*.

The active aim of the studies was to experiment with potential methods to improve habitat management. The overall research framework outlined different variables including both ecological and socio-economic factors. The habitat variables tested included slope aspect, litter depth, canopy density and soil depth. Socio-economic factors and potential methods to improve the habitat management were identified through an assessment of factors that contribute to institutional arrangements. These included rule-making, local participation, fencing and stronger tenure through regulations that closed selected hillsides to outsiders. The variables of watering mushrooms and harvest techniques were also identified as cross-cutting factors that needed to be assessed. A total population of farmers from Han-Chinese and Yi cultural groups lived in the 16 villages of the study area. Income from mushrooms represents 37 per cent of household income in this area, with 50 per cent of villagers involved in seasonal mushroom harvests. Active participation of the farmers in both research design and research process enabled the success results that suggest how to artificially adjust the ecological conditions (e.g. litter depth and canopy density) to significantly increase mushroom production, and while the community institutional building provide the foundation for effective management. In addition, research benefitted from local empirical knowledge in improving harvest techniques.

In co-ordinating the collaboration of different disciplines within the project, the inter-disciplinary research became a knowledge generation process, since integration and innovation of knowledge serve significantly to enhance social capital and collective capacity. In contrast to 'traditional' experts from 'hard' science controlling research, farmers and other stakeholders were actively involved in the entire research process from problem identification, research design and experimentation, to monitoring and evaluation. This increased understanding of the complex socio-ecological system and enabled the farmers to control and make decisions related to the on-farm research process. This farmer-led research strengthened a sense of ownership of the research process and led to better project implementation and monitoring. Participatory research experiments showed that due

Figure 9.6   *Harvesting* Telephora ganbajun *is possible on a rotational basis*

Photograph: He Jun

to its growth pattern, *Telephora ganbajun* could be harvested between three and six times, depending on different treatments (He et al, in press; Figure 9.6).

As a result, the quantities harvested increased by 43 per cent and income by 86 per cent compared to 2006, before the research started. Through adopting our approach, the county government has expanded the integrated approach and harvest methods to 4460 hectares of forest land, with a harvest of 113.7 metric tonnes of *Telephora ganbajun* worth an estimated US$2 million. In this way, we demonstrated how interdisciplinary research can function in the process of co-generation of knowledge and as the platform for knowledge exchange and communication. This is significant in the context of policy decentralization and reform through the integration of indigenous knowledge and extensive local participation in forest management and biodiversity conservation.

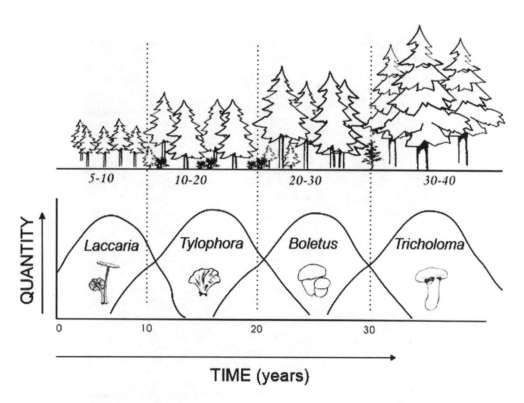

Figure 9.7   *Diagram showing links between forest successional stages and populations of popular macro-fungi in southwest China*

Source: Kunming Institute of Botany

One of the challenges is that new factors can change the situation entirely – often without our knowing it. Invasive species are a good example as they can have an impact on fungi, including highly valued macro-fungi. In China, for example, the invasive weed *Eupatorium adenophorum* has spread rapidly since it was introduced in the 1940s (Zhu et al, 2007). Local people believe it is detrimental to *Thelephora ganbajun* populations, which is likely given the known anti-microbial chemistry of several *Eupatorium* species, but no studies are known on these impacts at this stage.

ACCESS AND BENEFIT SHARING

The intention of 'access and benefit sharing' under Article 15 of the CBD was to ensure benefits to people from use of biological diversity through links to commercial markets and new technologies that in turn provided incentives for conservation and sustainable use. Rhetoric and reality were very different, however. In a recent assessment, Tvedt and Young (2007) found that:

Figure 9.8   *Invasive species, hidden impacts. A. Since the 1940s, the introduced weed* Eupatorium adenophorum *has spread through southwest China, including into prime habitats used by mushroom collectors; B.* Thelephora ganbajun, *a species that mushroom pickers say has been affected by the* Eupatorium *invasion.*

Photograph: He Jun

> *At present, the provision of 'access' has not yielded any significant benefits to the access provider at the level of national implementation; while the compliance of users with benefit sharing is infrequent, in part because users feel that they do not receive anything of value in return for their compliance. While provider countries, stakeholders and NGOs seek to impose stronger requirements, sanctions and other measures on access to genetic resources, users (especially researchers and others directly collecting resources in developing countries) bear the brunt of the failure. These user burdens include the possibility of high-profile claims of 'biopiracy', but also less known burdens.*

In terms of mycology, the access and benefit sharing (ABS) component of the CBD has worsened the situation. As Hyde (2003) points out:

> *The CBD that offered promise, had both good and bad affects. Countries became aware of the value of their biological resources and began to protect them. This meant that it became more and more difficult to obtain permission to collect fungi in various countries, and thus there was less rationale for mycologists in developed countries to train and collaborate with local mycologists. Developing countries lacked the resources to train mycologists themselves and most locally funded mycologists were poorly equipped, to the extent that they lacked research quality microscopes and even the basic recent mycological literature. The result was, therefore, a decrease in the number of mycologists in most developing countries. The CBD in most countries, therefore, failed in its promise to promote biodiversity study.*

There are opportunities for policy reform based on past experience of what has and has not been achieved by ABS policy (Tvedt and Young, 2007). For example, the Secretariat of the CBD has been developing a new Strategic Plan of the Convention on Biological Diversity for the period 2011-2020. In South Africa, practical solutions have been suggested to ABS legislation with alternative models for biodiversity prospecting that may have wider application (Crouch et al, 2008; Wynberg and Taylor, 2009).

RECOMMENDATIONS

Taxonomy, collections and curation

Hyde (2003) has already recommended that mycologists should lobby the national 'focal points' who have been appointed to carry out country taxonomic needs assessments for the Global Taxonomy Initiative (GTI) (see www.bionet-intl.org) to ensure that fungal systematics are given priority. Good taxonomy provides an invaluable tool for interdisciplinary work, e.g. research conducted in Venezuela (Dennis, 1970). Well-curated national or regional collections based on good quality specimens (Chapter 2) are also essential. Hawksworth (2003) has already suggested a series of codes of practice for fungal genetic resource collections, mushroom collection, good taxonomic practice and good cultural practice, so it is not necessary to repeat them here.

Systematic planning and priority setting

This should identify which sites are most important for conservation (Margules and Pressey, 2000) as suggested by Hawksworth (2003) as well as for local livelihoods (such as miombo woodlands (Chapter 1), temperate forests in the US (Chapter 4) and the Himalaya (Arora, 2008; Christensen et al, 2008)). It would also be helpful to attain more effective networking and form interdisciplinary partnerships for effective development and implementation of conservation and sustainable use strategies. These are discussed below.

More effective networking

Hyde (2003) sums up the terms of more effective networks eloquently:

> *Most important of all, as an orphan group, all mycologists should support each other in any way possible. This can include: positive reviews of grant applications; reviewer help to improve manuscripts rather than negative rejection, supportive references in promotion applications, and collaboration and training. There is no room for bickering or territorialism between mycologists. There are enough fungi for everyone to study without having an effect on the scientific advances of others. We are at a critical point, with existing expertise rapidly disappearing. The future of mycology is in the hands of the small number of fungal systematists remaining and we cannot, therefore, be complacent.*

Interdisciplinary partnerships

There are at least three reasons why it would be useful for mycologists to form inter-disciplinary partnerships:

Conservation and resource management plans for fungi need to take an integrated, ecosystem approach

This has been discussed earlier in this chapter, with work by Molina et al (2003) and Lehmkuhl et al (2007) as good examples. There is no better place to test theoretical approaches to biocomplexity that the real world. Multiple spatial and time scales not only illustrate biocomplexity, but pose research opportunities in two main ways. Firstly, in terms of how we perceive and study patterns and processes of interacting ecological, social, cultural and economic systems at multiple scales. Secondly, the resolution or scales at which measurements, models or experiments are conducted. These issues are well known in ecological studies and also need to be addressed in ethnoecological and ethnomycological research.

Systematic conservation planning faces a 'taxonomic bottleneck'

Even in the case of macro-fungi, there are very few mycologists to deal with mega-diversity of fungi. This challenge is particularly acute in developing countries. What is possible for mycologists in Europe or North America is more difficult to achieve in the tropics. In Europe, national action plans have been developed at a national scale, with a focus on threatened fungus species. These are in Estonia (for 19 species of fungi, with monitoring at 56 sites), Finland (10–15 species), Sweden (for 27 non-lichenized fungal species), Switzerland (for 150 red-listed species) and the UK (50 species) (Senn-Irlet et al, 2007). In North America, particularly in temperate coniferous forests of the Pacific Northwest, detailed conservation plans have been developed taking an ecosystem approach and managing for habitat heterogeneity (Carey, 2003; Lemkuhl et al, 2007; Molina et al, 2001). The tropics are even more challenging. In Panama and Mexico, respectively, it is estimated that only 3.6 per cent (Piepenbring, 2006) and 3.5 per cent (Guzman, 1998) of fungus species in those neotropical countries are known. At a global scale, there are so few mycological systematists that at the current rate of description of new fungi a total inventory would take 1290 years (Hawksworth, 2003). Despite these constraints, developing general fungus conservation strategies are possible, as Cuba has done (Portales et al, 2005). Taking a 'higher-taxon approach' with macro-fungi is one way of getting a better idea of where to focus conservation effort (Balmford et al, 2004).

Another is to get the benefits from 'citizen science'. In Australia, for example, *Fungimap* (www.rbg.vic.gov.au/fungimap/home) involves both professional and amateur mycologists in networking for conservation purposes as well to learn more about fungi. Although folk taxonomic knowledge is declining as woodlands disappear in some parts of the world such as Burkina Faso (Guissou et al, 2008), people in other locations retain a good knowledge of mushroom folk classification, from Cameroon (van Dijk et al, 2003) and Malawi (Morris, 1984) to Mexico (Shepard et al, 2008). Ethnomycological studies (see Chapters 3 and 4), with folk taxonomy linked to good specimen collecting for formal identification (Chapter 2) can help expand our knowledge for fungus conservation and sustainable harvest strategies. Systematic surveys of which species are sold in local marketplaces, using ethnobotanical methods (Cunningham, 2001) can also play a role.

Implementation strategies: Operational models and the need to involve local stakeholders

It is important to identify key locations for conservation efforts, but this will provide relatively little information on how conservation initiatives should be implemented. The real test of conservation initiatives, whether for particular habitats or species, depends on the extent to which they have encouraged and empowered different stakeholders to implement sustained conservation action (Yaffee and Wondolleck, 2000). Based on their work in southern Africa, Knight et al (2006) lament the fact that 'science is informative about where one needs to do conservation, but silent on how to achieve it'. As a result, they make a strong case for the development of operational models for implementing conservation action in priority conservation areas, suggesting that these should aim for two goals. Firstly, to establish social learning institutions that link to conservation planning initiatives as experiments and secondly, for conservation planners to work with various stakeholders in a process of mutual learning. This should include links to enterprise development through sustainable use (Figure 9.9). In common with most cross-cultural research such as ethnobiology, this requires good people-skills and a respect for different forms of knowledge. This applies as much to conservation in general as to conservation of fungi. It is also a way in which local knowledge can bridge

BOX 9.4 MUSHROOMS AND ECONOMIC RETURNS UNDER DIFFERENT MANAGEMENT REGIMES

Brian E. Robinson

Competition over open-access resources often results in overexploitation, the so-called 'tragedy of the commons' (Hardin, 1968). This occurs because individuals do not consider the ways in which their harvests reduce the supply available to others looking for the same resource; eventually all must search harder for fewer resources until it is hardly worth the effort of searching. Economically speaking, individuals do not internalize the loss they create for others by consuming more resources. Two sources of economic loss are usually present in these situations. Firstly, overexploitation causes degradation of the resource, creating a loss in revenue. Secondly, as resources are depleted, the time spent searching for or extracting the resource is less productive, increasing the cost of harvesting.

For wild-harvested mushrooms, degradation in the traditional sense does not necessarily occur – studies have shown that picking mushrooms does not influence their future availability (Egli et al, 2006). (Although the biological impacts of mushroom harvesting are debated, several long term studies have found sporocarp removal to have no detectable impact on future sporocarp emergence (Norvell, 1995; Egli et al, 2006).) However, competitive harvesting for valuable mushrooms can still induce collectors to pick fruiting bodies before they grow to their optimal size. The search for immature mushrooms becomes a more labour-intensive 'race to the bottom,' thus increasing the cost (in time) of harvesting.

In northwest Yunnan, China, this kind of overexploitation is clear in the harvest of *Tricholoma matsutake*, a valuable mycorrhizal species sold for export to Japan. Most of the rural residents in this region harvest from local village-managed forests. Immature matsutake can be sold for about US$5 per kg in local village markets, while mature specimens (typically 5 to10 days old) sell for closer to US$15 per kg. Mature mushrooms are therefore more profitable because they sell for a higher per-weight price and weigh more, making the average revenue from mature matsutake six times greater than immature matsutake.

Figure 9.9a shows the distribution of the age of harvested matsutake from two villages in northwest Yunnan from data collected in the summer of 2008. Residents of Village A harvest from a private forest plot, whereas Village B residents are free to harvest anywhere within their communal forest. Over half of Village B's harvests are less than three days old, while the mean harvest age for Village A is about seven days. Further, although the average harvester in Village A collects far fewer mushrooms (seven mushrooms per day) than Village B (43 per day), s/he makes about 9 RMB per hour spent harvesting compared to 3 RMB per hour for the communal-access village.

Figure 9.9b shows the relative revenue obtained from these harvest distributions. The total harvest revenue (the area under the revenue curve) attained by Village B is 46 per cent that of Village A, giving an estimate of the revenue lost from open access. Thus by mitigating the revenue loss alone, Village B could nearly double its profits by adopting a 'private access' type distribution. (This does not account for decreased costs from utilizing less labour, so this estimate of revenue gain certainly underestimates the potential increase in profits.)

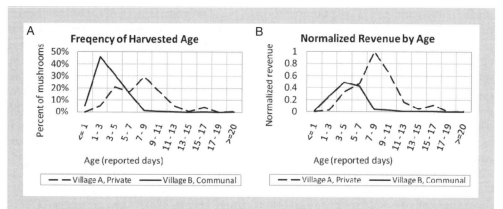

Figure 9.9 *Harvest distribution: A. Frequency of harvested age; B. Normalized revenue by age*

Despite the clear financial gains from regulating harvesters, many villages in northwest Yunnan have not implemented rules to regulate harvester activity. Why would villages let this 'tragedy of the commons' continue? Management involves large time-costs in organizing, devising, enforcing and adapting rules. Whether the benefits for management outweigh these costs hold the key to the villagers' opportunity: cost of time, village population, the productivity of the village's forest and the ease of monitoring and enforcement. Perhaps more importantly, villagers might not have profit maximization as a collective goal, but rather aspirations for egalitarian access to resources or mitigating intra-village conflict, either of which might be contradicted by property division or collective rules.

gaps in formal scientific knowledge. Local people also often have a good knowledge of the habitat preferences of macro-fungi, how they respond to disturbances (from fire or logging for example) or the use of macro-fungi as bio-indicators. Local knowledge is also important in understanding the nuances of land and resource tenure that are necessary for long-term success of conservation and sustainable use strategies (Box 9.4).

Develop paths out of the 'regulatory maze' of the CBD's access and benefit sharing policy

People have used macro-fungi as food and medicines for centuries. Good examples are *Cordyceps sinensis, Ganoderma lucidum, Lentinus edodes* and *Inonotus obliquus*. In the 21st century, biotechnology enables new commercial products to be developed from many well-known fungi (Wasser, 2002). The genus *Pleurotus*, the medicinal fungus carried by the Neolithic 'ice-man' 5000 years ago (Peintner et al, 1998) is used as a source of polysaccharides, hydrolytic and oxidative ligninolytic enzymes extracted from cultured mycelia (Gregori et al, 2007). Several mushrooms from several species used in traditional medicinal systems in Asia are potential sources of active ingredients to treat human health problems. Mycelial cultures from *Phellinus baumii* are a potential source of an anti-diabetic product (Hwang et al, 2007). Others are sources of anti-tumour polysaccharides (Zhang et al, 2007). In addition, there is commercial interest in endophytic fungi, which have not been the focus of this book, but which also produce a diverse range of compounds commercially used in agriculture, forestry, medicine and industry (Stobel, 2002). The problem is that one person's 'bioprospector' is another's 'biopirate'. As a result, ABS policies have even limited academic collaboration on fungus taxonomy (Hyde, 2003).

Writing policy may seem complex enough to the lawyers, lobbyists and politicians involved, but implementation in the real world is the real test. As Wynberg and Taylor (2009) point out, the ABS component of the CBD created a regulatory 'maze', limiting access, but with few benefits (Tvedt and Young, 2007). This has had a negative effect on studies of plants (Crouch et al, 2008), fungi (Hyde, 2003) and primates (Check and Hayden, 2007). Although this complex policy issue is far from being resolved, there are opportunities for policy reform and Laird and Wynberg (2008) have made recommendations on steps that might be taken. Hopefully these will be taken into account as the Secretariat of the CBD develops a new 'Strategic Plan' for the period 2011–2020 and a policy 'vision' for 2050.

A better understanding of trade and the values fungi

The values and trade in fungi need to be better understood at three levels: firstly, the extent of international trade; secondly, national economic values; and thirdly, in terms of values at a household level across a range of sites. Improving this understanding has important policy implications and there certainly is room for improvement. In terms of international trade, the Harmonized Commodity Description and Coding System, known as the Harmonized System (HS) is the main trade tracking tool used by 190 countries. The HS is not only the basis of customs tariffs, but also facilitates the collection and analysis of international trade statistics. About 5000 commodity groups are involved, but the classification of fungi and other natural products could be improved. Fragoso and Ferriss (2008) have recently made recommendations on how this can be achieved. At a national level, many countries underestimate the value of the trade in mushrooms and fungi, as much of the trade is through the informal sector. As Susan Alexander and her co-authors point out in Chapter 4 for the US, economic assessments are not designed to account for the informal sector or micro-enterprises whose workers are busy seasonally or intermittently. Even further below the 'radar screen' are harvesters who lack the legal authority to work in the United States. As a result, the US Census probably underestimates economic activity related to wild fungi and other non-timber forest products (McLain et al, 2008).

More micro-economics studies at the household level that cover all seasons of the year would be useful for several reasons, not least because they might raise awareness among policymakers of the links between the uses of fungi and people's livelihoods (see Box 9.4). As the PEN questionnaires are now available in seven languages, this offers a great opportunity for a collaborative project to gather data using the same methods across a range of sites. It would be useful to do this as a cross-continental comparison in ectomycorrhizal woodlands and forests. The PEN methods would also be useful as a research and monitoring tool to study 'before and after' change in villages where small-scale commercial production is taking place through cultivation. The best lessons for mushroom production are in China, the world's largest exporter and consumer of mushrooms. This has been achieved over the past 50 years, through co-operation between the government, mycologists and 15 million local farmers. Technical guidelines for the PEN questionnaire method are available for download at the PEN homepage (www.cifor.cgiar.org/PEN).

Enterprise development for local livelihood conservation

Across the world, policymakers are looking for sustainable models for rural development or incentives for conservation of biodiversity. Enterprise development based on commercial mushrooms can have positive conservation outcomes (Garibay-Orijel et al, 2009 and Figure 9.10). However, to be effective there are several challenges that need to be overcome.

Firstly, many small-scale producers are rapidly losing market share as modern markets replace informal sector markets, which predicts a worsening situation for rural producers (Vermeulen et al, 2008). Practical support is necessary if small-scale producers are to become reliable business partners; this could occur through 'anticipatory policy' and a 'three-way deal' between policymakers, business and civil society organizations.

Secondly, many rural producers are unable to access the international market, even though they harvest commercially valuable species (Christensen et al, 2008).

Thirdly, an understanding of how existing value chains are structured is necessary for well-informed enterprise development. Local and national markets are easier to access, as requirements for quality control and traceability are generally lower than those for international market access.

Finally, quality standards and traceability are important to sustain high value markets. When they are not in place, prices can tumble, market share can be lost and health problems can occur. One example is lead-poisoning from consuming *Cordyceps sinensis* (Wu et al, 1996), almost certainly a result of unethical traders putting slivers of lead into the body of this high value fungus to increase its weight and consequently their payments. This only works in the short term, affecting credibility and prices in the longer term. It has also stimulated *Cordyceps* traders to have small metal detectors that they run over the caterpillar fungus bodies to ensure this doesn't happen. The necessity of quality control is exemplified by the price crash in the matsutake market in Yunnan in 2002 when pesticide residues were detected in matsutake imported into Japan from China (Menzies and Li, 2010). In that case, the quality control response was at the level of the harvesters as well as provincial guidelines. In some countries, independent food standards agencies are directly involved in developing standards at a national level. In New Zealand, for example, there is legal control over truffle export quality through the New Zealand Horticultural Export Authority. There is international support for this process, such as the Swiss Import Promotion Programme (SIPPO) (www.sippo.org). Different forms of certification (FairTrade, organic, FairWild or through the Forest Stewardship Council (FSC)) may also be an option, but the costs and rules may prove to be a real challenge to rural producers. An excellent example that has wider application for linking enterprise development with community-based forest management is the model approach developed by Garibay-Orijel et al (2009).

Figure 9.10   *Steps in a longer journey towards achieving conservation goals through local community participation in natural resource-based enterprises that provide an incentive for community-based management in landscapes outside 'strictly protected areas' (after Knight et al, 2006)*

Better access to published research

The cost of journal subscriptions is prohibitive for individuals and even university libraries in many developing countries. Use of internet resources such as www.scholar. google.com is useful. There are admirable online resources, including websites such as *Cyber Truffle* (www.cybertruffle.org.uk), a guide to specific references, or the *Index Fungorum* (www.indexfungorum.org), which enables us to search for fungi by their scientific names. The development of websites that hold thematic e-library resources related to mycology in PDF format would be useful. The bibliographic database organized by the Poverty and Conservation Learning Group (PCLG) might be a good model to follow (see www.povertyandconservation.info).

Curriculum development

In my experience, many undergraduates have an overwhelming interest and enthusiasm in relevant research that addresses applied problems with a robust theoretical background framework. This offers a great educational and capacity building opportunity. Curriculum development in ethno-ecology, with ethnomycology as a component, offers an opportunity to meet the need to produce a new generation of trained professionals who will be employed in research, development and conservation organizations where they will study and apply interdisciplinary sciences theory in the context of local and indigenous peoples and their land. Attaining a 'critical mass' of people in interdisciplinary science can be achieved in several ways:

BOX 9.5 COMMUNICATING RESULTS:
A DVD ON COMPETITIVE VS.
COLLABORATIVE HARVEST OF MATSUTAKE

Xuefei Yang

Matsutake are the most valuable mushroom for people's livelihoods in northwest Yunnan, but in many cases they are an open-access resource. As a result, matsutake collectors face many problems, including resource competition which results in poor harvest methods. Collaborative harvesting and benefit sharing is promoted as an ultimate objective for sustainable use and management.

Different community-based management models were tested through research in northwest Yunnan and recorded in a documentary film. In June 2008, this film was shown at a workshop on the feasibility of establishing collaborative harvesting methods and moving away from open access in Zhongdian (Shangri-La) County. Five cases from Jiangpo, A'dong, Sanchun, Lizui and Wujie were shown to illustrate different pattern of resource use from competition to collaboration and benefit sharing. All workshop participants in Jidi were greatly inspired by the video and realized the advantage of the collaborative and contracted management approaches.

However, when it comes to the best solution of local community, no one thought that the approaches from Lizui (collaborative) and Wujie (privatized) were feasible to Jidi. This was explained by, firstly, a lack of strong local institutions to protect and manage such a big open access ('no wall') area from outsiders or unmanaged harvest. Secondly, the proposed 'participatory' management approach outlined in the film needed to be balanced with sufficient benefits to households. Thirdly, the complex topography character made the common-property resource management costly.

In terms of lessons learned from the use of this film, there is no doubt that it was an effective tool to communicate research results. However, what works in some areas may not be feasible in others. Nevertheless, it stimulated very useful discussions that will be remembered on the long road to sustainable use.

- Synergistic academic relationships between university departments, producing frequent and substantial interactions between faculty and students.
- Research studies that encourage interdisciplinary research team participation, including work with local and/or indigenous resource users and landowners.
- Identifying problems and solutions from an interdisciplinary perspective and using methods which also draw on local and indigenous knowledge (for example, Chapters 3 and 4).

Communication of research results

Effective communication of research results is a key to bridging the gap between research on one hand and policy and practice on the other. Hawksworth (2003) has suggested the need to prepare a brochure aimed at international and national funding agencies that focuses on the importance of fungi to human welfare and environmental health. Sunderland et al (2009) have also suggested other innovative ways of communicating research results to bridge the gap between conservation biologists, fellow scientists as well as field practitioners. Examples are use of open-access journals. Another is through websites such as "Advancing conservation in a Social Context" (http://www.tradeoffs.org/static/index.php). Equally important is the need for scientists to communicate the results of their research into a more understandable form that is directly relevance to local people. Scientists rely on the written word, but for a different audience, other means can be more effctive. Research results can certainly be communicated in many ways to diverse audiences, e.g. through film in video and DVD format (Box 9.5).

Good research, good communication strategies and good partnerships certainly go hand in hand. It is my hope that, in a small way, the 'mycelial connections' will spread out from this book to build stronger links between biodiversity, ecosystem services and people's well-being in the future.

REFERENCES

Arora, D. (2008) 'The Houses That Matsutake Built', *Economic Botany* 62, pp278–290

Carey, A. B. (2003) 'Biocomplexity and Restoration of Biodiversity in Temperate Coniferous Forest: Inducing Spatial Heterogeneity with Variable-Density Thinning', Forestry 76, pp127–136

Check, E. and Hayden, T. (2007) 'Strike threat over jailed primatologist', *Nature* 448, pp634

Christensen, M., Bhattarai, S., Devkota, S. and Larsen, H. O. (2008) 'Collection and Use of Wild Edible Fungi in Nepal', *Economic Botany* 62, no 1, pp12–23

Claridge, A. W. and May, T. W. (2006) 'Mycophagy among Australian mammals', *Austral Ecology*, vol 19, no 3, pp251–275

Crouch, N. R., et al (2008) 'South Africa's bioprospecting, access and benefit-sharing legislation: Current realities, future complications, and a proposed alternative, *S. Afr. j. sci.* [online], vol 104, nos 9–10, pp355–366, www.scielo.org.za/scielo.php?pid=S0038-23532008000500009&script=sci_abstract, accessed 31 July 2010

Cunningham, A. B. (2001) *Applied ethnobotany: People, wild plant use and conservation*, Earthscan, London

Dalgleish, H. J. and Jacobson, K. M. (2005) 'A First Assessment of Genetic Variation Among Morchella esculenta (Morel) Populations', *Journal of Heredity*, vol 96, no 4, pp396–403

Dennis, R. W. G. (1970) *Fungus flora of Venezuela and adjacent countries*, Kew Bulletin add., Series 3, Royal Botanic Gardens, Kew

Egli, S., Peter, M., Buser, C., Stahel, W. and Ayer, F. (2006) 'Mushroom picking does not impair future harvests – results of a long-time study', *Biological Conservation* 129, pp271–276

Evans, S. E., Marren, P. and Harper, M. (2002) *Important Fungus Areas: a provisional assessment of the best sites for fungi in the United Kingdom*, Plantlife, London

Fragoso, G. and Ferriss, S. (2008) 'Monitoring International Wildlife Trade with Coded Species Data', *Conservation Biology* 22, pp4–7

Garibay-Orijel, R., Cordova, J., Cifuentes, J., Valenzuela, R., Estrada-Torres, A. and Kong, A. (2009) 'Integrating wild mushorooms use into a model of sustainablemanagement for indigenous community forests', *Forest Ecology and Management* 258, pp122–131

Gates, G. M., Ratkowsky, D. A. and Grove, S. J. (2005) 'A comparison of macro fungi in young silvicultural regeneration and mature forest at the Warra LTER Site in the southern forests of Tasmania', *Tasforests* 16, 127–152

Guissou, K. M. L., Lykke, A. M., Sankara, P. and Guinko, S. (2008) 'Declining Wild Mushroom Recognition and Usage in Burkina Faso', *Economic Botany* 62, pp530–539

Guzman, G. (1998) 'Inventorying the fungi of Mexico', *Biodiversity and Conservation* 7, pp369–384

Hardin, G. (1968) 'The Tragedy of the Commons', *Science*, vol 162, no 3859, pp1243–1248

Hartnett, D. C., Potgieter, A. L. F. and Wilson, G. W. T. (2004) 'Fire effects on mycorrhizal symbiosis and root systems architecture in southern African savanna grasses', *African Journal of Ecology* 42, pp328–337

Hawksworth, D. L. (1991) 'The fungal dimension of biodiversity: Magnitude, significance, and conservation', *Mycological Research* 95, 641–655

Hawksworth, D. L. (2001) 'The magnitude of fungal diversity: The 1.5 million species estimate revisited', *Mycological Research* 105, pp1422–1432

Hawksworth, D. L. (2003) 'Monitoring and safeguarding fungal resources worldwide: The need for an international collaborative MycoAction Plan', *Fungal Diversity* 13, pp29–45

Hawksworth, D. L. (2009) 'Mycology: A neglected mega-science', in M. Rai and P. D. Bridge, *Applied mycology*, CAB International, Wallingford, UK, pp1–15

He, J., Zhou, Z., Yang, H. and Xu J. (in press) *Integrative management of commercialized wild mushroom: A case study of* Thelephora ganbajun *in Yunnan, Southwest China*, Environmental Management

Hong, T. D., Ellis, R. H. and Moore, D. (1997) 'Development of a Model to Predict the Effect of Temperature and Moisture on Fungal Spore Longevity', *Annals of Botany* 79, pp121–128

Hwang, H. J., Kim, S. W. and Yun, J. W. (2007) 'Modern biotechnology of *Phellinusbaumii* – From fermentation to proteomics', *Food Technology and Biotechnology* 45, pp306–318

Hyde, K. D. (2003) 'Mycology in the future in the Asia-Pacific region', *Fungal Diversity* 13, pp59–68

Knight, A. T. et al (2006) 'An operational model for implementing conservation action', *Conservation Biology* 20, pp408–419

Laird, S. and Wynberg, R. (2008) *Access and benefit-sharing in practice: Trends in Partnerships across sectors*, CBD Technical Series No. 38, Secretariat of the Convention on Biological Diversity, Montreal

Lehmkuhl, J. F., Kennedy, M., Ford, E. D., Singleton, P. H., Gaines, W. L., and Lind, R. L. (2007) 'Seeing the forest for the fuel: Integrating ecological values and fuels management', *Forest Ecology and Management* 246, pp73–80

Liang, H. H., Cheng, Z., Yang, X. L., Li, S., Ding, Z. Q., Zhou, T. S., Zhang, W. T. and Chen, J. K. (2008) 'Genetic diversity and structure of *Cordyceps sinensis* populations from extensive geographical regions in China as revealed by inter-simple sequence repeat markers', *Journal of Microbiology 2008*, 46, pp549–556

Lindenmayer, D. B. and Franklin, J. (2002) *Conserving forest biodiversity: A comprehensive, multi-scaled approach*, Island Press, Washington

Margules, C. R. and Pressey, R. L. (2000) 'Systematic conservation planning', *Nature* 405, pp37–47

Masaphy, S., Zabari, L., Goldberg, D. and Jander-Shagug, G. (2010) 'The Complexity of Morchella Systematics: A Case of the Yellow Morel from Israel', *Fungi* 3, pp14–18

Maser, C., Claridge, A. W. and Trappe, J. M. (2008) *Trees, Truffles, and Beasts: How Forests Function.* Rutgers University Press, New Jersey

McLain, R. (2008) 'Constructing a wild mushroom panopticon: The extension of nation-state control over the forest understory in Oregon, USA', *Economic Botany* 62, pp343–355

Menzies, N. and Li, C. (2010) 'One Eye on the Forest, One Eye on the Market: Multi-tiered Regulation of Matsutake Harvesting, Conservation and Trade in North-western Yunnan

Province', in S. A. Laird, R. McLain and R. P. Wynberg (eds) *Wild Product Governance: Finding Policies that Work for Non-Timber Forest Products*, Earthscan, London, pp243–264

Miller, S. C. (2005) *Cultivation of Morchella*, United States Patent 6951074, www.freepatentsonline. com/6951074.html, accessed June 2010

Mirua, L. (2007) 'A sacred glacier disappears in China', *Climate Change: The Nature Conservancy*, www.nature.org/initiatives/climatechange/features/art19699.html, accessed June 2010

Molina, R., Pilz, D., Smith, J., Dunham, S., Dreisbach, T., O'Dell, T. and Castellano, M. (2001) 'Conservation and management of forest fungi in the Pacific Northwestern United States: An integrated ecosystem approach', in D. Moore, M. M. Nauta and M. Rotheroe (eds) *Fungal conservation: issues and solutions*, Cambridge University Press, Cambridge, pp19–63

Morris, B. (1984) 'Macrofungi of Malawi: Some ethnobotanical notes', *Bulletin of the British Mycological Society* 18, pp48–57

Negi, C. S., Koranga, P. R. and Ghinga, H. S. (2006) 'Yartsagumba (*Cordyceps sinensis*): A call for its sustainable exploitation', *International Journal of Sustainable Development & World Ecology* 13, pp1–8

Newton, A. C., Davy, L. M., Holden, E., Silverside, A., Watling, R. and Ward, S. D. (2003) 'Status, distribution and definition of mycologically important grasslands in Scotland', *Biological Conservation* 111, pp11–23

Nix, H. (1997) 'Management of parks and reserves for the conservation of biological diversity', in J. J. Pigram and R. C. Sundell (eds) *National Parks and protected areas: Selection, delimitation and management*, University of New England, NSW, Australia, pp11–36

Norvell, L. (1995) 'Loving the chanterelle to death? The ten-year Oregon chanterelle project', *McIllvainea*, vol 12, no 1, pp6–25

Noss, R. F. (1990) 'Indicators for monitoring biodiversity: A hierarchical approach', *Conservation Biology* 44, pp355–364

Parmasto, E., Perini, C. and Rahko, T. (n.d.) *Attempts to Introduce Fungi into Nature Conservation Activities*, www.nerium.net/plantaeuropa/Download/Procedings/Parmast_%20Perini_Rahko. pdf, accessed 31 July 2010

Peintner, U., Pöder, R. and Pümpel, T. (1998) 'The iceman's fungi', *Mycological Research* 102, pp1153–1162

Peterson, R. L. and Farquhar, M. L. (1994) 'Mycorrhizas – integrated development between roots and fungi', *Mycologia* 86, pp327–335

Piepenbring, M. (2006) 'Inventoring the fungi of Panama', *Biodiversity and Conservation*, vol 16, no 1, pp73–84

Portales, J. M., Figueroa, S. H., Sierra, Á. M., Minter, D.W. and the Instituto de Ecología y Sistemática (IES) (2005) Estrategia para la Conservación de la Diversidad Fúngica en Cuba, www.cybertruffle.org.uk/cubacons/Index.html, accessed June 2010

Prasad, P., Chauhan, K., Kandari, L. S., Maikhuri, R. K., Purohit, A., Bhatt, R. P. and Rao, K. S. (2002) 'Morchella esculenta (Guchhi): Need for scientific intervention for its cultivation in Central Himalaya', *Current Science* 82, pp1098–1100

Richards, R. T. and Saastamoinen, O. (2010) 'NTFP Policy, Access to Markets and Labour Issues in Finland: Impacts of Regionalization and Globalization on the Wild Berry Industry', in S. A. Laird, R. J. McLain and R. P. Wynberg (eds) *Wild Product Governance: Finding Policies that Work for Non-timber Forest Products*, Earthscan, London, pp287–308

Saito, H. and Mitsumata, G. (2008) 'Bidding Customs and Habitat Improvement for Matsutake (*Tricholomamatsutake*) in Japan', *Economic Botany* 63, pp257–268

Scheidegger, C. (2003) 'Eriodermapedicellatum', in *IUCN 2010. IUCN Red List of Threatened Species* [Version 2010.1], www.iucnredlist.org, accessed on 17 June 2010

Senn-Irlet, B., Heilmann-Clausen, J., Genney, D. and Dahlberg, A. (2007) *Guidance for Conservation of Macro fungi in Europe*, prepared for the Directorate of Culture and Cultural and Natural Heritage, Council of Europe, Strasbourg

Shepard, G., Arora, D. and Lampman, A. (2008) 'The Grace of the Flood: Classification and Use of Wild Mushrooms among the Highland Maya of Chiapas', *Economic Botany* 62, pp437–470

Stobel, G. A. (2002) 'Gifts from the rainforest', *Canadian Journal of Plant Pathology* 24, pp14–20

Stott, K. and Mohammed, C. (2004) *Specialty Mushroom Production Systems: Maitake and Morels*, Publication No. 04/024, Rural Industries Research and Development Corporation, Canberra, Australia

Sunderland, T., Sunderland-Groves, J., Shanley, P. and Campbell,B. (2009) 'Bridging the Gap: How Can Information Access and Exchange Between Conservation Biologists and Field Practitioners be Improved for Better Conservation Outcomes?' *Biotropica* 41, pp549–554

Thomas and Bunnell (2001) cited in D. B. Lindenmayer and J. Franklin (2002) *Conserving forest biodiversity: A comprehensive, multi-scaled approach*, Island Press, Washington, DC

Trappe, J. M. and Claridge, A. W. (2010) 'The hidden life of truffles', *Scientific American* 302, pp62–67

Tvedt, M. W. and Young, T. (2007) *Beyond Access: Exploring Implementation of the Fair and Equitable Sharing Commitment in the CBD*, IUCN, Gland, Switzerland

Van Dijk, H., Onguene, N. A. and Kuyper, T. W. (2003) 'Knowledge and Utilization of Edible Mushrooms by Local Populations of the Rain Forest of South Cameroon', *Ambio* 32, pp19–23

Venturella, G. (2006) 'Pleurotusnebrodensis', in *IUCN 2010. IUCN Red List of Threatened Species* [Version 2010.1], www.iucnredlist.org, accessed 17 June 2010

Vermeulen, S., Woodhill, J., Proctor, F. J. and Delnoye, R. (2008) *Chain-wide learning for inclusive agrifood market development: A guide to multi-stakeholder processes for linking small-scale producers with modern markets*, International Institute for Environment and Development, London/ Wageningen University and Research Centre, Wageningen, The Netherlands

Wasser, S. P. (2002) 'Medicinal mushrooms as a source of antitumor and immunomodulating polysaccharides', *Applied Microbiology and Biotechnology* 60, pp258–274

Winkler, D. (2008) 'Yartsa Gunbu (*Cordyceps sinensis*) and the Fungal Commodification of Tibet's Rural Economy', *Economic Botany* 62, pp291–305

Wu, N., Yang, K. C., Wang, C. M., Lai, J. S., Ko, K. N., Chang, P. Y. and S.-H. Liou (1996) 'Lead poisoning caused by contaminated *Cordyceps*, a Chinese herbal medicine: Two case reports', *Science of the Total Environment* 182, pp193–195

Wynberg, R. and Taylor, M. (2009) 'Finding a path through the ABS Maze – challenges for regulating Access and Benefit Sharing in South Africa', in E. C. Kamau and G. Winter (eds) *Genetic Resources, Traditional Knowledge and the Law: Solutions for Access and Benefit Sharing*, Earthscan, London

Yaffee, S. L. and Wondolleck, J. M. (2000) 'Making collaboration work: Lessons from a comprehensive assessment of over 200 wide-ranging cases of collaboration in environmental management', *Conservation Biology in Practice* 1, pp17–25

Yahr, R. (2003) 'Cladoniaperforata', in *IUCN 2010. IUCN Red List of Threatened Species* [Version 2010.1], www.iucnredlist.org, accessed 17 June 2010

Zhang, M., Cui, S. W., Cheung. P. C. K. and Wang, Q. (2007) 'Antitumor polysaccharides from mushrooms: A review on their isolation process, structural characteristics and antitumor activity', *Trends in Food Science and Technology* 18, pp4–19

Zhu, L., Sun, O. J., Sang, W., Li, Z. and Ma, K. (2007) 'Predicting the spatial distribution of an invasive plant species (*Eupatorium adenophorum*) in China', *Landscape Ecology* 22, pp1143–1154

Index